Changing Sources
of Power

Changing Sources of Power

American Politics in the 1970s

Frederick G. Dutton

McGRAW-HILL BOOK COMPANY
New York   St. Louis   San Francisco   Toronto
Düsseldorf   London   Mexico   Sydney

To All the Young People Who Will Be
Voting for the First Time in This Decade

To complain of the age we live in, to murmur at the present possessors of power, to lament the past, to conceive extravagant hopes of the future, are the common dispositions of the greatest part of mankind. . . . [But] there is something particularly alarming in the present conjuncture. . . . The great parties which formerly divided and agitated . . . are known to be in a manner entirely dissolved. There is hardly a man in or out of power, who holds any other language: That government is at once dreaded and condemned; that the laws are despoiled of all their respected and salutary terrours; that their inaction is a subject of ridicule, and their exertion of abhorrence; that rank, and office, and title, and all the solemn plausibilities of the world, have lost their reverence and effect; that our foreign politicks are as much deranged as our domestick economy . . . that we know neither how to yield nor how to enforce; that hardly any thing above or below, abroad or at home, is sound and entire; but that disconnexion and confusion, in offices, in parties, in families, in the nation, prevail beyond the disorders of any former time: these are facts universally admitted.

—EDMUND BURKE, 1770

Contents

Preface

After the 1968 Presidential election, many old-timers concluded that beneath the surface appearances not much had really been changing after all in American politics. The White House changed partisan hands, but the two major parties emerged about as closely matched as at any time in the past, with the Democratic coalition down somewhat but with still by far the largest single bloc of Americans loosely identified in polls as Democrats, just as has been true for the last four decades. The Presidential candidate of one of the two main parties had emerged out of the Cold War and the other from the New Deal. The only perceptible new vote nationally developed on the Wallace right, not among the black or young or other less conventional forces. And seniority continued to reign on Capitol Hill regardless of what happened at the White House.

A contrasting view held by a number of generally younger observers is that the '68 election shows the long-dominant base shaped by Franklin Roosevelt is now fragile and fading and a whole new political era is struggling to emerge—perhaps to the right, perhaps to the left. They point out that the Democrats not only lost the South but also attracted the lowest support among organized labor's rank and file on Election Day since before F.D.R.: 56 percent. And that occurred despite the most expensive voter drive in history by union leaders among their own members. The effort finally brought back around 15 percent of the labor vote, but the unprecedented exertion which went into recouping that group suggests the depth of the potential defection. The Democratic party's vote among under-thirty voters fell below 50 percent for only the second time since before F.D.R., with part going to Nixon and a smaller but still significant segment (13 percent of the twenty-one- to twenty-four-year-old voting group) supporting Wallace. The only other time was when Eisenhower was decisively re-elected in 1956—but even his first massive victory did not sweep along most of the new voters. Negroes overwhelmingly voted Democratic in '68, but their turnout in the North was the lowest in several decades. Over-all, as respected pollster Louis Harris concluded, had Wallace not been in the race that year the Democrats could have lost by ten million votes.

Further, in the view of the younger observers, much of the country did not really vote for either major party or Presidential candidate, but rather against. The winner gained the smallest plurality in over half a century, and he was the first Presidential candidate in 120 years not to carry with him enough of his own party's legislative candidates to gain a majority in at least one house of the Congress. Even while the GOP was capturing the Presidency, the portion of the electorate identifying itself to pollsters as firmly Republican was the lowest in over a hundred years: below a third of the electorate. And this was the first time in at least that long that the group of voters declaring themselves "independent"—over a fourth of all voters—was almost as large as the base of one of the two major parties.

The new critics also note that the voter turnout in '68 was low compared not only to the previous Presidential election but, more important, to recent increases in the adult population, especially in the more populous states. New York, for instance, had over 900,000 more people of voting age than only four years earlier, but almost 500,000 fewer voters than before. California had almost a million more residents of voting age but less than 30,000 additional voters. Illinois had 200,000 more adult citizens but 200,000 fewer voters. Michigan and New Jersey each had over 250,000 additional adults but fewer than 10,000 more voters than four years earlier. The turnout in many other states was comparable. Nixon received a million fewer votes while winning in '68 than he did when losing in 1960. In net effect, these younger observers argue, the long-prevailing political arrangements—embracing both the Democratic and Republican parties—have been losing an important part of their hold, and the tumultuous social, technological, and other changes taking place were only temporarily papered over with ballots.

The difference in outlook between the older and younger observers similarly persists as to the outcome of the Congressional and other elections in 1970. Looking at the results, tradition-minded commentators have emphasized the continuing dominance of the two major parties, the decline in campaign interest among young people and the newer forces as they became more the target than the hope of much of the country, the tentative revival of the Democratic base as the nation experienced economic difficulty, and emerging of Democratic Presidential possibilities more in the mold of the recent past than anything really new. Younger observers, in contrast, have stressed the pervasive disinterest of much of the older as well as the newer group in the last elections and current politics; they compare that with the intense interest of many young people in the public problems confronting society. The percentage of voter turnout in 1970 was not only well below 1968 (as it almost always is in off-year elections compared to Presidential years) but also when compared to the previous off-year elections, in 1966. The country remains closely divided and sluggish at the level of state government; the federal structure is split between a Republican President and Democratic Congress, with only modest progress anticipated at the federal level by practically everyone. The younger observers tend to write off the prevailing arrangements about as cavalierly as the older society minimizes and derogates the newer tendencies and views.

For practicing politicians and anyone else who would seek to chart and either ride or affect the course of this decade, the implications of the 1968 and 1970 elections should be put somewhat differently from both the usual older and younger perspectives. The over-all closeness of those elections and the size of the untapped voter pool make clear that all the support that can be mustered from both traditional and new sources are needed now to win elections *and govern*. Anyone who would rely on only one or the other base takes on a considerable handicap and probably cannot sustain power and a national direction in any viable historical sense. Simply the incremental importance that the more recent developments and groups have attained, even if minimized, indicates a slippage by the older political order and the adjustment it must make sooner or later, however grudgingly. Certainly, there was little in the 1970 election results to confirm conservative columnist (and former Nixon campaign aide) Kevin Phillips' theory of an "emerging Republican majority." And the centrist prospect about which political statisticians Richard Scammon and Ben Wattenberg have written, with the great middle sector of the electorate "the real majority," seems more a gloss for stalemate and indecision than the means of achieving stability or an invigorating sense of national direction. What the country really faces is not a simplistic surge right, or an undivided center majority, or a leftward preordination, but the relentless politics of pluralism, uncertainty, contention, and choice.

After the 1968 election, a widespread assumption developed among a number of political writers that the outcome of that Presidential contest would likely hold for two terms, so substantial had become the influence of the White House and the explicit or latent disarray in the rest of American politics. But the profound challenges facing a Chief Executive are also now greater than ever before. And the newer elements are altering the mix of forces in the public arena more rapidly than at any time since at least the 1930s. In the long run, that is far more important than the equivocal 1970 election results and what one side or the other may try to read into this or that immediate policy success, political setback, or personality tea-reading.

Even in periods of considerably less social turmoil and change than this one is experiencing, history indicates that the prospect for winning two Presidential terms is not especially encouraging. Thus, as a result of fate or more deliberate processes, only two of eight Presidents in the last half century were re-elected—one in four. And in the last century and a half (since the Era of Good

Feeling—it is interesting the nation has not since produced a time that could be described at all similarly), only eight of thirty-one Presidents have been elected a second time: roughly one in four. Whether a shift in national leadership takes place as a result of the next Presidential election will depend in important part on what happens between now and then and what the choice finally is. But some vigorous long-range factors and patterns are also at work and must be taken into account.

This inquiry seeks to look at those forces so that the next Presidential election or two can be viewed in a larger context than simply the contention between the two major parties or among the better-known prospective candidates and their supporting casts. What is most important are the *historical lines of force* to which they are likely to be responding early or late during this decade. Especially in a period of divided government, there is need to recognize that what so tentatively prevails now will probably be under serious challenge as the seventies move along. The insurgency is not confined to one particular party or part of the political spectrum; it is stirring throughout this society. If the older America has more votes, money, experience, and guns at present, the new elements have still-unfathomable energy, growth, imagination, and time on their side.

The objective of this discussion is not prediction but an exploration of the more important possibilities, probabilities, and near-certainties in the shifting arrangements of power in the United States. The concern is with not just more or less of what already exists, but also what could well be different over the course of the seventies. The tendency when looking ahead is to slip off into the more bizarre and volatile fringes, quite without regard to their proportional role or probable historical effect. But the interest here is primarily in the mainstream as it is developing in its own diverse and often turbulent ways. Besides the many galvanizing agents of change at present there are also, of course, a number of constants, as what Robert Heilbroner has called "the inertia of history" and "the heritage of the human condition." The concern of this inquiry, however, is with "the growing edge of the present."

Unforeseen events and individual personalities will inevitably exert a great and often decisive effect on the coming politics. But even they operate in a setting of already-evolving groups, attitudes, values, interests, institutions, and other influences, simultaneously responding to and reshaping them. And most public figures and developments in the day-to-day news are actually only out-croppings of more fundamental forces at work. It is possible that within the decade the country will experience revolution or, more conceivable of late, jarring repression. It is probable, however, that we shall fight out our differences, fears, and hopes within the broad and expanding frame of reference of the country's develop-ment to date.

A difficulty with much of the recent discussion and practice of politics is that the more dramatic developments surface on tele-vision and tend to be assimilated into the thinking of the articulate and active elements long before they seep down into the main part of American society. They lose much of their freshness and become clichés even before they are absorbed and have effect in the main base. This has led to premature predictions of success by those most interested in change and to what in the end is an equally premature discounting the same unfolding by politicians and writers resistant to much alteration.

Another difficulty results from the considerably different ways that even the word *politics* is currently being used. The older group tends to separate political factors from social, economic, cultural, and other considerations. For the new group just about everything is politicized, whether admitted or not. What is in issue is not just a word but different ways of seeing the same things, especially in their relationships with each other. Any contemporary look at politics must consequently take into account the fact that the arena itself is becoming larger and more diverse than ever be-fore. The older group generally wants to talk about elections and the electorate, the President and the Congress, governors and state legislatures, contributions and campaigns, and at times administra-tive and related governmental matters. Many younger people are preoccupied with culture, morality, communications theory, flux, and the interior individual as they seek to get at what happens. This is enlarging, surrounding, predetermining, diffusing much of the battle area. That may not be the most direct way to win an immediate election, but it is a soaring strategy for prevailing over the course of a decade or a generation.

Looking beyond the latest crisis and present rash of problems poses a task more complicated and demanding than the electorate has generally been willing to face. Even more, it raises dilemmas for the country's public leaders considerably beyond their usual ways of thinking and operating. The age-old political practice of promising early and dramatic results—really the merchandizing of almost instant history—becomes increasingly risky as well as irresponsible as most of the problems and society itself become more massive, intricate, and locked into place by a rapidly lengthening technological, educational, and other lead-time. At the same time instant mass-death in a nuclear exchange has become an ever-present possibility, just about everything else of significance takes longer and longer to get done. The prospect is not good, however, for politicians unwilling to pledge and produce fairly quick and visible results. A persisting challenge will be how to develop short-term solutions within a longer-range strategy—in effect, how to phase-in the future with both rational validity and political promptness. That may rarely be an easy exercise. But it cannot be put off if the democratic process, or simply human choice, is to cope with the developing situation.

Probably never before has there been a greater need to undertake quite deliberately what a recent study of contemporary religious stirrings called "the search for a usable future." The past has always worked its will well ahead, and it will continue to do so. But never has the future been so fundamentally affected by so many current developments. Beneath the much-touted recent political reaction and widespread public apathy, there is also a considerable regeneration of American society struggling to break through. Some is on the left, some on the right, and much in the middle, even in the major parties. The early practical political prospect may be between a little more or less than what the coun-

try has had in the 1960s and at the outset of the 1970s. But deeper
and different developments are also forming. As a broad array of
quite specific new forces approaches, we should be trying to perceive, sort out, affect, and relate to what may still be a few or
more years away.

CHAPTER 1

The Ordeal of the Old Order

Each age is a dream that is dying,
Or one that is coming to birth.
—ARTHUR O'SHAUGHNESSY

Before the many forces ascendant in American society are examined, perspective on the public environment into which those forces are intruding is needed. The widespread social and political turmoil of the last half-dozen years and more has generally been considered in terms of the Vietnam war, the unrest of the young, black militancy and the responding backlash, a breakdown in law and order, an erratic economy, and dissatisfaction with much of the leadership by both major political parties. But more fundamental historical processes are at work. Amid the spreading disquiet, old attitudes, assumptions, and arrangements have been widely clung to with greater and greater rigidity and at the same time found to be less and less reassuring—until at last, though still holding onto the White House, Congress, and other key bastions through the traditional two-party system, they are becoming more remembered than real, more vestigial of what is going than seminal for what is coming.

The two sculpting experiences of our national life and politics during the last half-century have been the Great Depression and World War II. The consequences of those events, their conditioning effect, still underlie many of the personal as well as public premises of the long-prevailing Democrats and the more recently empowered Republicans—and, most important, of tens of millions of voters. Lyndon Johnson, as one fairly recent example, came into politics as a young man in the 1930s. Richard Nixon, like Johnson the son of an economically failed father, came of age in the 1930s and into politics in the forties. What they and their contemporaries felt and did under the pressure of those decades crystalized into the social and political viewpoints and institutions which today's restive forces are coming up against and which now generally resist change.

Yet how vastly different American society has become compared to the decade of the Depression! Then well over a third of the work force at one time or another found itself without a job for a considerable period; almost all of the other breadwinners had their paychecks severely slashed and feared that they, too, could suddenly be without any means of support. By 1932, men's wages in Pennsylvania, for instance, had plummeted to less than 8 cents an hour for general contracting work, 6 cents for brick and tile work, and 5 cents in sawmills. Store clerks in Boston, Chicago, and Los Angeles worked for a nickel an hour. "I've wrote back that we're well and such as that," commented one individual cast adrift at the time, "but I never wrote that we live in a tent."

Large-scale unemployment made for a dog-eat-dog economy. Thus, at one factory, several dozen men showed up to answer a one-job want ad. The supervisor looked over the group, singled out one man and said he would pay him $15 a week. Another applicant called out that he would do the work for $10 a week and got the job. Summing up the impact of the Depression from the close vantage point of 1937, Robert and Helen Lynd wrote in their classic study of "Middletown" that they found a streak of meanness and suspicion in people not present when the same individuals had been interviewed before the crash. "The experience," the Lynds noted, "has been more nearly universal than any prolonged recent emotional experience in the city's history; it has approached in its elemental shock the primary experience of birth and death."

Even without the economic collapse, the country was only modestly developed compared to now. Then over one out of every three housing units in the United States lacked flush toilets. Now fewer than one in twenty do. Then over half of all households cooked on wood, coal, or oil stoves. Now fewer than one in twenty do. According to the 1970 census, as many families now have TV sets as toilets. And one in three families have two or more TV sets, or color television. Now almost as many families have refrigerators, washing machines, vacuum cleaners, radios and electric irons as modern cooking ranges. Almost endless similar contrasts could be drawn. It can be argued that such comparisons are too materialistic. But so, largely, were the driving ambitions, public attitudes, and politics which came out of that time.

Compared to the Depression, World War II was almost shallow and benign in its immediate effect. It generally firmed up the political ties and trends formed during the thirties. The outbreak of hostilities in Europe in 1939 and Roosevelt's decision to make America "the arsenal of democracy" quickly brought to a close a decade of hard times. The war boom liberated millions of families from unemployment and privation and millions of others from penny-pinching and the pall of a stalled economy. Almost 300,000 U.S. soldiers were killed, but that slaughter touched only a small fraction of the people and the accompanying prosperity benefited practically everyone.

The conflict itself was looked on as "a war of liberation"—a motivating phrase which nationalists and Communists of the economically less developed world have since appropriated as their own. American life resurged in the global struggle with a sense of personal usefulness, individual pride, and extra cash. For the vast numbers who had been "imprisoned by depression and poverty," Caroline Bird noted, "the war meant getting out of the house, out of town, out where the action is. They were needed, and the work was not made up to keep them occupied." In his case study *Democracy in Jonesville* in the last half of the 1940s, W. Lloyd Warner concluded: "Verbally and superficially they disapproved of war, but this is only partly revealed in their inner feelings. In simple terms, most of them had more fun in the second World War, just as they did in the first, than they had at any other period of their lives."

For contemporary purposes, however, the war is most relevant for its grim afterbirth: the cold-war power struggle between the principal victors; a national taste for and dependence on a "defense"-sustained prosperity to handle the serious economic flaws which provoked the Depression and have been unevenly staved off but never really solved since then; a technological emphasis which shot up even more sharply than the birth rate of that time; a mounting reliance on force, on violence, as the nation's main leverage both on the rest of the world and on ourselves; and, finally, the nuclear age. Those developments reinforced the broad social and political interests and institutions which had coalesced in the Depression and World War II; and the principal deployments of power which came out of those experiences have dominated most of the public battlefield ever since.

Increasingly, however, that order of things has caused a sense of oppression among large numbers of people, especially many of the young. Equally important, the arrangements and people who were conditioned to them are now generally well along in their own life cycle. The aging of the old political order is most readily seen in the evolution over the years of the great majority coalition forged in the 1930s in the Democratic party. This coalition has been the main organizing factor in the country's public life during the last four decades. As reflected in the Presidential election returns, which are the principal explicit decision American society makes, the strength of the coalition dropped very perceptibly from the high point reached in the mid-thirties to the bare but tenacious holding-on by Harry Truman in 1948. The falloff was decisive after Truman. John F. Kennedy's narrow election in 1960 and the lopsided but maverick and quickly expended Johnson victory in '64 indicated the wobbling persistence of the Democratic coalition.

But the era that congealed with Franklin Roosevelt has become so erratic that any claimed continuum is contrived.

More fundamentally, both parties have long been losing their once-distinctive profiles. The Eisenhower years in particular reduced the substantive differences by largely continuing intact the programs of the New Deal and the Fair Deal. Kennedy started a new delineation for the Democrats with a fresh public style, a developing critique of the domestic society, and—just six months before his assassination—a more conciliatory approach to the world, in his future-charting American University address, which prepared the way for the Partial Nuclear Test Ban Treaty and a start toward a downturn in the arms race. Lyndon Johnson made a reflexive return to the earlier period with his idealization of Roosevelt, Texas Populism, and a remarkable legislative record modeled on the New Deal during his first several years in the White House. But his and, to a lesser extent, J.F.K.'s attempted "consensus politics" were largely an extension of the effort made in the 1950s by Eisenhower to blur party and ideological lines. The blurring contrasts with F.D.R.'s and Truman's frequent attempts to sharpen the differences in fairly fundamental ways. The change in emphasis is one of the more revealing political developments of the last twenty years. In effect, the strategy of the minority party to overcome its built-in disadvantage was adopted in considerable part by the one-time majority party.

The really critical difference, however, between the epoch-creating efforts of Roosevelt and the prevailing politics during the last half of the 1960s and the threshold period of the seventies, under both the Democrats and Republicans, lies in the approach taken to the fundamental problem of social change itself. Roosevelt's genius was in welding together and giving direction to the new and powerful economic and social forces which were then stirring. He was elected on an orthodox platform but quickly realized that conventional methods could neither end the Depression nor hold off the social stresses that were building up. To cope with the situation, he helped bring a substantially larger proportion of the working class and even some of the poor into the electorate; he also institutionalized and expanded the public role of organized labor and other groups. In effect, he politicized major new forces within the over-all balance of power and thus changed the main relationships there. He was unable to relieve the basic economic ills until World War II came along, and defense work did that for him. But by then he had already vented the more urgent pressures for change and kept the nation from either rigidifying or flying apart. Equally important, he used the opportunity to motivate most of society's restive elements on behalf of themselves and the larger society as well.

In contrast, the recent national leadership in both political parties has largely sought to contain another time of vast restlessness and change within already well-dug channels. Lyndon Johnson was seeking to broaden and deepen those channels to some extent until the Vietnam war pre-empted most of his and the country's attention and priorities. Nixon's welfare proposal constitutes another such initiative with modest possibilities. But neither the Democrats nor the Republicans have yet either proposed or pragmatically worked out an effective strategy to provide a significantly larger public role and fresh institutional arrangements for the social groups which are stirring today. Instead, those groups have simply been told again and again to work within the system. At the same time, with a few limited exceptions, like eighteen-year-olds voting, the system itself has refused to open up more, as it did with Roosevelt.

A tentative working insight into the nation's present politics is suggested by the fact that, at least in the approach taken to the underlying problem of social change, the period since the mid-sixties is comparable in a sense to the Hoover years. Historical analogies can be only approximate, and there are profound differences, of course, between the two times. But a brief look at that earlier passage can perhaps help suggest some of the underlying posturing and clashes of our own period from a more detached perspective. Then as now, debate and change abounded, and the older and established groups sought to rally against perverse developments of a very fundamental nature. The deepening troubles were endlessly attacked with sturdy premises out of the past, but rarely with fresh ideas or a basic re-examination of the existing ways and relationships. Then the underlying pressure came primarily from contending economic classes. Now it is being exerted by a huge generation of young people, a racial underclass, an affluent and liberating upper-middle-class element, and a lower-middle class insecure amid all that is altering.

Then as now, the traditional gods and customs of the Republic were invoked again and again against anarchy, mob rule, and much that was merely new and different. At the same time, a sharply heightened dislike, then disbelief, of politics and politicians, gathered, developing into a deep-seated "sense of estrangement," as Arthur Schlesinger, Jr., some years ago described the mood of that time. For large numbers of Americans the so-called power structure, the roster of influential Americans, seemed more remote than ever.

Just as the national leadership of both major political parties has done during the last half-decade, Hoover called over and over for confidence, unity, stability, and the will to persevere. At the outset of his Presidency, he appointed a distinguished panel to advise him on the health of the economy, and it counseled against any structural change. If that study were changed to cover the health of today's over-all society, the same conclusion could be found uncritically recited in scores of government reports in recent years, though the alienated forces at hand make the prescription of no institutional improvements even more questionable now than then.

Almost four years and a whole economic debacle after Hoover received that task-force study, he still held to it. Influential publishers like Mark Sullivan backed him up; in 1932 Sullivan was insisting "Nobody doubts the Depression is ended." In its election-eve issue that year, *Time* magazine declared: "After many a false alarm, business seems in the act of struggling to its feet." The president of the National Association of Manufacturers proclaimed that autumn: "The overshadowing problem of all problems is crime, which bestrides our nation like a colossus."

Undeniably sincere and concerned over the country's plight, Hoover persisted with the basic policies and principles of an earlier time despite their demonstrated inadequacy to deal with the dilemma. Even with hunger lines across the nation, he long refused to make federal funds available to help feed the unemployed, claiming handouts would only destroy people's moral fiber. He watched unmoved while the Federal Reserve raised interest rates, though the action made it more difficult for hard-pressed U.S. banks to get funds from the Federal Reserve System for domestic needs. But when a banking crisis then developed in Michigan, he had the chief of the Secret Service send over three hundred men to watch for anyone spreading "unfounded rumors" about banks in the area.

A firm supporter of high tariffs, Hoover denounced reciprocal trade agreements proposed to help stimulate international commerce; he called them "a violation of American principles." And he came to regard much of the criticism against himself in a similar light. His private secretary, Theodore Joslin, later wrote that Hoover considered the attacks against him and what he stood for "as unpatriotic. He felt himself fighting, not just for the established order, but for the survival of American institutions."

In a speech in 1932 Hoover observed "Thank God we still have a government in Washington that knows how to deal with the mob." When the "bonus army" of World War I veterans came to the nation's capital that year, Hoover refused to see them and finally had them forcibly ousted with only an hour's notice, harried—like the blacks and young white protesters recently—by tear gas. Hoover insisted the "invasion" of Washington was made up mostly of hoodlums and Communists, plus only a scattering of veterans. He stuck to that claim even after an investigation by the Veterans Bureau was unable to substantiate it. Those earlier demonstrators were actually so rightist—their *B.E.F. News* praised Mussolini and Hitler—that some Communists who sought to infiltrate the group had to appeal to the District of Columbia's police commissioner for protection. Meantime, out around the country, many people who read in the newspapers about the march concluded it was bent on igniting a revolution.

In many large cities, "unemployed councils" sprang up, and hunger marches were staged. In Detroit the unemployed banded together so effectively that over a hundred policemen had to be called out to evict a single Polish family. Farmers, too, did not hesitate to take matters into their own hands. In a number of rural areas, sheriffs were driven away from mortage sales with shotguns. Lawyers, bank representatives, and local law-enforcement officials were frightened off from other foreclosures with threats of being strung up. After a trip through the Midwest, "Mother" Bloor, one of the leading Communist agitators of that time, said, "I never saw anything like the militancy of those farmers."

Students sympathetic to the working class and against "the exploiting capitalists" organized the American Student Union to encourage strikes against obsolete university policies. A group of New York ministers qualified for membership in the AFL by forming the Ministers Union of America, Local 1. Groups of college girls tried to relate to the times in an early, do-it-yourself version of VISTA by working among the poor during summer vacations. But a frequent response to them is indicated by the comment of a coal miner to an Eastern coed who went to a poverty-stricken Appalachian mining community: "They don't hate you. They hate what you stand for—and you do stand for it, and you can't get away from it." In summing up the attitude of many young people, Eric Sevareid, then a young man out of the University of Minnesota, sounded very much like Mario Savio at Berkeley three decades later: "It was all a mess. We refused to accept it as inevitable, untouchable. Men were *not*, regardless of all the determinists, the helpless victims of uncontrollable forces. . . . Men could take hold of the system and direct it."

Many confrontations of that time had a quite contemporary ring. In one of the most famous, nearly three thousand marchers took out from Detroit on a freezing, windy day to parade several miles to the Ford plant in Dearborn. They went to demand that

Henry Ford take back some of the many men who had been laid off. Ford had previously moved his plant outside Detroit, partly to avoid paying taxes toward the $25 million a year the city was spending on those in need. The march was organized by the United Auto Workers and the Unemployed Council of Detroit, both with some Communist sponsors at the time. The group moved peacefully through Detroit, where a permit had been obtained and a police escort was provided. But no permit was carried for Dearborn, and the marchers were confronted by waiting police as soon as the city line was reached. The demonstrators were promptly challenged, then tear gas was used. Wind quickly blew the gas away, but the incensed marchers stoned the police. The police chief was knocked out; his men were badly mauled, but they held their fire as instructed. At that point, however, Ford's head of security, Harry Bennett, rushed up in a car and insisted on getting out of it despite police objections. He was immediately assaulted by the marchers with bricks and stones. The police opened fire in return. The crowd broke and ran.

Each side later claimed the other had shot first. But no guns were found on the marchers, and independent accounts subsequently agreed the police had fired point-blank into the crowd. Four demonstrators died, fifty were hospitalized; fifty more who were wounded refused to go to the hospital in order to avoid being interrogated. All of the wounded had been shot in the back, side, or legs except a press photographer whose camera had been shot out of his hands. The police who received medical attention had suffered blows only from sticks and stones or bricks.

Ford spokesmen and the Detroit *Free Press* blamed Communists for inciting the trouble. The Detroit *News* placed the responsibility with the marchers for failing to get a permit from Dearborn. City officials talked of charging the protest leaders with criminal syndicalism or murder of the demonstrators who had been shot by the police and died—if a legal way could be found to do that. The U.S. Immigration Service conducted raids in the area to try to find any deportable aliens. The American Civil Liberties Union entered

the picture and placed the "responsibility for the tragedy...
squarely upon the shoulders of Henry Ford." It threatened to sue
him, defend anyone indicted for speech alone, and contest the
constitutionality of a 1931 Michigan statute allowing the police to
determine that an assembly was unlawful and escape liability for
the death of anybody killed while they were breaking it up. A
grand jury investigation eventually put the blame on the Dearborn
police but cleared Ford. The march aroused so much public sympathy that the Communists went out of their way to get as much
of the blame as possible.

In the early stages of the great national crisis of that time, the
higher ranks of organized labor were as slow to respond as they
have been in this period of stress. The editorials of AFL President
William Green in the *American Federationist* barely conceded the
presence of mass unemployment before the middle of 1930 He
also joined with Hoover and a unanimous business community in
resisting a dole, charging it would turn a man into "a ward of the
state." At labor's national convention in 1931, Green attacked
those who "are exploiting the workers" but successfully fought
against the endorsement of compulsory unemployment insurance
urged by Teamster representative Dan Tobin and other spokesmen
from the floor. Even as late as 1932, the chief lobbyist of the AFL
told a Senate committee: "The leaders of our organization have
been preaching patience."

One of the nation's leading economists, the University of Chicago's Paul Douglas (an all-out Democratic party regular in his
older years), organized a League for Independent Political Action
in 1929 and heralded it as the nub of a new radicalism. In 1932 the
group held a convention in Cleveland and endorsed for President
Socialist Norman Thomas, whose main appeal, like that of Senator
Eugene McCarthy many years later, was to the educated middle
class, not the working masses. In response, John Dos Passos wryly
commented against the grim backdrop of the Depression, "I should
think that becoming a socialist right now would have just the same
effect as drinking a bottle of near beer." Texas Senator Tom Con-

nally declared that year: "If it was constitutional to spend $40 billion in a war, isn't it just as constitutional to spend a little money to relieve the hunger and misery of our citizens?"

The present circumstances are more complex and subtle than was that earlier period. But already the unsettlement has lasted longer, though generally been felt less hard than in Hoover's time. America should now be far more capable of thoughtfully meeting a national testing of turmoil and change than was the poorer, less educated, more constrained society of the Depression. Yet there is strong sentiment of late to hold to ways of thinking and governing rooted almost entirely in the last four decades, or to turn still further back to many of the WASPish views and values of a still earlier time. Certainly neither major party, nor each of us personally, is completely free of such backward-clinging.

History, however, is now hardly about to turn back or even mark time, no matter how much that might be wished or willed. As signaled by the moonwalks in a technological way and by the urban and campus ferment in a social sense, this society is already taking off on still another great surge matched only a few times in the past, and possibly never before. To attempt to hold back politically can only intensify the potential strains and danger. At a minimum, much of the country's fresh, still-forming vitality and vision could be lost or lastingly damaged in such a repression. And when the newer dynamics finally break through, as they almost surely will in one form or another if only with the passing of time, they could be even more alienated in their ultimate effect. The need now is for a public transition such as that from Hoover to Roosevelt—in short, the crossing of a great historical threshold. But that involves both an individual initiative in attitudes and the heart and institutional implosions which let in fresh air and bring about some at least somewhat-changed relationships.

Looking at the few really basic watersheds in U.S. political history, Samuel Lubell noted twenty years ago in *The Future of American Politics* that the first requisite for the country to move from one fundamental era to another is a loosening of the old ties.

That is almost always a fairly long and finally painful process. But for one epoch to end and another to open there must also be vast technological, social, or other changes in our national life, the coming of a new generation not bound to the earlier loyalties and eventually a great, crystallizing happening or series of happenings. Those last three requirements, however, are not enough by themselves. For the country has experienced massive change, seen generations come and go, and been wracked by staggering events, all without an underlying political upheaval necesarily taking place. First, there has always had to be the ordeal of the old order—the phase in which we are now caught up. But "once the old ties had weakened sufficiently," Lubell observed, "the second stage of lasting change emerged fairly quickly."

How to reconcile the two periods overlapping in the years immediately ahead—a resurgent past and an insurgent future—presents a demanding and perhaps decisive test for the country's political system and particularly those who would claim to lead it. It will not be enough for our principal public men to equivocate, wait, and compound an historical impasse—mostly running hard in place and issuing statements, even sentences which ride off in a number of different directions at the same time. The country considers its political figures in many ways: what they are like personally; what their more recent economic, social, and foreign policy views are; and much more. But there is also need, increasingly, to scrutinize them—and ourselves, too—for an ability to help open up the future.

Thus, when a particular individual discusses pressing issues, is he really trying to get his audience to believe that he will somehow transport it back to an earlier, easier time? Or is he preoccupied mostly with the fleeting present and why so little can really be done now? Or does he also eventually get around to the likely conditions and hard decisions for the years ahead?

Which policies and leaders most energize the nation's young people and other restive Americans, and get the most out of them—for themselves and the entire society?

• Most difficult of all, what will be the more likely consequences of what we are now doing, or not doing, five or ten years hence? And how can we each best affect that?

There is a constant dying and creating of futures, the French philosopher Bertrand de Jouvenal has written. We need to keep reaching out to try to influence the alternative futures available to us much earlier than we have been doing. But, of course, the population explosion, environmental pollution, arrival of the nuclear age, and so many other problems that have developed during the last third of a century should have already made that quite clear.

CHAPTER 2

The New Voters and the Numbers Game

Of all the new input into American politics, the liveliest and largest is the unprecedented wave of young people that barely started entering the electorate near the end of the 1960s but will be rapidly expanding its share of political power throughout the seventies. This decade will witness the political arrival of by far the biggest population wave in U.S. history. The sudden baby boom which followed World War II is now coming of age and will soon be moving massively into the electorate. Richard Scammon has emphasized that the age of the average voter will drop only a little in the mid-forties age range as a result of the younger influx in the next few years. But the psychological momentum of various groups as they expand or contract in their social effect, and the psychological age of the over-all society, often overshadow the numbers involved.

Politicians and historians long were fascinated by, at times almost preoccupied with, the succeeding waves of immigrants who crowded to this country. For decade upon decade the precinct captains of Tammany and the ward chiefs of Boston, Philadelphia, Chicago, and the other principal cities watched and worked with the newcomers with anxious care, quickly learning the customs, language, and needs of each new group. The politicians of the 1970s will have to become no less conversant with the customs, language, and needs of the egocentric if not ethnic group of fresh arrivals on the political scene. Harvard historian Oscar Handlin, a leading authority on the great immigrations of the American past, has commented: "Once I thought to write a history of the immigrants in America. Then I discovered that the immigrants *were* America's history." From today's vantage point, the new generation *is* America's future.

In 1964 just over 10.5 million young people became eligible to vote in their first Presidential election, a number reached by slow climb over the course of more than a century. In 1968 the number of first-timers abruptly jumped to just over 12 million. It will increase to over 25 million in 1972, including over 10 million eighteen-, nineteen-, and twenty-year-olds, eligible to vote for the first time in federal elections, and soon then in more and more state and local elections, plus a natural growth of roughly 2 million in those turning twenty-one since 1968. Over another 16 million first-time voters will become eligible between 1972 and 1976 and another 18 million between then and 1980.

In addition, the impact of all these young people will be heightened by the fact that, from one Presidential election to the next, roughly 5 million Americans of voting age die—and the overwhelming majority are older people. Together, the arrivals and departures between 1968 and 1980 will result in a change of roughly one out of every three people in the eligible electorate.

It should be remembered that this country's biggest baby boom in many decades opened in 1947 following close on the return home of the veterans from World War II. A million more babies were born in 1947 than 1946—that was an increase of over a third within one year. Even more remarkably, the birth date then remained high for almost a decade. Babies born in 1947 did not turn twenty-one until 1968, and they constituted only a small tip of the coming political mass.

Another way to look at the changing age mix with which the politicians will have to be working is that the age group thirty-five and older is increasing between 1970 and 1980 by about 6 million, while the age group which is below that and will be able to vote is increasing by about 22 million. Still another way to try to get perspective on the potential is to state that the sector of eligible voters under thirty-five when John F. Kennedy was elected in 1960 was just under 30 percent. In 1970, it was still just barely over 30 percent. But with the eighteen-year-old vote, the eligible group under thirty-five jumps to almost 35 percent in '72 and 38 percent by 1980.

The impact of the coming group of eligible voters will be greatly enhanced by the fact it follows the numerically thin population group born between World War I and World War II. First, those who are now senior citizens gained a larger share of the electorate at the expense of that wave. Now the younger group will do that. The broad middle group's share of eligible voters fell from not quite 56 percent in 1960 to 53 percent in 1970. It will be about 50 percent in 1972 and about 47 percent in 1980.

The country's senior citizens' increasing political leverage during the last third of a century provides an indication of the potential of the post-World War II baby crop. Ever since the 1930s, U.S. politics and government have been giving steadily mounting attention to the upper end of the age spectrum—to social security, medicare, special tax advantages for the aged, nursing homes, and a widening variety of benefits at both the federal and state levels. Much of the original impetus was the Depression-born objective of getting older people out of scarce jobs and into retirement. After that need had faded, the continuing concern was rationalized largely in terms of the welfare philosophy of the New Deal and as a matter of a basic right. But down at the political bedrock, politicians also kept their eye on the burgeoning growth in the number of senior citizens.

That sector's share of the adult populace climbed from 8 percent in 1930 (close to its share of all adults since before the turn of the century) to 15 percent in 1960, when it just about leveled out. The figure reached about 15.5 percent in 1970 and should be near that in 1980. It will probably stay close to that to the end of the century, even with expected improvements in life expectancy. The total number of older people will continue to rise but not their expected share of the population. Any further increase in the political influence of the group will probably have to be generated out of a projected general improvement in its economic status.

The upsurge since 1930 in the portion of the over-all populace occupied by senior citizens, it is worth noting, has been due in large part to the aging of the young adults who made up most of the huge wave of immigrants coming to the U.S. between the turn of the century and World War I. Thus, while less than a tenth of the total native population is now over sixty-five, well over a third of our foreign-born populace has passed that age. As those immigrants die off, they are closing out one of the most colorful chapters in the nation's history, and the elderly boom, as well as the base of the ethnic vote, is tapering off.

The increased share of the eligible electorate gained by the eighteen- to thirty-four-year-old group during the 1970s alone will be about as large as the additional slice attained by senior citizens during the last third of a century. If the long, slow expansion of the older group contributed to the pressure for the development of the social security system and other benefits for the aged, then the sudden growth of the younger voting group in the seventies should shake loose a whole cornucopia of public "incentives" and "opportunities" for the approaching generation. It may be argued that the needs of the aged were the real imperative for the development of new programs for senior citizens in recent decades, but politicians have never been reticent about developing new rationalizations for what will attract voters. The needs of the young in their family-forming years, and the need of the nation to develop its newer human resources to the fullest provide the makings for a whole pantry of fresh political appeals—educational, economic, cultural, medical, and recreational—as the leverage of the younger voters increases. The coming period is "the era of the young marrieds," as the Director of the Census Bureau expressed it in 1970. He pointed out that in the ensuing fifteen years the number of people in their twenties, thirties, and early forties will increase by 28 million, while the number between forty-five and sixty-five will barely change.

The main limitation on the early political power of the coming generation of voters is simply the fact that a smaller percentage of the eligible young people has usually bothered to vote, compared to the older age groups. During the 1960s, for example, only about half of those who were between twenty-one and twenty-four and qualified to vote cast ballots in Presidential elections. The turnout was around 66 percent for those twenty-five to thirty-four years old, but even that is still below the 75 percent participation by people thirty-five to sixty-five years old and only equals the turnout of those over sixty-five.

The traditionally lower voting record of those in their early to middle twenties is working to delay for a while the full political impact of the generation now coming of age. But the fact remains that the number of younger voters actually casting ballots will be substantially larger than ever before, and the turnout of the advance group which came of age in the latter sixties and the outset of the present decade will climb sharply with every succeeding election. That prospect, plus the cumulative effect of all those reaching eighteen each year, suggests that the first real impact of this generation could be felt in the 1972 Presidential election; in 1976 they will almost certainly be voting in huge numbers.

It is quite possible that the influence of this younger group will be perceptibly higher somewhat earlier than is suggested by past experience; it could come crashing in as a great political tidal wave despite the widespread recent discounting of it. Voter turnout increases with education, affluence, political awareness, and social influence, and those attributes are all demonstrably higher in the coming generation than in any other new voting group in history. Gallup and other pollsters have found that the group is already at least as interested in becoming politically involved as its elders and in some respects, including campaign work, contributing financially, and entering politics as a career, more so. A *Fortune* poll in 1969 found that over two-thirds of its sample of college students, and almost a third of the noncollege group of the same age, had already worked in a political campaign, taken part in a civil rights march, or otherwise been activist. More important, as such an enormous mass of potential voters accumulates, it will inevitably be appealed to more and more boldly in terms of its own interests and idioms. Franklin Roosevelt brought into the electorate of the 1930s a large number of older urban poor who had never before voted; they began to participate as their special needs and numbers came to be recognized. It can be expected that the political involvement of the young will similarly be sharply raised during the years ahead.

This involvement is one of the major opportunities of the coming period. History turns as much on lost opportunities, of course, as on those which are successfully seized. Yet historians, working after the fact, often write as if they are dealing in the inevitable instead of what actually had been only one of various alternatives. "In retrospect everything seems determined," Henry Kissinger wrote some years ago, "and the more remote an event, the more difficult it is to imagine the consequences of an alternative decision." Politicians, in contrast, are "obsessed not with the inevitability of their decisions, but with the obscurity and multiplicity of their choices" as Henry Kissinger put it. They must seek to sort out the floodtide of people and events before, not after, they rush by. The politics of the seventies offer one of those rare chances to rally a new following, or at least to provoke a different configuration, out of this immense sector of younger voters who are still at an impressionable and responsive stage. If an exciting individual or cause really stirs this generation, it could be activated in numbers that make irrelevant any past indicator of political participation among the young, and it would then become one of the few human waves of historic consequence. If this still unmarshaled mass is allowed to scatter, or a substantial part of it is politically turned off, it will pass by as one of the great lost opportunities in American politics and history.

In the 1920 Presidential election, when women were constitutionally guaranteed the right to vote for the first time (a third of the states already had female suffrage), an even larger wave of new voters came into the electorate, a factor that did not disturb the prevailing political patterns at all. But what has been called the "sex role dependence" of the overwhelming majority of women on their husbands' political attitudes kept them from having the assertive independence already apparent in the coming generation. That feminine dependence, tied as it was to less education, a more rural population, and greater male domination than exists at present, was far greater then than now. Women as a group are still less active politically than men, as reflected in their 10 percent lower turnout to vote during the last ten years. But the low turnout resulted primarily from slight participation by women at the lowest economic levels and in the older age groups. The gap between the sexes is rapidly closing in politics as in other fields, especially among young people.

The full potential of the new generation of voters is perhaps best indicated by the fact that the opening of every major realignment in U.S. political history has been accompanied by the coming of a large new group into the electorate and a fundamental reshaping of the voting populace. Jefferson and the new party which turned the Federalists out in the "revolution of 1800" succeeded in significant part by bringing into the electorate for the first time the "overawed, marginal . . . citizen who had just enough property to vote but who was loath to speak up against his 'betters,'" historian Thomas Bailey noted. Jacksonian democracy came to power with the massive shift of population westward and Old Hickory's mobilization of the rough-hewn settlers as the decisive balance in relation to the divided Atlantic seaboard states. In 1800 only one out of twenty Americans had migrated west of the Appalachians. By 1828, when Jackson was elected, one in three lived in the trans-mountain settlements.

The advent of the next major era, the long period of Republican dominance that began with Lincoln, was preceded by almost a doubling of the country's population between 1840 and 1860 and further vast migration, particularly into the Midwest. Those developments redistributed the country's populace and provided a huge pool of new voters. "If it is true that the pre-Civil War parties were overwhelmed by their inability to dam back the passions stirred by the slavery controversy," Samuel Lubell wrote, "it is also true that they were unable to channel the flood of new voters." The political polarization which then occurred under the shock of the Civil War, with the new Republican party almost fortuitously in power, imposed partisan attachments on a regional basis still apparent a century later. That is an example of how a political pattern, once crystallized, often persists long after the participants and forces which brought it into being have passed from the scene. The major contours are usually discernible even after the next great upheaval deposits a whole new epoch on top of it.

The impact of the numbers of young people about to move into the U.S. electorate is suggested most clearly of all by a look at the forces which prepared the way for the political chapter that began with Franklin Roosevelt. From Lincoln to F.D.R., the majority of people considered themselves Republicans; the politics of seven decades had to revolve around that pervading fact, including the politics of the only two Democratic Presidents of the period, Cleveland and Wilson. Yet the beginning of the end of the long Republican majority is rooted not just in the highly publicized stock-market crash of 1929 and the economic turmoil which followed but also in population developments much earlier and more fundamental.

Immigration swelled sharply from the 1890s to World War I, with the proportion of foreign-born in the U.S. population reaching an all-time high in the 1910 census. The birth rate of the foreign-born had long exceeded that of the more numerous and politically dominant native, white, Protestant stock. But this last great tide of immigrants finally placed their group in a position to breed to power. By 1910, a majority of the school children in over three dozen large U.S. cities were the sons and daughters of a foreign-born parent. The portion rose to two out of three in New York, Chicago, and a number of other places. Concurrent with the coming to maturity of this large group in the 1920s, six and a half million rural, largely younger Americans with low living standards were drawn to the cities to make up for the foreign sources of cheap labor shut off by World War I and the restrictive national immigration policy which followed. Of those, four and a half million settled around New York, Chicago, Detroit, and Los Angeles.

Even without the Depression, these population changes, Lubell pointed out, "forecast a major political upheaval sometime between 1930 and 1940. . . . Massed as they were in the states commanding the largest electoral vote, their sheer numbers would topple any prevailing political balance." In 1920 the Republicans held a majority of over a million and a half among the registered voters in the country's dozen largest cities, but by 1924 that had dropped to just over a million, then by 1928 to zero. Even while Herbert Hoover was swamping Al Smith for the Presidency that year, the Democratic vote in a number of the more populous cities was climbing. The unskilled, underdog, urban masses were, in effect, overtaking the established Republican forces in key areas well before the economic deluge at the end of the decade. Lubell concluded: "The really revolutionary surge behind the New Deal lay in this coupling of the Depression with the rise of a new generation, which had been malnourished on the congestion of our cities and the abuses of industrialism. Roosevelt did not start this revolt of the city. What he did do was to awaken the climbing urban masses to a consciousness of the power of their number."

Who, if anyone, may be the F.D.R. of the emerging generation and what the great event or events will be which forge it into its eventual political configuration only the years ahead can make clear. Perhaps no one man or development of real significance will break clear; perhaps only hobbled leaders and indecisive events will jostle the new electorate confusedly about. But neither the magnitude of the Depression nor the towering influence of Roosevelt was foreseeable at the outset of the 1930s. There is so much thrust and distinctiveness already apparent in this new generation that it could precipitate major public personalities and developments quite on its own.

The forces science has unleashed in the world and in the human mind will also probably cause within the course of a decade an event or events that galvanize both the new group and at least one or two dominating figures. In this century, the world birth rate, wars and social struggles, strong men and madmen who can shake not just a castle or country but almost simultaneously practically every part of the world, provides the elements for a convulsive epoch. The final political catalyst must be the key individuals who sort out and personalize—*lead* is the word of the egoists—these circumstances. But no one can be the Franklin Roosevelt of the seventies, or what Jefferson and Jackson and Lincoln were to earlier periods, unless he first discerns the historical tides already moving and then, with a sense of their own inner timing, harnesses or at least sales with them.

Both history and statistical studies of voters during the last third of a century suggest that the public outlook of most people tends to take shape by their twenties and is more likely to become rigid than to loosen after that. The 1960s and early seventies are thus a particularly critical period in the public forming of this new generation. That longer-term development needs to be kept in perspective amid all the transient political hoopla which attracts so much press coverage. It must also be remembered that political campaigns, like the daily run of news, have generally been found to crystallize and reinforce public opinion much more than to convert it. Equally important, the size of the group in the over-all electorate whose minds are changed from the beginning to the end of a campaign must be divided among converts going in opposite directions. The relatively small margin by which many elections are decided makes even the net difference in that two-way traffic important. But that is usually secondary to the turnout on election day from within each candidate's own base of strength, particularly that of the largest party. The usually quite narrow play of all those short-term political factors underscores the importance of the first-time voter. For that group will be at its highest strength in over half a century during the decade. First-time voters, in fact, will probably account for well over 10 percent of the electorate in the next Presidential contest.

The political ties of the overwhelming majority of people have been found in the past to be set much more by private conditioning—family, neighborhood, marriage, employment, close associates —than by more remote public developments and campaign charades. But there is now a greater tendency than ever before among young people to declare their independence from the private as well as the public influences which have predetermined social and political attachments in the past. The sharp break today between many parents and young people, for instance, will likely reduce the "politics by inheritance" which has long preset as many as 60 to 75 percent of new voters. The Gallup poll in recent years has found that more young adults in their twenties characterize themselves as independents (40 percent) than as Democrats (30 percent) or Republicans (a little over 20 percent), with the remaining 10 percent declining to indicate from among these three choices. The proportion of independents among college students is even higher. The leverage of the independents is thus at an all-time high. This is now also true in the older age groups, though at a much lower percentage level. American society has increasingly esteemed political independence; and, for good or bad, the new generation is both reflecting that and setting the pace for the future.

The large number of new voters and the high level of independence among them reinforce the probability that a critical passage in the politics of this country is at hand. There are more impressionable, movable votes within reach in both an actual and relative sense than for a number of decades. The main part could go right, left, turn off, swing erratically, divide inconclusively, or become a personal following. But it will almost surely be felt, positively or negatively. A clear-cut coalescing within this large sector even close to that of the New Deal generation could give it a significant measure of political power not only for the 1970s but well beyond. It is only a coincidence that this group will be moving into the electorate just as the New Deal generation's ranks are thinning and its public influence is slackening. The groups on which Lincoln and the long Republican dominance were built disappeared long before that era ended. But this time there *could* be a quite literal passing of the political torch from one cornerstone generation to another.

CHAPTER 3

The Politics of the New Generation

The potential public impact of all the young people coming of age in the 1970s lies not in just their numbers but in the distinctiveness of much about them. "This is not just a new generation," *Time* noted in naming the group a collective "Man of the Year" before it was even twenty-one years old, "but a new kind of generation." Historians are usually obsessed with continuities, but these are not always controlling. Peter Gay, discussing the eighteenth-century French Philosophes in his book *The Enlightenment*, traced how past ideas made a substantial contribution to the education of those committed rationalists but did not determine their selectively built-up belief—finally dogma—that unfettered use of the critical mind would lead man to a better future. In far more fundamental ways, this generation has been built of revolutionary technologies and rapidly changing conditions in their immediate world.

These young people know the Depression, World War II, and most of the cold war only as episodes in history textbooks. They have been shaped instead by the greatest material outpouring for almost an entire society that the world has ever seen, capped in the 1960s by the longest-sustained prosperity this country has yet had. And so the conditioning and the expectations they bring into the electorate are as different from the Depression-rooted attitudes and insecurities as the ICBM is from the Model T.

Compared to any past generation, a fairly small portion of this group had to do menial labor for long hours in the early and middle years of adolescence. The majority will become more pocketbook-minded as they move further into their working and family-rearing years. But in contrast to earlier generations, this one is significantly less economic and more social—with the accent on social conscience for some and social status for others. Over-all, they have primarily a "doing and using" rather than "working and saving" outlook.

A really precipitous downturn in the national economy could sharply temper the easy economic attitudes of many of these young people. This country has never been stoic about panics and depressions in the past, and the new group could react in an ugly way to a long and severe recession or an effort to curtail its living standards for other priorities. The young people of the booming 1920s had to face up to the economic debacle of the 1930s and did so with considerable hardiness. But the affluence of this last decade has been far greater, longer, broader-based, and more built into people than was the affluence of the 1920s. Many members of the new generation feel that in some way they have a "right" to and a "guarantee" of good times. That outlook may be faulted by economic conservatives, but it is a political fact of life which politicians may disregard at their peril.

"The shagginess and chosen poverty of student communities have nuances that may be tremendously important to the future," Paul Goodman has commented. "We must remember that these are the young of the affluent society, used to a high standard of living and confident that if and when they want, they can fit in and make good money. Having suffered little pressure of insecurity, they have little need to climb, just as, coming from respectable homes, they feel no disgrace about sitting a few nights in jail. By confidence they are aristocrats—en masse." There is little evidence that many will be rejecting either "affluence" or "things" in the coming years. But this group has already shown a considerable selectiveness amid its shagginess. The young from working-class and poorer families are often more career-determined, more organization-adjusted than the pace-setters of the student communities. But the same liberating tendencies are clearly discernible there, too, even if less dramatically. What is happening beneath the beards and beads and all the other garb is a rearranging of preferences and purposes—and that still has to be sorted out in the American economy, value structure, and political system.

Almost as important as the economic conditioning is the fact that these young people are, quite precisely, the first baby crop to be nurtured by television. TV went public just as the first of them arrived on the scene. In 1946 the U.S. had fewer than 17,000 sets; five years later it had well over 10 million. By the early 1960s, when this group was in adolescence, the nation had over 45 million sets. That medium, especially since it was new and novel, more often than not played the role for this generation formerly filled by grandmothers, fairy tales, and most of the rest of what occupied children once upon a time. Television brought them face to face with "live" gunplay and monsters—and in heavy doses—at a very early stage of their development. Not long afterward it tuned them in on an adult society both bewildering and exciting, brutal and indulgent, especially compared to school lessons and parental pieties. Television gave these young people a precocity and unusually complex perception.

And it affected not just the *content* of their thought but *how* they think as well. As Marshall McLuhan and others have written, a child before a TV set is conditioned differently from a child undergoing the straight-line, tightly ordered, set mental discipline of the printed page. Television watching is not a passive experience; the viewer unconsciously has to make instant sense out of the flickering two-dimensional, moving mosaic. And in doing that, especially if still young and impressionable, he very soon acquires an appetite for involvement in depth. TV plays heavily upon the senses and evokes instant awareness. The new generation cannot really be understood, much less communicated with, without taking into account the interior "participation" and nonverbal personal levels encouraged by television.

Still another important conditioning experience for this group has been its greatly accelerated education. The first of these young people were barely halfway through grammar school and the rest of them not yet even there when the Soviet launching of Sputnik I in 1957 suddenly triggered an unprecedented speedup and enrichment of almost the entire educational system in the United States. One result is summed up in these comments of a New England educator: "I recently looked over my final exams of some years ago. If I gave those tests today, the students would laugh at them—they would be so easy. On the other hand, if I had given today's tests then, the students probably wouldn't even have tried them—they would have been so hard."

Ironically, the intensified education of this group was largely a response to America's cold-war alarm over the Soviets being first to put a man into space; yet most of the generation is the least aroused over communism of any major sector of the U.S. populace since at least the early 1940s. Opinion surveys indicate that more and more young people are simply dismissing talk about a Communist threat as irrelevant. In that they are products not of the Cold War but of the thaw which occurred during their later schooling. To the extent that anticommunism is a propellant or rationalization for American action abroad, much of the new generation, especially its more educated elements, merely turns off. New premises will probably have to be constructed if the brighter and more concerned of this group are really to be stirred in support of any extensive U.S. concern with the world over the longer course ahead.

The overwhelming majority of the eligible new voters have been provided not only a greatly accelerated and enriched education but also more years of it than any previous group. The new generation on which the New Deal built had the equivalent of an eighth-grade education; the group coming to maturity at the end of the sixties and in the early seventies will have received the equivalent of a little more than a high school education. The consequence is that while a general public appeal in the 1930s had to be aimed primarily at a person who had not gone further than grammar school, politicians in the period ahead will have to contend with an individual with at least a high school diploma—a vast difference in terms of organized instruction about history, government, other parts of the world, abstract mathematical and other thinking processes, and many other matters. Yet even those extra years of schooling do not take into account today's substantially higher educational standards, the impact of the mass media, and the greater sophistication of present-day society. For the nation, the economic, social, and political implications of those advances can be calculated only in terms of light years.

A closer look is needed, however, to see the full effect of the rising educational achievement as it bears on the younger, middle, and older groups of voters. The heavy majority of senior citizens now voting have had a grammar school education. The clear majority of the rest of the voters have had a high school education. But a majority of the new voters of this decade will have had at least some education beyond high school.

What is happening at the upper level of the educational range, in fact, may be particularly relevant since this group is usually the most influential. Barely over 10 percent of the high school graduates of the 1930s went on to college. By 1950 over 20 percent were attending at that level at least for a while. In the 1970s, well over half will go on for some college education. The actual number of university students jumped from less than three million to eight million during the last ten years alone, and almost half of all college freshmen now hope to continue their education beyond a four-year degree. Between the mid-1960s and the mid-1970s, more master's and doctor's degrees will have been awarded than in the preceding half-century.

In the great college boom under way, more young people than ever before are pushing beyond the educational level and thus likely beyond the economic and social potential of their parents. The Census Bureau has reported that almost a third of the students now getting a higher education come from families whose head never completed high school. The warning cry a century ago was "Go West, young man." Now it is "Go to college." Notwithstanding the widespread resentment against campus unrest, the college diploma is increasingly seen as the great equalizer and key to opportunity, just as "free soil" was for the homesteaders of the nineteenth century and Ellis Island for the immigrants. And it is worth underscoring that over two-thirds of all the young people who are currently obtaining a higher education are working to meet a part of their costs, and a fourth of them are entirely self-supporting.

David Riesman and Christopher Jencks have suggested that the central political question in the academic revolution taking place is whether or not all the additional education is actually promoting equality in American society. They give a tepid affirmative answer but argue that the equalitarian effect has been overstated because the new mass higher education is divisible into first-class and second-class schools, with all the social, cultural, and political consequences which ensue from that. Both equality and elitism, however, are unmistakably working their will, even if unevenly.

Probably the principal obstacle to more social upgrading through education lies in the motivational differences between most children from middle- and lower-income families during the elementary and secondary school years. The first group generally attends schools strongly oriented toward further education; the second group usually goes to schools which do not particularly encourage additional, much less advanced, training. Also, the first group is inculcated very early with the middle-class fear of a social fall; the second group more readily accepts the frustrations which come when upward mobility is thwarted. Most of the political attention to education in recent years has been on the integration of Southern schools, but a far more fundamental problem remains the differing class consequences of the schooling made available for the young from middle-income and lower-income families.

The direct political impact of the general educational upgrading going on is nevertheless important and fairly immediate. For better-educated individuals vote and participate in public affairs much more than the less educated. In recent Presidential elections, barely over 50 percent of those with an eighth-grade education have voted. Over 75 percent of those with a high school education have voted, and over 90 percent of those with at least some college training have cast a ballot. Of almost equal importance, additional schooling increases the likelihood that an individual (largely because of his increased status rather than any intellectual considerations) will urge others to be for a particular candidate or cause, and thus he will in at least the simplest way act as an "opinion leader." Only about a quarter of those with a grammar-school diploma have met that test during the last two decades, but almost half of the group with some higher education qualified. The higher educational level of the young generation should help assure its substantial political activity regardless of the staying power of its youthful activism.

Important but less measurable is the probable effect of more schooling on the quality of the public dialogue and candidates who run for public office. In-depth opinion studies show, predictably, that better-educated voters tend to have a sharper perception of immediate events and issues and a fuller understanding of the political system and the historical context into which they fit. Less educated voters usually give only the most general and passing attention to such matters, being moved more by personality, party label, and the mood of the period than by particular issues. The better-educated tend to be more specific, selective, systematic, and "ideologically oriented." More education thus tends to shift the grounds on which elections turn. This could have increasing effect on campaigns and eventually enhance the usually negligible leverage which election mandates have on the governing process. Of all the forces at work on the new politics, the educational dynamics and divisions are clearly among the more influential.

Another basic conditioning aspect of the new generation of voters is that very early its members saw the civil rights struggle through television if not at first hand. Most, though certainly far from all, of the group came through that turmoil with attitudes at least several decades ahead of their parents. A Gallup Poll of the nation's college students shows that element considers racial problems the greatest single social challenge this age group will face. A study by L. F. Sheff reported (contrary to the situation in the older populace) no evidence of greater prejudice or ethnocentrism among young conservatives in the North than among the rest of the young people there. There is unquestionably a hard-core segment of young whites who are militantly antiblack; they have surfaced in George Wallace's movement and the white mobs of Cicero, Milwaukee, and other urban centers. But the proportion of whites under thirty who are antiblack is demonstrably smaller than among the older group. Even some of the younger voters who were for Wallace in '68 were concerned less with his racial connotations than his stance as a fighter and his role as the most anti-establishment candidate available that year. More significant in the long run is the fact that from the civil rights conflict came an early moral commitment by a considerable portion of this generation, confrontation tactics by the activist minority, and a re-emergence of the political dissent which has since flooded into practically every corner of American life. The civil rights struggle, in fact, is almost certainly as significant for its politicalization of both the young whites and the young blacks as for such tangible progress as it has yet led to for most Negroes.

The Vietnam war further insistently shaped much of this generation. It provoked a grating mixture of disillusionment and compromising rationalizations in a heavy portion of the young. "Most young people don't believe in it," one educator commented, "but most serve. I shudder to think of the cost the war is taking in the loyalty and commitment of our young. This is the biggest price we're paying." Some of the young, however, paid a bigger price. The age of the average draftee during the last half-decade was under twenty-one; and over 60 percent of the U.S. casualties were eighteen to twenty-three years old. The draft itself, as an immediate pressure on millions of young men already vaguely against war and frequent television witnesses of the mortal nightmares of Vietnam, has probably contributed more directly to the hostility and unsettlement of this age group than any other single factor. Nothing more starkly reflects how the nation has been emasculating itself at home in order to maintain military strength abroad.

This is also the first generation which has grown up entirely within the setting of the nuclear age—"We're the bomb babies" some of their demonstrators have declared. For the entire aware life of these young people, before their television eyes, the great political systems of the world have been straining for supremacy. And many of the group have taken more seriously than their elders the idea, as expressed by journalist John Poppy, that a "situation in which a decision by a man can undo everything evolution has built over three billion years gives moral questions and questions of sanity a new vitality."

The year 1968 brought the first Presidential election which the vanguard of this group watched with any sense of proximity. And the nation's public processes intensely engaged many of the more concerned ones on behalf of Senators Eugene McCarthy and Robert Kennedy. Then swiftly the door slammed shut as much of that group viewed events, and politics retreated into some of the more manipulative and crass of its older ways. Whether right or wrong, this influential group feels that this state of affairs is continuing largely unabated. For a wave of young people already fairly widely politicized, the long-term consequences have been less of cynicism (although that has been ample) than of further radicalization, less discouraged turning off than determined turning on. One warning sign was the fact that while the rest of the country turned to the Presidential campaign in the fall of '68, many college newspapers across the nation remained preoccupied for months with rehashing the events of Chicago that August. And the gap between the pace-setters of the college press and the regular society has remained very wide since then. Both the press and most student groups considered the campaign activity among young people for the 1970 Congressional election not at all impressive, and many politicians quietly went out of their way to minimize evidence of student support in the face of an apparent anti-youth backlash. Yet the extent of political work by young people was still at an all-time high for an off-year election, with surveys showing 15 percent of the college students doing some campaign work that year—well over three times higher than the figure for the adult electorate.

The view of much of the younger group about more traditional politicians of the time-tested school of conventional convictions and reassuring homilies drops somewhere below contempt. Political analyst Haynes Johnson wrote after a coast-to-coast tour interviewing young people in 1968 that they bear "a political consciousness shaped by the New Frontier and shattered during the Great Society." The response of the more vocal element to the Nixon administration has hovered somewhere between apathy and agony, though less over the policies than the life style of that administration—or its "death-like pall," as one campus editorial commented. Quite predictably, a popular "campaign button" on many campuses has been *Harass Your Local Politician*.

Out of all the protean conditioning is coming a generation which those who have worked with it most closely thus far (the nation's educators) generally assert is far and away the most fiercely independent, perceptive, and self-motivated they have ever seen. It is also obviously the most disruptive and demanding yet to arise in American society. From the outset it has been shaped by what Eric Hoffer, a voluble critic of the group, has called the "experience of change." And while, as Hoffer comments, "one used to think that revolutions are the cause of change, actually it is the other way around: change prepares the way for revolution."

The prospective political energy in this generation is suggested by the fact that even before coming to maturity, its vanguard members helped set the pace for the two predominant controversies of the last decade: the civil rights struggle and the Vietnam war protests. These young people have also forced the most searching reappraisal of higher education in the U.S. since the borrowings from the German universities in the last quarter of the last century. And the concern of this group with the college environment has been political as much as educational in nature. Yet for all the criticism of the university by students, a *Newsweek* survey found they still rank that institution more favorably than they do family, business, religion, or the present political parties, which are deep at the bottom of the list.

The particularly virulent assault on the nation's leading universities has gone directly to the exercise and distribution of power within the educational establishment. And the university is only the first of the larger environments into which this group is moving. Nationwide college polls have found well over half of the university students seeking "a greater voice" in the running of their school. "The student," says Dr. Harold Taylor, a former president of Sarah Lawrence College, "has become the most powerful invisible force in the reform of education—and, indirectly, in the reform of American society." There is even a theory that the young activists are the latest addition to the uneasy galaxy of power elites in this country. Those who ridicule this because of the new group's lack of corporate resources, dues-paying organizational following, or electibility fail to recognize the wells of power opening up through sheer commitment, mass numbers, the magnetism which attracts the mass media, and the informal cultural networks taking shape.

Another possible indicator of the potential social and political energy in this generation is provided by the hundreds of thousands of college students (the "constructivists," they have been called) who have regularly been volunteering part of their free time to tutor underprivileged children and do social service work. Gallup reported near the end of the sixties that a majority of all college students had done some social work, with a substantially higher proportion of the campus demonstrators thus committed than is true of the nondemonstrators. The group which is intensively involved in social work constitutes a small part of the total generation, but the proportion is still at an all-time high among this country's young people. And the socially involved in the older populace constitute a much lesser fraction of that larger society.

What is perhaps most remarkable about the huge, pace-setting college group is not its proportionally few but determined protesters and constructivists but the fact that significant numbers of the rest at the more influential universities have rallied at critical junctures on major issues, ranging from the racial controversy and educational reform to the draft and free speech. As recently as 1966, Samuel Lubell found only one in ten of all college students were active rebels; the Educational Testing Service reported the ratio then was one in twelve. In 1968, however, Gallup found one in five had taken part in college demonstrations. At the end of the decade, he reported, nearly one in three college men and one in four college women said that they had "participated in a demonstration of some kind." In 1970 a clear majority had joined in one or more protests. A Harris poll that year also found a third of the college students saw some effectiveness in violent tactics—but three-fourths thought other protests and demonstrations are effective. An educator at a large private Western university put the campuses in perspective in saying: "The American university student of today is involved, he cares, and he has left the sandbox of student activities for good."

A fundamental trait of not only the leadership group but of most of the new generation, and one likely to contribute to its influence, is a deeply instilled imperative to experience and to have effect *now*. David Riesman has written that these young people are the instigators of "a revolution of immediacy." But it is a key impediment to their working within a gradualist system either willingly or well. One university president has remarked that "In some of these young minds, patience is a dirty word." This is partly the result of the usual impatience of youth, but the forced nature of this group is also a consequence of the hurried pace of much of contemporary life. A recurring criticism by those who have worked closely with these young people is that they have no sense of history. In the words of one bitter academician, "They think Jesus Christ died in 1939." A coed at Emory University in Atlanta, however, perhaps summed up their attitude more accurately: "I don't think we read and digest and believe very easily, but once we get fully convinced, look out!" There has lately even developed among some of the activists a strong sense of an historical mission.

Many in this age group have sought more kinds of experience "sooner, younger" than their predecessors, and that vanguard has an unmistakable sense of nearing power, fed by a growing consciousness of the generation's size and by all the attention the mass media have given to protests and marches for many years. Far more important, the tribal self-awareness among these young people (their talk is full of *we* and *us*) has been heightened by mass advertising appeals over the course of many years to the $25-billion-a-year teenage market—to "the Pepsi Generation," for instance, during their adolescence. Aware of all the attention and their numbers, many are entering the electorate not meekly but brashly.

In a very elementary sense, a large proportion of these young people come seeking more power and freedom. Or, as one of them has said, they demand both "to be taken into account" and "to be let alone." To ignore these two elemental drives is to miss the main political point about them. They have been rushed to the age of assertiveness and independence faster and earlier than any previous group, and they have been made quite aware of their herd strength. At the same time, more and more of them have been pursuing a higher education. That has put a larger portion of this generation—in fact, the most vocal part of it—under crowded, institutional restraints in later, more restless years than ever before. For many of them, the result is antagonism on top of assertiveness on top of precociousness.

Increasingly they have not asked but taken liberties and authority. It is this striking feature which gives their numbers such life and thrust. It introduces into the electorate not only fresh views and energies but also the most basic kind of struggle with established patterns, without regard to whether those are economic, social, political, religious, or moral—or liberal or conservative. There is distrust of the present and disregard of the past, a challenging and testing and desire to experiment beyond what this country has ever before had to cope with and assimilate. What is most fundamentally being put in question is hierarchical authority—which just happens to be the working principle of the schools, the church, the trade unions, the family, business, and most other institutions.

Study after study has shown that the rebellious and critical element contains a very large proportion of the most perceptive, creative, and intelligent of this generation. Even in terms of the Silent Generation of the 1950s, General Electric found in a ten-year study of 400 employees who had been recruited in 1956 that the "conformists" have not made nearly as good a record as the "unsatisfied individualists." A *Fortune* poll at the end of the sixties found that less than a fourth of even the conservatives among recent college groups are ready to "easily accept outward conformity for career advancement." The percentage was substantially less among the other college students. Some of the more advanced corporations, especially in the computer, electronics, and other advanced fields, are already adapting their recruiting, employee relations, and working arrangements in key job areas to the new generation. They are offering not just higher pay and better conventional fringe benefits but also more independence of effort, opportunity to innovate and criticize, flexible job conditions (including hours and compensated time for social work of the employee's own choice), and other circumstances that will attract the more able and productive of the coming group; more than most others they are responsive to new and different impulses among many of the young.

The widespread hope that the challenges being mounted by the more active young people will ease up after this age group grows a little older, misunderstands the deeper sources of the forces which are stirring. The activism, a study at the University of California concluded, "appears to represent a relatively enduring personality disposition rather than an isolated, impetuous, ephemeral behavioral act." The power-seeking in the new generation, it seems, is as real and determined as that of earlier social groups who pushed their way into the country's political structure, from the unpropertied freemen early in the nation's history to the offspring of the 1900-to-1914 immigration wave that provided the generation base on which Roosevelt built. The new group is proportionally larger compared to the rest of the populace than were either of those earlier historical waves, and it already has a stronger beachhead within this society than those earlier groups initially had.

That profound forces are feeding the unrest of the young is made clear by the fact the rebellion is not confined to this country, but characterizes much of the huge post-World War II generation throughout the world. A United Nations study reported student demonstrations in 1968 in more than fifty countries. A turbulent wave is unmistakably straining to break through the retaining walls of the established order in democratic and authoritarian societies alike, in Communist and non-Communist countries, and in developed and underdeveloped regions. "They brought into play ultra-leftists, anarchist ideas, often echoing those of Mao-Tse Tung, in an effort to cause confusions and disorient ardent but politically inexperienced young people, divide them and turn those who fall under their influence into blind tools of provocation." That attack against young troublemakers might have been made by the head of the FBI, but it came from *Pravda*.

Relatively quiet periods can be expected in youthful activism from time to time. On a short-term basis, it is even possible to discern cyclical outlines in which winters are calmer on most campuses than springtimes; political off-years have tended to be less strenuous than election-years, especially Presidential election years. Practically any brief calm in recent years has quickly been interpreted by the press and many campus administrators as proving that at long last the age storm is really passing. But the underlying social mobility and other forces feeding the restlessness and appetite for change give every sign of increasing, not abating. Even with some of the countervailing factors now at work, within the younger generation as well as in the larger society, it is likely that the level of youthful assertiveness will be substantial throughout this decade. Kenneth Keniston, one of the most perceptive analysts of the newer tendencies among young people, predicts that the activist phenomenon will probably be apparent through at least the end of this century.

A comparison of the new generation and the "Silent Generation" of the 1950s—the most passive in many decades—provides useful constraints and cautions. That earlier group had enjoyed considerable prosperity, been exposed intensively to television, lived much of its formative period in the nuclear age, and received more education than previous groups. Yet it has generally proved to be more security-conscious, conformist, and less stirred—in fact, at practically the opposite pole from the latest group. Why the difference? There is, of course, no precise or sure answer. But in general, the same influences came to bear on the Silent Generation less sharply and at a much later stage of development than with the present noisy swarm. The conditioning of those of the 1950s also included, very early, some of the Depression decade and World War II, then the full blast of the Cold War, and finally the Korean War and Joseph McCarthy period. All of those factors were repressive influences on the public climate in which the young people of the fifties took shape; there were no important opposite factors comparable to the cultural liberation and the virulent protests of the sixties and the outset period of the seventies. Nor did they have anything like the numbers and tribal sense of the new group.

The Korean episode was an experience to which the Silent Generation submitted uncritically. But this latest generation encountered the Vietnam war only after its independence and tendency, then its *will*, to dissent had taken hold. In addition, the whole climate of the country during the Korean and Vietnam expeditions was vastly different. The overwhelming majority of those who were finally called went along in both situations. But the Vietnam involvement crystallized social criticism, including that among some who served. The contrasting conditioning and characteristics of the two groups suggest how much broad social and public developments can affect young people, then reverberate through them long afterward.

A look at the high school students of the last few years suggests that the recent college militants and "hippies" have been having an even greater influence, in personal styles and social outlook, on much of that malleable younger set than on anyone else. Most of the recent high school students have heard the endlessly throbbing tribal drums of the new culture; and some of the more vivid of the recent college activists and hip ones have set the baseline in tastes, attitudes, and modes of behavior from which the next wave of young people are moving on, including a great many who will never go to college. The recent young pace-setters have been exceptionally bizarre for American society, and they are being imitated even beyond the usual excesses of adolescent mimicry in search for personal definition. Through that process, their most prominent qualities are changing norms, even becoming clichés fairly rapidly. Fads come and go, of course; but in individual dress, sexual activity, social concern, use of pot, and political awareness, the current high school group has been found to be well ahead of even the recent college activists at the same age.

A substantial minority of recent secondary students have staged demonstrations over a wide variety of causes. It has been estimated that roughly half the country's high schools have experienced social and political protests of varying kinds in the last half-dozen years. *The New York Times* reported that between 500 and a thousand underground newspapers were being printed in the country's secondary schools in competition with the regular school papers at the outset of the seventies. In 1969 the Harris poll found half of its sampling of high school students "disaffected." A *Fortune* survey that year summed up what is happening this way: "The ideas that have kept colleges in turmoil this year are spreading beyond radical students to the rest of American youth, including those not in college." In net effect, the old order has likely already lost much of the war for a critical part of the next wave coming on.

Like every generation, the new one moving into the electorate in the seventies contains many different social and political groupings. Its far fringes include neo-Nazis, Maoists, Marxists, and Guevarists, though these are mostly labels for poses rather than commitments. There is also a plethora of fairly new organizations —a constantly reviving American phenomenon noted as far back as de Tocqueville. They range from the vastly overpublicized but once seminal Students for a Democratic Society and Weathermen on the left to a legion of far-right groups and a small but dogged Sexual Freedom League. All of these groups are active, sometimes frenetic. But they are still limited to a very small percentage of young people. Also, a much smaller proportion of young people is being turned on by the established hierarchies of the two major political parties, organized labor, and the churches than has been the case for many decades.

An advance political breakdown of the main part of this generation might take as its principal categories none of those organizations, and certainly not the young Democrats and young Republicans or liberals and conservatives, but what might imprecisely be called "the existentialists" and "the philistines." There will obviously never be a national political convention, party platform, or $100-a-plate dinner under either of these banners. But they allow for consideration of the new voters free of the tired traditional labels, which should be either abandoned or basically redefined for the seventies. The suggested groupings represent attitudes and influences more than individuals in the new generation. But they also point to trends and likely tensions and countertensions of power in American society.

The existentialists are the vital, vocal elitists and activists of the new generation, very much the smaller of these two principal groups but the forward edge, "the prophetic minority," as they like to think of themselves. They are often pictured as disheveled and long-haired; and many of them do seem to believe, as John Fisher wrote, that "there is some relationship between being emancipated and unbuttoned." But the group also include a much larger number of well-combed young people with views and values well beyond those which have determined the American past and dominate the present. These futurists are not just the still-growing New Left or the Hippies, the more concentrated political and cultural distillates of what's been happening, but a much broader phenomenon in U.S. society and the part that is increasing most rapidly in both numbers and influence.

The existentialists are committed to racial progress and bringing the poor into the economic and social mainstream, and they have a growing identification—*a sense of the species*—with the rest of mankind. They reject what some of them have charged is this country's "gun-toting nationalism on a worldly scale." Most of them also dispute the special emphasis on Christianity, the right of parents, teachers, and public officials to make decisions for others, and the essential decency of the present society. But to see the group in terms of those antagonistic points of departure is to miss its main thrust, which cuts across the entire mainstream of American life.

The existentialists seek not just a "liberal more" or "conservative less" of what the nation has been doing for many years, but quite different directions. They define the good life not in terms of material thresholds or "index economics," as the New Deal, Great Society, and most economic conservatives have done, but as "the fulfilled life" in a more intangible and personal sense. They reject what they consider the compromises of the "sellouts" and "occupational idiots" who pursue what William James long ago called "the bitch goddess Success," or what a more recent hip one called the "ant trip," the organized world of work.

For a massive generation which will be living with rapidly increasing automation and could find the search for meaningful leisure as trying as the search for meaningful work has been in past times, such a turning of things upside down may not be as absurd as many older people think. Nor, in the nuclear age, is another key response of a number of these young people, as summed up by Geoffry Gorer: "Mankind is safer when men seek pleasure than when they seek the power and the glory." The existentialists' attack, however, is more immediate than these vaulting simplifications. Just as the New Deal sought to solve the frustrations and failures of a Depression-wracked society, they seek to get at what they believe are the distinctive frustrations and failures of an affluent society. They see those not as wants which private prosperity or new laws or public spending can really resolve for the majority of Americans, but as problems of fairness and morality and life style which challenge the generally unquestioned assumptions of this society.

The existentialists are also concerned with processes more than programs, with "moving" things rather than "set" things—a not illogical shift for a generation which has lived in a period more in flux than any other in human history. They find the past and its lessons generally remote from the storm of sensations bombarding them; so they turn to present perceptions more than to history, to empirical action instead of the conventional wisdom, and to a multilevel search for an expanded being in place of the earlier emphasis on rationalism, which they perceive was never really attained or lived very much, anyway. There is, of course, a heavy dose of untested idealism in their outlook. And they still have jobs, children, and a life to put together ahead of them. But at a minimum, large numbers of these young people are committed, as one observer summed it up, to a "deliberate, aggressive attempt to create a different world from that of their parents." In fact, according to *Fortune* in 1969, "65% [of the] college students want a life different from that of their parents—and so do 57% of the young people who do not go on to college." Most of the older population takes offense at such presumption. And yet, as Robert Kennedy commented, "If the young scorn conventional politics and mock our ideals, surely this mirrors our own sense that these ideals have too often and too easily been abandoned for the sake of comfort and convenience. We have fought great wars, made great sacrifices at home and abroad, made prodigious efforts to achieve personal and national wealth, yet we are uncertain of what we have achieved—and of whether we like it."

The existentialists of this generation have felt most strongly of all that what the country and world now need is "love"; and among the many labels they have taken on, the one which stuck most widely is "The Love Generation." But "love" is given the broadest, even vaguest possible meaning, and they criticize the older sector for narrowly equating love with sex and then getting "hung up" with that. As one campaign button popular on a number of campuses in recent years expressed it: *Put a Little Love in Your Sex Life.*

A study prepared at the end of the sixties by the Institute of Sex Research (the former "Kinsey group") concluded, "The so-called [recent] sexual revolution has little to do with the preconceptions of the young but a lot to do with the preconceptions of the old, particularly their anxiety and fantasies about the young people enjoying something they missed." The survey found college students "considerably more sexual" than those of twenty years ago, when the famous Kinsey report reducing sex to statistics was published. But the latest figures are viewed as largely reflecting an earlier start of dating and courtship patterns. Dr. John Gagnon, one of the study's authors, summed up a key conclusion: "There's a kind of cooling off of sex as an important organizing tendency in life for these young people. . . ." A minor sign of the changing times may be the comment of a manufacturer of tin buttons during the recent big button craze: "It's the adults who buy the sexy buttons. The kids go more for humanitarian inscriptions like 'Warmth' and 'Ankh,' the ancient Egyptian symbol of love." One twenty-three-year-old writer expressed what these young people are seeking this way: "They're after love: not a Valentine limerick or a pop song refrain or a proposition . . . but like an emotional handshake from the self to the other, it's a drawing-in, an oxygenation of the soul. It is too nonspecific to be a goal, but as in the Christian concept of grace or the Buddhist nirvana." The annoyance of many older people with such gropings is reminiscent of Samuel Butler's comment that most people are disturbed by anyone who either questions or practices religion.

Many of the young existentialists actually seem to be neither especially affectionate nor compassionate, neither tolerant nor forgiving, as the tone of so many campus protests makes clear. But these young people are deeply concerned with community as well as with their interior selves—community based on "the whole man" and a relationship with every other human being, not a voluntary association of like with like and certainly not a meritocracy, which they see as but another version of the hierarchical order they seek to escape. Some of them make a fetish of being authentic and committed rather than simply belonging. And they overwhelmingly seek humanity at first hand rather than humanity categorized through a system of institutions on standardized terms. Over-all, the group combines a democratic inclusiveness with an ethic of experience-seeking.

Some observers have expressed concern that these new adults are "opting out of the political picture; they seem to be limiting their actions to the range of their perceptive selves," as Democratic Senator Walter Mondale of Minnesota put it. A small minority are indeed dropping out—a process that estrangement among many young people over the Vietnam war grievously aggravated. But the disengaged element is still very minor compared to the vast sector which, as in every generation, is simply indifferent to what society is doing. And most of the older populace find that latter group of young people positively comforting. Sharp differences exist, of course, between the hippies and political activists, although to an important extent the hippie turnoffs have only been acting out in their own way in an early period of their lives what the activists are verbally explicit about: a rejection of the present society, its values, ploys, and power system.

Most of the more active young people are actually too committed to both inward and outward experience to turn off for long. Joan Baez, the protest folk singer who was one of the early voices of this generation, has claimed: "Moralizing has been a failure for 6,000 years ... the only person you can make aware is yourself." Yet she has organized a school to teach nonviolence as a catalyst for change, repeatedly "given witness" in civil rights, free-speech, and antiwar demonstrations, gone to jail several times as a result, and championed her young husband while he was imprisoned for opposing the Vietnam war. Senator Mondale's concern fails to take into account the range of commitment and experience which many among this generation seek. To dismiss that group as essentially apolitical or antipolitical is to misunderstand the fundamental questions they pose, the disgust large numbers of them have come to feel for the current construction of American society, and the provocative role many of them are bent on.

Instead of turning off, many of the activists will far more likely be tough, articulate leaders and social, cultural, and political agents in the coming years. Community by community, they will be providing much of the public cut and thrust both substantively and tactically. Their interest will generally be less in winning immediate elections than in relentlessly pressing for a fundamental recasting of values and direction, for they see elective politics as only a very limited part of the politics of social change—one of the crucial shifts taking place in American society.

It is fundamental to the public prospect that the values of these young people cannot be fulfilled primarily through governmental action or a power hierarchy. The real revolt is against government, mass politics, pragmatism, gradualism, and long-prevailing liberal methods as much as against the private organization world and its establishment. That is why, within loose and often almost anarchic organizations, much of the group has fastened onto the concept of "participatory democracy." F.D.R. railed against trickle-down economics; much of this latent new constituency would turn trickle-down decision-making and trickle-down power upside down. That may sound like a put-on, but this impulse is one of the few serious efforts now being made to breathe fresh life into self-government and individual freedom and make them vigorous again in the face of an increasingly depersonalized, intensively organized society.

Some critics have claimed to see a parallel between the ideal of participatory democracy and the concept of the people's democracy in Communist countries. They like to point out that the founding fathers rejected direct rule—"mobocracy"—as unbridled and unworkable in a country as scattered and diverse as even the original colonies. The more sophisticated of the new activists, however, have few illusions about being able to undo the organic arrangements very soon, if ever. The overwhelming majority are simply groping for some less-structured alternative to the institutionalized America in which they believe they and their fellow citizens are being subjugated. They seek mostly to bring about greater personal involvement than the minimal participation which prevails in the present politics and society. For them, just casting a vote every couple of years serves neither their humanity nor their view of what a citizen's responsibilities really should be.

Whether or not quixotic, their instinctive, not just intellectual, want is to rescue the individual from a mass society of superorganizations and recover the human condition from technological domination. These young people generally accept and take easily to the spreading technologies, but a considerable number are resisting the "technologicalization" of man. The group wants to refurbish and reinvigorate individuality, and to do it through the vagaries of commitment and the imprint of each person who will speak out in either protest or affirmation—and put his body, not just his mouth, on the line. A sympathetic older observer might say they believe in the force of example, but it would be more accurate to say they are simply following the force of being themselves.

Among a small fraction of this wave, there is a growing and self-contradictory resort to force. The change in tone of some in the Love Generation is reflected by the declaration of one underground paper: "To love, one must live; to live, one must struggle; to struggle, one must resist!" That shift in tenor could have critical implications for the period ahead. It underlies the rash of bombings and the charge by some older critics that this generation has an authoritarian potential in its herdlike vehemence. The latter criticism, however, fails to understand the deep want as well as the commitment of the overwhelming majority of this age group, including almost all of its activists, to genuine individuality and social freedom. The resort to physical force among a few is surely less a peculiar characteristic of this generation than of the national culture out of which these young people come and—more specifically—a response to the older society's efforts to order, educate, draft, curb, and otherwise compel them into the older ways.

All the individuals involved would vociferously object, but there is in the young existentialists a certain amalgam of the New Deal liberal (without his economic determinism), Barry Goldwater (without his Air Force proclivities), and Henry Thoreau (without his recluse side). The mixture includes some incidental overlap. But it is primarily a reworking of historic materials in the American make-up, especially of individualism and idealism, and turns importantly on the kind of ambiguities and contradictions through which politics endlessly tries to reconcile divergent groups and put together new and shifting majorities. In traditional terms, there is in this younger sector a passionate commitment to the individual—but to the full and sensitive individual; in essence, to a less competitive individualism, not the acquisitive, domineering, elephant-skinned "rugged individualism" of economic history. The accent is on personal "identity" and "authenticity," not the social adaptability extolled in the New Deal ethic. The psychological and verbal imperative is "principle," but as each individual sees it, not as society does. In such ferment, pressures for change in the basic tissues of U.S. politics and policy are at work. "An incredibly American generation in our midst," Michael Harrington has noted, "has become radical by taking the house platitudes seriously."

Liberals and conservatives who think in traditional terms may challenge how the younger group can reconcile putting a new emphasis on individualism and "privatism" with seeking the social leverage and public resources required to make real progress on the racial problem, helping the poor, and similar goals. The existentialists are fumbling with that dilemma themselves and look heavily to further cutting military appropriations as their program. But consistency and adequacy of concept have never been mandates of politics or hallmarks of any particular period, and there is little that indicates they will be in the approaching epoch.

The philistines—the other loose major group in the ranks of the coming young people—are by far the more numerous but less active of the two. A considerable part of this group will not even vote unless very strongly stirred. Most of the philistines, however, will conscientiously comply with what they consider their minimum public duty; and the majority will uncritically follow the immediate partisan ties of their parents. Most of the present horde of young people, as sociologist Seymour Martin Lipset has summed them up, are politically passive, socially conservative, morally conventional, and largely preoccupied with private pursuits. A *Fortune* survey in 1969 provided this perspective: "Among [college] students 81 percent of the radicals and 77 percent of the reformers have been activist, but only 59 percent of the conservatives have been [a distinct minority on the campuses]. In all categories of noncollege youth, including 80 percent of the conservatives, the majority has been politically inert. Nowadays it is the conservatives and the less educated who are the political 'dropouts.'"

Much of the press has reported a new conservative surge among young people during the last half-dozen years, including on the campuses, but there is no important statistical evidence of that. There have been occasional efforts at encouraging the organization of fairly rightist student groups with money from sympathetic older elements, and James Buckley's successful Conservative Party campaign in New York in 1970 for a U.S. Senate seat made effective and exciting use of some younger people. But all that has been as a trickle, not the mainstream, of this age group.

Opinion studies of those turning twenty-one in the early 1970s have shown that a clear majority thought the U.S. could not prevent wars but should keep trying; would not participate in civil rights demonstrations and considered those either ineffective or damaging, but supported human rights in the abstract; believed in private enterprise "but thought some people could not make it no matter how hard they tried"; wanted a life of adventure but listed as their main goals "a good-paying job, money, success"; and judged themselves honest and upright but admitted they had cheated in school. They could readily identify a number of current TV stars but could not recall ever hearing of Ho Chi Minh even at the height of the Vietnam conflict.

This philistine majority is made up of those who pursue the traditional "American dream"; in so doing they are carriers of continuity, not agents of change. They divide on a wide range of values and viewpoints but usually reflect only the already respectable alternatives. Even in their diversity they are not the newness in the new generation. They show, as Donald McCoy wrote of Calvin Coolidge, a "reluctance to recognize the problems underlying dissidence ... [and to] fight to head off the problems of the future." A large proportion has unquestionably been repelled by the more extreme activism of a small minority of their contemporaries in recent years, and that has had a very slight conservative effect on some of them. But even such unrelenting critics of the newer tendencies as Lewis Feuer and John Roche concede the unwillingness of most of this age group to take on those they disagree with in their own generation. More often than not, the philistines actually seem to pull back from either opposing "the old men" or committing "generational treason."

Perspective must also be kept on the fact that the philistine group is substantially more educated, aware of the outside world, fad-influenced, self-assertive, self-indulgent, and change-propelled than the main part of any previous generation. It is inextricably caught up in the new influences at work even while trying to give the "correct answers" wanted by parents, teachers, and prospective employers. Even without the very considerable influence being exerted by the wave-making existentialists, the philistine majority forewarns of a fairly swiftly moving society and a whole new politics of change. If the electorate of the seventies were tracked with a simplistic political speedometer, most older voters would likely show "slow" to "moderate" headway, the philistines "fairly rapid" progression, and the existentialists "fast acceleration." For those who like a leisurely pace, the prospects are hardly reassuring.

An over-all view of the main groups in the new generation is suggested by excerpts from the 1969 poll by *Fortune* magazine:

	Those with no College	*"Practical" in College*	*"Forerunners" at College*
Favor more freedom to debate and disagree openly	68%	73%	92%
Cannot easily abide by laws they don't agree with	43%	35%	48%
Believe there are more things to fear politically than the threat of communism	47%	64%	82%

	Those with no College	"Practical" in College	"Forerunners" at College
"We should set our house in order before we police the rest of the world"	91%	83%	86%

Another *Fortune* survey of this age group, published later in 1969, reported: "Surprisingly, noncollege youth takes nearly as critical a view of society as college youth. . . . When asked if they thought the American way of life was superior to that of any other country, only 18% of the students and 33% of the nonstudents agreed."

There are some observers, of course, who look on the coming influence of the new generation as simply "the youth myth," as Kenneth Crawford has called it. And conservative columnist Henry J. Taylor has contended that in politics, as in life, youth is merely a condition to be left behind, not a possession. That hopeful, or desperate, older view is contradicted, however, by what the major voting studies of recent decades show is the life-long persistence of the distinctive early public and, particularly, political characteristics of other generations. The last redoubt for those wary of this horde of young people would seem to be the more realistic expectation that if the coming power of the new generation is not mythical, may it at least not become monolithic.

What, in net effect, may be the actual impact of this flood of young people on the politics of the seventies? What will be the over-all thrust of the new generation when all of the differences among millions of mercurial young people have to come down to the frustrating, oversimplified, either-or choices on a ballot, or to just whether they will even take part in such decision-making? Reduced to the confines of actual politics, a new generation, like the rest of the electorate, inevitably divides and responds to many causes, many men. How it splits and regroups in a particular election depends so much, of course, on who the candidates are, what the public mood and problems may be, and whether immense events have intervened to bend or shake the times. After those critical factors are at least approximately recognized, however, a generation as huge, distinct, and assertive as the coming one still has a life and velocity of its own which must be fed into the calculations of a decade. This enormous group will influence as well as be influenced—it will batter as well as be battered.

The years ahead will almost certainly show politicians that diverse approaches are open with this mass of new voters. But the essence of politics is to try to perceive and affect the mold before, not after, it has hardened into history—and not discursively, but as those who go to the public must seek to frame it. If all the uncertainties and variables about the new group could be even partially reconciled in advance, in what would amount politically to an optimum appeal, that in turn might suggest clues about some of the principal pressures which will be working on American politics in the new decade and then, possibly, something about the changing nature of those politics and the nation itself. Tentative premises would at least wrap the enigma whole for working purposes, though propositions which might produce a viable majority would hardly satisfy either the radicals or the reactionaries among us.

- As a starting point, it would seem that while the dominating slogans of national campaigns have long been variations on *Prosperity!* and *Peace!* new battle cries capable of reaching younger voters may evolve out of *Live!*—perhaps even *Love!* (or even *Ankh*). And, by implication, live and love it up a little.
- While the prevailing personal goal of Americans in recent decades has been *security*, the objective may gradually shift not back to the older cry for *opportunity* but to *fulfillment*.
- While there have been pretensions recently of striving for the Great Society and a law-and-order society, the growing want among young people is simply a *humane society*.
- While there has long been a preoccupation with *national* purpose, the rising concern is again with *individual* purpose. And not even *purpose* so much as *being*.

- While most practical attention has long been on *special-interest politics*, the scope must be expanded in not just rhetoric but substance to include the elusive and difficult *politics of values*. And while the primary emphasis of politics and government has long been on *programs* and *laws*, the balance is unmistakably shifting toward a concern with *process, variety and spontaneity*.
- While the public frame of reference has long been *city, state, and nation*, the loyalty evoking increasing response is *mankind*.
- While the public pace which has long been extolled is *gradual progress*, there will be increasing insistence on *now*.
- And while the principal attention has been on the *Democratic* and *Republican electorates*, the vital new focus will be increasingly on the *independent electorate*, and whether to try to encourage or blunt it.

CHAPTER 4

The Generational Struggle in Politics

On the actual political firing line, the most important example of generational politics thus far is provided by California, "the land of political pop" as it has been called. That state, setting aside its many kooks and special causes, is as close as this country has to a large-scale laboratory of social and political change. California's huge immigration since World War II has drawn on all parts of the nation and the various urban-rural, racial, and income divisions in fairly indicative proportions. Perhaps most relevant, the state has more young people than any other part of the country, and they are generally more mobile than anywhere else. With California lacking deeply rooted traditions and a stabilized social or political structure, new public attitudes and trends often break through there quickly and dramatically. Admirers have called it the turned-on state. One of its British critics once remarked that it is "rather much." But from either perspective it is, as George Leonard said, "a window into the future."

Generational politics exploded in California not just on the periphery but in the political mainstream well before, and more severely than, they have erupted in the rest of the country. The 1964 campus explosions at Berkeley were only bearded, sandaled show-openers played up by the mass media. Ronald Reagan's decisive election as governor in 1966 and his re-election in 1970 were built on a number of factors, chief among which was his war against the assertive young as symbolized by campus disruptions. Extensive opinion polling in the state in the last half-dozen years has consistently shown a strong public reaction against "long-haired kids," "loose sex among a lot of young people," "restless students," "disrespect for authority," and related attitudes expressed with vehement feelings. Politics have a way, moreover, of merging and muddying disparate issues and forces. It is not just that politicians by intention or ineptitude often tend to be fuzzy. So is public psychology sometimes, and so are some of the principal problems. Thus the so-called youth issue grew by association. A widespread public attitude in the state was summed up by one independent political writer: "There is no explicit connection whatever among the Watts riots, the Free Speech Movement at Berkeley and a random mugging on an Oakland street. But in the deep symbolism of California politics, there is a very clear relationship. All three are very personal threats from strangers, who are, typically, very young."

Ironically, some of the more vocal radicals have repeatedly welcomed the prospect of a triumphant Reagan as a means of dramatizing what they consider the hypocrisy and inadequacy of the state's long tradition of moderate and progressive politics. They have charged that the old approach could neither head off the insurgent ultraconservatism nor meet the really critical problems building up—including, in their view, racial and generational antagonisms, the lack of a vigorous public commitment to peace, the environmental blight, and the failure to find answers to the widespread disquiet with life even in the midst of rampant affluence. Partly as the result of a virulent strain of recent radicalism, California has experienced a fairly severe case of political reaction in the last half-dozen years, with the active newer forces generally uninterested in results within the reach of immediate compromises, the traditional interests resurgent and strong, and middle-of-the-roaders in both parties trying to thread their way through the crossfire.

California's social and generational tensions are still strong and likely will continue to be for much of the decade. But the conservative ascendancy was partially blunted in the 1970 election results and could be strongly challenged in the coming years. A large proportion of the new generation will be moving into their family-forming, settling-down years, when they will probably seem less abrasive and blatant in the view of others. Also, at least a partial accommodation to new influences usually goes on in the middle, moderate part of the general electorate after a certain time lag. The most important single factor working to turn the tide, however, may simply be the rapidly expanding number of young voters. One and a quarter million young Californians are now turning twenty-one every four years. Each of these increases amounts to over 10 percent of the eligible electorate, a substantial segment by any test; and the cumulative effect could be awesome.

Politicians and factions that pit themselves against the younger group and try to ride the reaction in either California or the nation could pay a substantial price over the course of the seventies. That is quite apart from the moral implications of public leadership which goads or simply fails to excite and energize young people, especially the brightest and most active. To the extent that major characteristics of the new group are singled out and symbolically made a whipping boy, such as its restiveness or considerable break with orthodoxy, much of this self-conscious younger tribe could come together almost as a reflex. If a substantial portion crystalizes for or against a particular party or viewpoint, the consequences could be serious. The temptation for many conservative leaders and Republican tacticians will be to persist in playing the short-term game well into the decade, and to identify primarily with the grumbling of older voters. But a successful historical strategy must relate both to the immediate and to the longer-range forces and prospects. Keeping the early, reactionary phase of the generational conflict in perspective with the increasing numbers of young people will present a critical test for both major parties and any individual who would assert a significant and fairly lasting role.

Conservatism and its principal institutional embodiment, the

Republican Party, actually have a rare opportunity with the new voters as a result of the unmistakable individualism and resistance to big government among much of the new generation, including its most active members. An assumption has taken hold during the last four decades that the majority of young people are almost instinctively "little liberals." But the longer stretch of history shows that this has not always been true, and marked tendencies against the stereotype are apparent now. Conservative politicians will have mostly themselves to blame if they stick rigidly to their present aging styles and constituencies and do not raise issues which reach out to this huge new group. William Buckley, racing up Park Avenue on his Honda 50, shows that at least the manner of even the Right need not be antique. A real "opening to the young" by conservatives would require their returning to first, if not fresh, principles and abandoning the clichés in which the political right usually gets bogged down. But such courting would probably attract a larger share of the new voters than the GOP has won for many decades.

Whatever the relationship between conservatives and the new generation turns out to be, the political emergence of the younger group seems almost sure to unsettle still further the now-traditional liberalism represented by Franklin Roosevelt and Harry Truman from 1932 to 1952 and by Lyndon Johnson's policies more recently. Lapses in communication and understanding between many Democratic leaders and a considerable sector of young people in the last half of the sixties badly frayed the normally ardent relationships between Democratic liberalism and the young during the coming group's political formative years. The more articulate young people now see liberals as sometimes talking a good game but only infrequently playing it and therefore, worst of all in their view, full of hypocrisy—people who daily put aside their social convictions for careers and comforts that leave them shallow and dull. These same young people see the long-dominant liberal politics of compromise and consensus as the real engines of the existing order— the *status quo* of slow change in a world and technological era demanding radical change to meet profoundly new conditions. Pragmatism, moderation, and reasonableness, these young critics contend, are but means of rationalizing "the horrible deliberateness of policy," as in the slow de-escalation of the Vietnam war and the nuclear arms race. "There are times of moral enormity," Martin Perety has argued, "when cool reasonableness is a more pathological and unrealistic state than hysteria."

The young activists charge that "the liberal establishment" (one of their endlessly recurring phrases) has been trying to run both the domestic society and the rest of the world according to premises at least several decades out of date. They view the welfare state, the main contribution of modern liberalism, as a manipulative bureaucracy primarily concerned with the blue-collar whites who could most readily be rallied to the Democratic Party in the 1930s. The new activists complain over and over that, even in the poverty program, liberals came to grips only in a token way with the third of the nation most in need. When that program was enacted in the middle 1960s it was massively ignored on many campuses and was attacked on others as an "insensitive" attempt to placate the downtrodden at as little cost as possible and leave the rest of the country undisturbed and indulgent. More recently, the young critics have emphasized that the poor have been the first to be cut back under the press of military budgeting, business subsidies, and "prudent" fiscal policies.

Whatever the merit of such polemics, the result is a severe psychic jolt for traditional liberals who long ago came to believe that they had an almost exclusive stewardship over the American conscience, the American downtrodden, and the American young. Now the activists of the new generation are seeking to cut them off from all three. Worst of all, the newer element is not willing, at least not yet, to work out its differences in the practical ways to which established liberals became accustomed as they grew older, more prosperous, and—by their lights—burdened with the responsibility of winning elections. Traditional liberals, as well as most conservatives, have sought to raise the necessity for social compro-

mise to the status of a natural law, ignoring the historical fact that
democracy has sometimes been invigorated, even rescued at several
important junctures, by more unsettling courses.

The defection of the activist young from the liberal coalition
is not crucial immediately in terms of actual votes. But that group
is the most political of the new generation, and it would normally
provide much of the cadre of the liberal system and Democratic
Party in the years ahead. Of more urgent importance, this element
contains many of the most effective bridges to the rest of the new
generation and the racial minorities, and it tends to be a bellwether
of what has come to be oversimply known as the "ideological liberal vote" among teachers and other semi-professional white-collar
groups. All these other elements are indispensable to the liberal
and Democratic base. Pragmatists may argue that such elements
really have nowhere else to go, but the rising disaffection on the
left (as on the right) constitutes a grave danger for doctrinaire
politicians who count on compromise and pragmatism to maintain their base. A bold nineteenth-century maxim of Thoreau's is
turning out to be one of the determining impulses of the new
forces: "Any man more right than his neighbors constitutes a
majority of one already."

The hard fact is that the approach of the new generation contains irreversible pressures for a sweeping reappraisal of some of
the most basic goals, methods, and power arrangements of liberalism and the national Democratic Party. At a deeper level than the
histrionics at the 1968 Democratic National Convention, bitter
fights and basic changes in the Democratic coalition are likely inevitable during the seventies, with trouble-breeding dissatisfaction
certain to persist whatever the outcome of the first round. No
rhetoric or self-reassuring can extricate Democrats from the fateful
family brawl they face sooner or later. One of the party's main
constituencies for a number of decades has been younger voters,
and it will soon be larger than ever before. Like all other political
movements, the Democratic Party will have to go to this natural
source of support, not wait for the increasingly independent young

vote to come to it. The exhorting verbalisms and limp handholding of the past simply are no longer enough. Communicating with the new group will require involvement, principle, style, patience, action, and substantial acceptance of the independence of the young.

The distinctiveness of a key part of the new generation from both the conservatives and the traditional liberals suggests that what could be coming into the American political system is a third force: a loose gathering of attitudes and tendencies (among not only the young but also a substantial portion of the economically liberated upper-middle class, too) which does not readily fit into either of the two main present groups, as amorphous as those are. There is much overlapping among these three sectors, and what they have in common is more important in the long run than their differences. But the controversies and politics of the coming period will likely emerge largely out of their clashes. Many voters and candidates will combine qualities and views from at least two of the three sectors, and some voting blocs and problems will have to be considered entirely outside such structuring. But these three very approximate clusters still provide useful insights for the unwieldy purposes of a mass society and national politics.

A generational insight into American politics has generally been neglected in the past amid the preoccupation with economic classes, ethnic groups, sectionalism, partisanship, special interest pressures, and other fairly explicit factors. But all of those are being eroded by affluence, education, the mass media, and other processes at work in this country. Each of the earlier "determinants" has a role to play in the politics of the seventies. But in a time of rapidly changing conditions and great, jagged events, the once slow and fairly steady procession of history is being broken up into shorter, ever sharper zig and zags; and with that, the conditioning of each generation veers in a somewhat different direction. A new "generation"—really a semi- and even mini-generation—seems to be coming along in a social and psychological sense about every six to twelve years. "It is no insignificant trend of contemporary history," Midge Decter observed, "that in the rhythm of assigning epochs, the decade seems to have replaced the century."

The substantial changes which can take place between succeeding human waves even within the same family were noted for political and other purposes in an earlier period of U.S. history in connection with the gap between many immigrants and their children who were born here. "What's happening now," Margaret Mead has suggested, "is an immigration in time, with the people over 40 migrants into the present age, and the children born into it the natives." Generational differences in the mainstream of society have been attracting the increasing attention of social scientists if not politicians ever since World War I, beginning with the convulsions that wracked Germany. But with the sixties the breach between the younger and older groups widened very substantially in this country as well as almost everywhere else.

With only a few exceptions, the nation has been run throughout its history mostly by men in their fifties and sixties. And they have usually sought to govern as if the country were still—or at least should be—as it was when they were much younger. What will distinguish the period ahead from the past is not merely the rapidly widening gap between how the world was when a person was starting out and how it is several decades later but also the increasing numbers and special leverage which the young are gaining against the ancient authority of their elders. We are likely to witness more and more of what Tacitus, in a context of patriotism, called "this praiseworthy competition with one's ancestors."

For practical political purposes the divergent courses of the main groups in the electorate are perhaps most readily suggested by the banners and shibboleths under which they may be marching and reacting. Stated in the imprecise political shorthand with which mass groups must usually be described and rallied, the differing building blocks of campaign rhetoric for the three constituencies might include these possibilities—in the order of conservatives, traditional liberals, and much of the new generation:

Far-out caricatures of the growing generational politics already exist in the New Left and the Far Right. Both, as might be expected, have been particularly pronounced in California. The New Left pushes radical innovation with strident bravado; the Far Right dogmatically asserts an American past that never existed. Both spring out of the moralistic, fundamentalist aspects of our national character and are often impatient with democratic procedures, the clash of ideas, and the complexity, even tentativeness, of life and society. The future effect of each is uncertain. But they indicate important tendencies at work with reduced intensity in the general electorate. Over-all they are relevant mainly as simplistic signals and seedbeds.

What dominates and divides not just the Far Right and the New Left but the generations is the quickening rate and complex quality of transformation pervading our time. The social and political divisions and the public mood of the seventies will almost surely have to be rendered intelligible and dealt with more and more in terms of massive flux. A polarization more important than the obscuring labels of conservatism and liberalism will be that between all those who cannot get beyond suffering what Alvin Toffler has called "future shock," an "unreadiness to meet the future when it arrives," and those with the counterview summed up by George Leonard: "A cherished, desperately embraced mainstay of the past bends, breaks—and nothing disastrous happens. . . . We realize how rigid and limiting our society is only when we begin to see how many changes can be safely rung on it."

Politics are hardly well suited to be the arbiter of a struggle over whether to recognize and give assent to historic alterations in human values and social relationships. Politicians deal best with the specific and concrete. In past times, other channels have incubated and filtered almost all the great transitions. But in our secularized, democratized, mass-media society, the political process is a principal channel in which the task of making sense is being undertaken. The radically new is beginning to impinge on the old too fast and in too great a volume to be assimilated or rationalized very much by other institutions before being injected into politics and government. The crucial immediate social tools, for good or bad, are not a burning religious insight or educational expertise but the massed funds, publicity, and energies in the public sector.

The politicalization of religious leaders, philosophers, and others perhaps capable of sorting out basic social and human means and ends has rarely been a happy passage in history. Politics and secular power have a way of bringing out the irrational and irrelevant, and often the vicious, in even the most philosophical, religious, and scholarly individuals and institutions. But in an era of swift underlying change, the most serious flaw in our politics may result not from the traditional troubles of greed and apathy but simply from the fact that the great bulk of the voters and political leaders are so removed in conditioning and insight from the forces immediately reshaping both them and the social environment. A basic need of the seventies will be for leaders who do not just produce more and more laws, appropriations, programs, and personal publicity, but who raise a persuasive and reconciling rationale of change and create an excitement for fresh pioneering beyond mere rhetoric.

How the contention between the spreading younger forces of change and the old order of American society takes shape as a practical political matter will depend in important measure, of course, on the shifting personalities and immediate issues and on possible recessions, wars, deaths, and other events in grand procession. The underlying conflict, however, might be suggested in advance by projecting a Presidential campaign between John Calvin, a logical nominee of the conventional wisdom deep in the American conscience, and bearded, disheveled Socrates, that most modern and timeless of men in the view of many young activists in recent years.

Socrates would likely find the public atmosphere of the early 1970s almost as stifling as that of Athens near the end of his own life, for that city was then suffering a severe postwar hangover from its setback in a far-off land as a great sea-ranging power at the hands of supposedly land-tied Sparta. At the start of this campaign, the Gallup and Harris polls would surely have to show the earnest, hardworking, businesslike Calvin a heavy favorite, especially against an opponent who had been charged with "corruption of the young" and "neglect of the gods that the State worships." The far-reaching social and other changes likely to go on in this country during the seventies, however, could draw the contest steadily closer.

Calvin might be expected to articulate the outlook of most of the older electorate with such cant as "law and order," new anti-smut laws, "old-fashioned morality," "Success! Success!," "Not merely hellfire but napalm," a special U.S. responsibility for not just the world but NASA's universe and Billy Graham's hereafter —and, for his youth division, "Keep Cool—with Calvin." Socrates, in order to broaden the narrow base of his initial following, would probably have to play upon the growing permissiveness and questioning spirit in contemporary life. Thus he might build his campaign around the simple rallying cry of "Why Not?" (as Robert Kennedy closed most of his speeches in his 1968 Presidential primary efforts).

The more Calvin inevitably pressed the country to "Obey!" and "Conform!" the more likely Socrates would be tempted to urge "Free Yourself." Sooner or later the latter's campaign aides could be expected to try to take advantage of the recent campaign-button craze declaring "Reality Is Relative" . . . "I'm-a-Hope-Freak" . . . and later maybe even "Burn Pot, Not People." After all, Socrates was no self-tormenting ascetic, but rather—as Plato described him—"all glorious within" and knew well "how to abound." Socrates liked to remind his listeners that men who could not be bad could not be good. Many young people, though few of their elders, would also identify acutely with his declaration when his life, not merely a political career, was in issue: "Life unexamined is not worth living." And the Greeks, as Merle Severy noted, "examined life by participating; anyone who did not was an *idiotes.*"

Calvin would lash out again and again for "Prudence" and "Piety," a reminder of one of the two basic charges against Socrates at his trial. Socrates, borrowing from a golden passage of human history even earlier than his own and seminal for not only Greek civilization but also ours, might respond that each age, and especially this one, must venture its own odyssey, "a timeless journey of love and loss, danger and self-discovery."

Socrates' principal campaign theme might finally come down to *love*. It is remarkable how close his conception was to the gropings of the recent Love Generation: beyond a narrow and intense identification with the body and the organizing of much of a person's entire life around a sexual relationship to a more diffused and spacious being. Plato tells of a symposium (literally "a drinking party" for the ancient Greeks) that included Socrates and the playwright Aristophanes. As recreated by classicist Paul MacKendrick, "Aristophanes, recovering from a fit of hiccups, tells how men were once spherical, with four of everything they now have two of, and two of everything they now have one of. Then Zeus split men in two, and ever since they have been looking for their other halves. This is love!

"Socrates, more serious, expounds the theory that has since been known as 'Platonic Love'; We must progress from love of a beautiful body to love of beautiful thoughts, laws, institutions, until we gain a mystic vision. . . ." If Socrates turns off the middle-aged and older order with such a theme, he is still a sensitive voice for many of the brighter and more active young people and for the growing want for more of the spirit in American society.

Calvin would run a highly organized but frenetic campaign, jetting furiously about the country and exploiting television fully to exercise and exorcise the electorate to a frenzied pitch by the weekend before the election. Socrates would almost certainly conduct a more relaxed effort, sitting it out much of the time in New York's Central Park, or along Los Angeles' Sunset Strip, or in Chicago where the 1968 demonstrations took place, simply asking questions, which would be more bedeviling than Calvin for many Americans. Socrates would have to conduct much the less costly campaign; for as Aristophanes noted, the philosopher-teacher always suffered "a neediness" which resulted from his preoccupation with the needs of his fellow men.

While Calvin almost certainly would attack relentlessly, Socrates would probably ignore his opponent. If an exception were made to that, it might, surprisingly, be to press Calvin where he would seem to be least vulnerable with American society—in his exultation of the Protestant work ethic. While Calvin preached *Work, Save, Invest—and Be Saved,* Socrates would deride such "worldly asceticism" and perhaps, with a touch of political opportunism unexpected of him, invoke against Calvin the Old Testament scripture that "the labor of man does not satisfy the soul" (*Ecclesiastes*). Pressed to justify such a heretical stand, Socrates would likely fall back on the conviction of the ancient Greeks that most work should be done only by slaves (quickly clarified by his campaign staff as "machines and computers") and that labor brutalizes man and keeps him from pursuing the practice of genuine virtue. Such a stand might seem like a poor shibboleth for the present age, but Socrates' aides would undoubtedly be satisfied that in presenting a choice between "labor" and "leisure," their candidate had scored with a rapidly growing sector of U.S. society.

Sooner or later the Associated Press would probably distribute to its newspaper subscribers a campaign picture of Calvin throwing rocks and another of Socrates sitting on one. The Chicago *Tribune* would lead the overwhelming mass of editorial support for Calvin while Socrates would perhaps receive only the tortured endorsement of *The New York Times* and, much against their better judgment, several Greek publications in this country that had also lately supported Spiro Agnew.

Calvin would almost inevitably bring his campaign to an election-eve climax with a pledge of "Work and Wealth." Socrates probably would be extended to promise "The Sky—and Freedom."

Which man, which approach, which philosophy would prevail? Even with Calvin the clear initial favorite, the contrasting appeals and styles of the two men could finally turn the contest into a compelling choice in the developing society.

Such a campaign is not suggested here to indulge in the politics of the absurd but because it raises in a fairly direct way the very real conflicts coming into focus. In the American past, the prevailing differences might long have been indicated by campaign models between the Presbyterian Calvin and almost any self-made, malleable Episcopalian senator or governor—or, by the middle 1930s, between Adam Smith and J. Kenneth Galbraith. Or after John F. Kennedy broke the religious barrier, between Pope John and whoever happened at the time to be the head of some large foundation.

But the emerging political relevance of Socrates, however wispish, suggests the continued stretching and reshaping of the country's public frame of reference. The longer-range politics of the seventies may be discernible as well through a subjective perspective like that as by a mass of election statistics and all the pollsters' careful calculations.

CHAPTER 5

The Hardening Impasse: South

If ever America undergoes great revolutions,
they will be brought about by the presence of
the black race upon the soil of the United States
—that is to say, they will owe their origin not
to the equality, but the inequality of conditions.
        —ALEXIS DE TOCQUEVILLE, 1840

Twenty years after de Tocqueville commented on the possibility of America's racial problem leading to revolution, the nation erupted in civil war. And the problem still was not solved. America lurched through the ordeal, learned the lesson of geographic and commercial unity from that struggle, then lapsed back with the underlying human implications barely acted on. Now another testing strains the nation on much the same underlying human values.

It would hardly seem that a broadly educated, affluent, and quick-to-moralize society like this one should be in danger of suffering still longer the agony over inequality which de Tocqueville saw stored up in the racial dilemma. The flurry of court decisions, sit-ins, marches, Presidential directives, and new laws during the 1950s and 1960s created a widespread impression that considerable headway was finally being made. Out of a variety of motives, many politicians have been quick to exaggerate that impression. But much of the white population has only been unsettled by it, and the overwhelming majority of blacks see progress toward the promise of equality verified only unevenly, if at all, in their jobs, schools, neighborhoods, and daily lives. A detached historical perspective requires recognition that important legal rights long taken for granted by the rest of the nation have in fact been reasserted by, and for, Negroes. And most blacks, like most whites, have improved their standard of living compared to a decade or more ago. But there is impressive evidence that the economic and social gap between the vast majority of blacks and whites is still very wide and has even widened on some important matters.

In the 1930s, nationwide, the average black man earned just over 40 percent of what the average white man earned. In the first half of the 1940s, under the stimulus of the World War II labor shortage, the percentage rose to over 60. Then it gradually dropped again to the low 50s and had only climbed back up to about the wartime level at the outset of the 1970s. Since then, the recession of the early '70s has hit blacks the hardest. If the difference between the size of the average black family and the average white family is taken into account, the income of the former is still below 60 percent. The implicit economic judgment there is that a black man is worth only about three-fifths of a white man—a contemporary version of the Founding Fathers' constitutional edict that only three-fifths of the slaves were to be counted in determining the population of the individual states when setting political representation.

In the North the median Negro family income is now two-thirds that of the white, but in the South barely over half. In addition, the majority of black families require two or more breadwinners to get up even to the income level that they do attain, while a majority of white families rely on only one wage-earner. Even in key Negro population centers outside the South, such as Watts and Cleveland, the relative and indeed actual income of Negroes was on the decline during much of the sixties despite booming affluence in the surrounding communities, and broad statistical measurements conceal the extent of abject poverty and social disorganization among the lower third or more. One sensitive indicator, the number of nonwhite families with a woman as the chief breadwinner, increased in the central cities from 23 percent in 1960 to 29 percent by 1970. Four out of every ten young blacks in the cities now grow up without one or both parents.

"I watched my boys go bad like milk you know is standing too long and there is no use for, so it goes sour. All those people out there, do they ever see how we live and what we have to take all the time?"

The unemployment rate of urban blacks during the last ten years has usually been two to three times that among whites, and often worse. If "subemployment" is included, a more meaningful measure since it includes economic dropouts and those working only part time but in need of full-time work in order to support their families, the blacks' joblessness has been over ten times that of the whites', sometimes reaching over 30 percent of the black labor force. The plight of young blacks is worst of all, with the unemployment rate even in the prosperity of the last half of the 1960s generally over 25 percent among the sixteen- to nineteen-year-olds on the job market. Joblessness in that group rose to 42 percent in the last quarter of 1970. And that in a nation with a policy of "full employment." The actual picture hardly suggests a happy conditioning for future social usefulness or personal tranquility. Over-all, the unemployment ratio between blacks and whites has narrowed very little for almost a decade and a half. The much-publicized drive for the private sector to create new jobs in the ghettoes has not really made a dent on the problem.

Still more serious trouble lies ahead. "The lower rungs of the economic ladder are being lopped off," Negro moderate Bayard Rustin has warned. The country's economy is rapidly automating its blue-collar jobs and has less and less need for an unskilled labor force, much of which is black. Yet the upgrading of the black labor force is coming slowly at best. At the beginning of the 1960s only

6 percent of the craftsmen in the highly organized building-trades unions were Negroes. At the beginning of the 1970s they still constituted only about 8 percent. Any economic downturn almost inevitably still hits the black community first and hardest for its less-skilled workers remain the last hired, first fired.

The dismal job prospect for so many young blacks results in substantial part from the failure of Negro education, although being improved, to keep up with the rapid upgrading of job skills. The proportion of young blacks completing high school rose from 36 percent at the start of the 1960s to roughly 60 percent at the threshold of the 1970s, but the proportion of young whites getting a high school diploma jumped from around 65 percent to almost 80 percent. And more and more machines require the skill equivalent of a high school graduate. On top of this, the average black student is behind the average white student in standard skills at every grade level, and the gap widens with more schooling; the black is a year and a half behind in the sixth grade and over three years behind in the twelfth grade. Former U.S. Commissioner of Education Francis Keppel has noted: "Clearly the primary and secondary schools have been doing their worst job for the children who need it most."

The number of black children attending substantially all-black schools actually increased every year during the decade and a half after the U.S. Supreme Court's desegregation decision, even as the commitment of the black community to equal and integrated educational opportunities moved from desire to demand. In effect, racial hostilities were being built into more and more young blacks for the rest of their lives—for the rest of this century, and beyond. The courts and educational authorities simply have not been desegregating students as fast as the whites have been separating out into the suburbs and the black enrollment rises in ghetto schools. If these longer-term trends hold, even the public schools of the Northern cities could be almost totally segregated by 1980. A vicious cycle is at work. School integration has usually been hurrying segregated housing—more, in fact, came into existence during the sixties than ever before—and segregated housing leads directly back to segregated schooling. The Washington, D.C., schools, for example, were integrated in the 1950s but the exodus of whites to the surrounding suburbs has left the District of Columbia, its population already over 70 percent Negro, with a public school enrollment over 95 percent black. At the same time, in contrast, just over 35 percent of the police in this heavily Negro city are black; 90 percent of the white policemen live in the Virginia and Maryland suburbs.

Perhaps the most telling human need is health. A national symposium of doctors and public health officials in the later sixties concluded that "despite advances in medical science, despite increased federal spending on hospitals and Medicare and research, the health gap separating Negroes and whites is growing still wider." One of the most basic yardsticks is infant mortality. In 1940 the death rate among nonwhite babies was 70 percent greater than for white infants; now it is nearly 100 percent worse. Almost 40 Negro infants die per 1000 live births, compared to 20 white infants. In the ghettoes the figure is 60 per 1000 for Negroes. Fifty percent of the Job Corps trainees there have never seen a doctor; 90 percent have not been to a dentist. The average ghetto Negro has a life expectancy seven years shorter than that of the average white.

Samuel Lubell, writing in the early 1950s, used the decreasing number of lynchings since the turn of the century as evidence of the headway Negroes were making—a rather perverse measure of progress. A better one is that the black community has now importantly decreased its illiteracy rate and improved its general economic position. But the white community has improved its over-all situation even more. And while reminders of white advantage used to keep to the white side of the railroad tracks, now they intrude by television into the poorest of Negro homes right along with the roaches and rats. "It is the system itself that is incapable of producing freedom for the 22 million Afro-Americans," Malcolm X said. "It is like a chicken can't lay a duck egg. A chicken isn't constructed in a way to produce a duck egg; and the political and economic system of this country is absolutely incapable of pro-

ducing freedom and justice and equality and human dignity for the
22 million Afro-Americans."

The emergence of the Negro middle class—up from about
7 percent of the black population in 1950 to just over 33 percent in
the early seventies—would seem to be an encouraging harbinger of
social progress. Yet that group is still generally unsuccessful in
gaining the equal treatment and opportunities education and hard
work were supposed to make possible. Daniel Moynihan reported
that in New York City the proportion of Negroes with professional or technical occupations already exceeds that of the Irish
and Italians. But it is also true that the overwhelming majority of
this new black elite are locked almost as rigidly as ever into Negro
neighborhoods and segregated schools. The average Negro college
graduate still makes $1000 less per year than his white counterpart
—and in the South less than the average white high school dropout.
The black middle class is now among the most alienated groups in
American society. New York Negro leader Percy Sutton has
warned: "I think you ought to know the bomb thrower of tomor-
row is not going to be the shirtless one or the slum resident; but he
will be the disenchanted son of the middle class black, the young
fellow who went to Yale or Harvard and wore Brooks Brothers
clothes but later discovered that despite all his training and his willingness to work within the system, the system was not willing to
work with him."

The deeply ingrained mythology of American politics denies
there is any problem too big or complicated for the nation to
solve, usually fairly promptly. But more than a century after the
Civil War and over fifteen years after the start of unparalleled if
uneven exertion on behalf of equal rights, the racial prospect is
still grim. For both whites and blacks it is causing political and
social discord, economic loss, physical violence, and a deepening
pessimism that goes beyond will and moral character to challenge
the American system's very capacity to do much about its most
pressing human dilemma.

The present juncture perhaps contrasts most suggestively with
the end of the main passage of Negro progress in the last century,

the first Reconstruction period. It finally closed in the "Compromise" of 1877 with a whimper, not a bang. That came after a close Presidential election in which the South played a key role. The blacks of that earlier time were then overpowered by the rise of the Ku Klux Klan and white Populism, and they were unprepared to do much about their plight. The North was glad to abandon the problem to the South; the white supremacists, after a few years in which opposing factions vied for "the colored vote," took command of what was still only a regional tragedy and sealed Negroes off with Jim Crow laws.

Now, however, the black population is deployed throughout the nation—it has even achieved a strategic concentration in the larger states—and its activists are as skilled, diverse, and demanding as any developed by the great social movements of the American past. Also, the North and West, both major parties, and the white middle class are each divided over the racial issue. And the South, while still yielding little decisive ground, is torn in national elections among the two main parties and the recurring lure of a third alternative—a dangerous diffusion for a region historically dependent on bloc power.

··

" 'Let a race of men come forth.' I sort of like that. I think that sort of says it."

··

The course ahead will be worked out more outside of politics than within it, with a multitude of considerations, worthy and unworthy, woven and tangled together over the years. But the various forces and frustrations will finally come to bear, however imperfectly, in recurring elections. And a number of primarily political factors will go into that along with the economic, social, moral, and other elements. In order even to begin to consider the difficulties ahead, a look is needed at the unfolding racial politics in both the South and North.

Today, if a traveler drives from the green valleys of Virginia down through the Deep South and on to the cattle country of Texas, he can end up, as journalist Gene Roberts has observed, with "the conclusions that racial segregation and discrimination are gone at last." But by changing his itinerary ever so slightly and instead of going to a few of the countless small-town cafés, motor courts, and neighborhood movie houses, he can come away "convinced that the South has not changed at all." The two journeys suggest the sharp contradictions at work in the New South. The area contains the country's most change-resistant society, and it is often arrayed against key tendencies of not only the twentieth but the nineteenth century as well. It clings to its regional identity when the rush of events is toward not merely national but cosmopolitan relationships; it insists on hierarchy when the historical imperative is more and more egalitarian. Nowhere is the age-old clash between the attitudes of the past and the aspirations of the future more explicit than in the South, especially in the racial tensions there. Yet it is not at all certain that the "future" will prevail over the "past" in that struggle. The situation presents an almost-classic example of two great historical forces encircling each other.

For whites and Negroes alike, despite all the paternalistic Southern claims to the contrary, the unavoidable issue is equality. Over four-fifths of the blacks want outright what around two-thirds of the whites seem determined not to allow: equal, freely chosen and integrated opportunities. And the activists in both camps have been ascendant. The proportion of Negroes who willingly accept the existing order has been declining for at least several decades. At the start of the 1960s the group still held nearly 20 percent of the black populace. Now it has well under 10 percent, and most of the remaining "Uncle Toms" are older, poorer, rural Negroes whose influence is practically nil. Similarly, the white Southern liberals who began to emerge out of the ferment of the 1930s and 1940s have suffered a long decline. That can be benchmarked from Senator Frank Graham's historic defeat in North Carolina's Democratic primary in 1950, when the racial issue was blatantly injected at the last minute in one of the South's more industrial and better-educated states. Graham was brought down not by an old-style spellbinder, but a conservative, cautious, corporation lawyer. Since the 1970 elections, there has been talk of a new wave of moderate leaders for the region. And that may be so. But the racial issue lies just below the surface; and an inescapable fact about the last two decades is that whenever the racial controversy has sharpened in the South, the segregationists have rallied and usually submerged all else.

The militancy in the South is most apparent among the region's young people—of both races. Every major study of Southern political behavior during the 1960s reported that the mammoth group of blacks in their late teens and twenties is, as a whole, by far the most ardently committed to integration and one of the two politically most active elements in the Negro community. The other is made up of those Negroes who were generally in their forties dur-

....

"The Man ain't gonna give it to you. You got to make it yourself."

....

ing the last decade. That group was at a young and formative stage in the years immediately after the Supreme Court outlawed the white primary and President Truman's Civil Rights Commission urged an end to segregation. Those developments triggered the first really intensive Negro political effort in the South in this century. The older group and the present young blacks—"a long, hot generation," columnist James J. Kilpatrick has described them—are dramatic examples of the effect of forceful public events on the impressionable young.

The young blacks' fever for integration, however, is fully matched by the intransigence of most of the region's young whites, who are perceptibly more aroused against desegregation than most of their elders. The most exhaustive statistical study ever made of Southern political behavior was conducted from the late 1950s to the middle 1960s by University of North Carolina political scientists Donald R. Matthews and James W. Prothro. In their resulting work, *Negroes and the New Southern Politics,* they concluded: "If the young [white] adults of the South represent the hope of the future, they may be the hope of the strict segregationists rather than anyone else ... [for] the youngest southern whites include more segregationists than the middle-age groups at every level of education." Only white Southerners over sixty were found to be as opposed to integration as the new group, and the new Johnny Rebs appear to be more bellicose at the outset of their years of political activity than were the older segregationists when they started out. Another straw in the wind was a poll of white Southern school children in early and middle adolescence, conducted immediately after the assassination of Martin Luther King in 1968; it found that roughly 60 percent were elated or indifferent about that murder. The young whites will undoubtedly settle down in the years ahead and broaden their outlook with experience and additional contacts outside the region, factors which have been found to have a moderating influence on the racial views of many white Southerners. But this latest crop has been deeply saturated in racial antagonisms at a critical stage of development; and much of the intense reaction will likely persist, like that of the young blacks of the middle and late 1940s who were affected by the civil rights stirrings of that period and who are still, in middle age, substantially more energized over this issue than the Negroes who came immediately before and after them.

Ironically, both the Southern whites and the Southern Negroes have concluded that those on the other side of the controversy are much less committed to opposing them than is actually the situation as reflected in public opinion studies and recent history. Only about one in five of the whites, as they daily see Negroes bend to the traditions of the area, have come to believe that most blacks genuinely desire integration and in fact "freedom *now*," though blacks have been preaching the almost instant arrival of the millennium for many years. And for all the "Never" buttons worn by whites in the South, less than half the Negroes there have concluded most whites really want segregation. Matthews and Prothro have warned: "As southern Negroes gain power and concessions in the region . . . they too fall prey to the selective perceptions and wishful thinking which in harsher days were almost impossible except for white people." A Gallup Poll in 1970 found that the portion of white Southerners who objected to sending their children to schools where some Negroes are enrolled had dropped from 61 percent to 16 percent in the previous seven years. But the opposition to most other desegregation still burns fiercely, especially in its political consequences.

Voter registration provides another insight into the racial maneuvering in the South through elective politics. Only 5 percent of the adult black populace in the eleven Southern states were registered to vote in the 1940s, before the white primary was voided. By the mid-1950s, 25 percent were registered. For the 1968 Presidential election, 62 percent were registered. At the outset of the seventies, that had already climbed to around 66 percent.

In the eleven Southern states, less than a million and a half blacks were registered in the first half of the sixties, but over three and a half million had registered in the early seventies. Black registration will almost certainly continue to climb during this decade, but it will likely not reach too much over 70 percent in the early to mid-1970s and perhaps around 75 percent by the end of the decade. Meanwhile, among voting-age whites, registration is also up, jumping 5 to 10 percent across the South just since the early 1960s and reaching roughly 80 percent region-wide in 1968. It probably will inch only a little above that during most of the decade. Over-all, at the outset of the 1970s, there were roughly sixteen and a half million registered whites and three and a half million registered blacks in the region.

Actual voting by both racial groups has also been going up in the South in recent years. In 1964, 43 percent of the blacks of voting age voted; in 1968 the proportion rose to 52 percent. In the same interval, the turnout of white Southerners rose from 65 per cent to 72 percent. The escalation contrasts with the fact that in the North, where political participation has usually been considerably higher among both whites and blacks than below the old

Mason-Dixon line, voter turnout fell for both groups between 1964 and 1968.

In the years just ahead, the black portion of the eligible electorate in the South will probably range from a low of about 15 percent in Texas, where the Negroes' share of the electorate actually exceeds their proportion of the total population (and they have generally voted fairly closely with the large Mexican-American bloc), to around 33 percent in Mississippi, where they make up just over 40 percent of the population. Negroes will thus still be only a far-back minority in the electorate of the Southern states. Over two million remain to be registered, and getting a politically inexperienced group actually to vote at all regularly is much harder than getting it registered. But Southern blacks are carving out a strategic if only incremental role for themselves state by state.

....

"Look, we started the whole civil rights business with two Presidents who both told Martin Luther King it's impossible. But the pressure of events made it possible. Confrontation is both inevitable and creative."

....

Raising the actual voting level among Southern Negroes to that of the white sector will require substantial improvements in the educational and economic conditions of Negro life. Differences in voting turnout between the two racial groups generally disappear when a reasonably adequate minimum family income is attained. But the median for all Negro families in the region has been below $4000 a year during the last ten years, and the real income of most Negroes there is rising too slowly to have more than modest political effect within this decade. Urbanization and industrialization also have usually been overrated as facilitators of Negro political involvement. There is one influence, however, that can be relied on to raise the level of Negro political participation in the coming years: the blacks' emergent sense of pride in themselves and their need to assert it. Legal obstacles first had to be cleared away for this feeling to be able to exert itself in formal political ways. But it is now a powerful dynamic, well launched and operating in defiance of long-prevailing determinants of political activity. Violence and intimidation, for instance, have had diminishing effect in retarding Negro politicking. In fact, they now tend to have quite the opposite effect, so long as blacks feel they have some local group of their own to back them up.

Over 90 percent of the Negro voters in the South have registered as Democrats, and they are now the most Democratic group in the nation. That is partly the result of the national party's civil rights stand over the years outweighing the grip white segregationists have on the Southern party, but the alignment is also a result of Negroes consciously seeking to concentrate their votes. As Democrats, they can participate in the primary election of the region's majority party and still have an opportuniy to vote in the general election for the Republican candidate if he offers a better alternative. It would make little sense, in contrast, for them to isolate themselves in the Republican primary; the Dixiecrat GOP is usually not only as segregationist as most white Democrats in the region but also opposed to the economic and social programs the black community so urgently needs and wants. In addition, if a majority of Negroes chose the GOP as their main base, they might inhibit its regional growth and thus lose the prospect of further splintering the white vote and occasionally playing a decisive role.

The black vote in the South has demonstrated an impressive capacity in the last half-decade to swing as a bloc between the two major parties and on rare occasion even to go outside both of them. In Alabama, for example, moderate Democratic Senator John Sparkman received over 70 percent of the Negro vote in 1966; the party's gubernatoriai candidate, segregationist Lurleen Wallace, got less than 35 percent on the same ballot. In 1968 a large portion of Alabama's black voters pulled off the more difficult exercise of supporting the national Democratic ticket of Humphrey and Muskie by casting their vote for it via a third party after Wallace had pre-empted the regular Democratic label for his Presidential candidacy and then went on to carry the state. In Maryland, an old border state, Nixon got hardly any black votes in 1968 and lost that state. But the moderate-to-liberal Republican candidate for the U.S. Senate that year, Charles ("Mac") Mathias, energetically wooed the state's Negro community, won substantial support from it, and was elected. In Alabama in 1970, many Negroes voted within the Democratic Party in an unsuccessful effort to block George Wallace's drive to gain the gubernatorial nomination, then went to a splinter party in the general election rather than support either of the major party candidates and elected twelve of its nominees to lesser posts. In South Carolina that year, in contrast, black voters generally stuck with the Democratic Party and helped its moderate nominee beat back the bid of Albert Watson and Strom Thurmond's rising Republican Party in that state. The key role of the black vote in that election led younger GOP leaders in the state to protest immediately afterward against Watson's hard-line campaign. South Carolina was only one of several states in which a number of Republican leaders since the 1970 election have counseled a more moderate party approach in the region toward the Negro vote.

Over-all, in 1970 black political candidates made greater gains than in any election since Reconstruction. Half of the estimated 650 Negro candidates in the U.S. that year ran in the South and border states. They generally did best at the state level, but in the border state of Maryland, a black was elected to the U.S. House of Representatives from a district not predominantly black. The number of Negroes in the lower house of state legislatures below the Mason-Dixon line jumped from thirty-seven to fifty-seven, and in the state senates there from nine to eleven. In Alabama two won in districts that had not elected a black legislator since before the turn of the century, and the same thing happened in three districts in South Carolina. Across the Confederacy four blacks were elected sheriffs, eight as county commissioners, twenty as school board members, ten as city councilmen, four as county councilmen, and four as aldermen.

Before the influence of the growing black vote is projected too far, however, perspective is needed on the three main political facts of life operating in Southern politics with regard to the racial situation. First, Negroes make up a declining proportion of the Southern populace—a third at the turn of the century, just under 20 percent now. Second, and in more specific political terms, in the great majority of contests black voters are not decisive at all. Third, when strong Negro support for a particular candidate becomes apparent, more white votes are likely to be driven off than black votes gained. A recurring difficulty for moderate politicians is how to cope with the opposition's inevitable whispering campaign or open charge of "nigger support" and the resulting white reaction which can overwhelm all other issues and emotions. Considerable skill has to be used to marshal the black vote in such circumstances. But it can hardly be expected that Negroes will be self-effacing any longer.

Ironic psychological warfare sometimes is evident. Thus, in Mississippi in 1967, Negro leader James Meredith "endorsed" archsegregationist Ross Barnett, the man who had invoked all of his powers as governor to try to block Meredith from entering the Ole Miss law school. That same year, black political leader Charles Evers privately advised aides of the more moderate (and unsuccessful) of the two Democratic candidates for governor of the state: "Tell him to pour it on [us] hard tonight. We can take it." In Georgia a few years earlier, in order to win more moderate voters, supporters of segregationist Lester Maddox arranged to have his opponent for lieutenant governor given several open Ku Klux Klan endorsements in the hope that would be "a kiss of death."

The great need in the South, of course, is for a lessening of the grip the racial issue has on practically all the voters, white and black. There is little possibility as yet, however, of putting together an effective and continuing biracial coalition. Poor whites

....

"As soon as a good, white American gets in a polling booth, that booth covers him like a Klan robe."

....

and lower-middle-income whites generally support the same economic liberalism as the black community, but the two racial groups
are irreconcilable on the overriding issue of integration. The upper-
middle-class whites, though still firmly segregationist, tend to be
less aroused over the question. But they generally have a primary
interest in opposing the tax-supported economic and social programs which would help raise up the poor whites and blacks.

An alliance of Negroes and white moderates to oppose a coalition of Populist segregationists and economic conservatives is recurringly proposed, but some serious students of Southern politics
doubt the wisdom of promoting it, even if the politics of the region
could be rechanneled this way. They argue that to do so would
almost inevitably aggravate racial tensions far beyond their present
level. The consequence for either side of losing, or more exactly of
refusing to accept defeat in an electoral showdown, could be explosive. They contend it is preferable to try to keep Negro voters
and the lower-income whites in the same party, where they may
eventually have to work out at least an uneasy accommodation,
and to encourage the growing sector of middle-class whites who
are economic conservatives but less extremist on the racial issue to
move into the Republican Party, where they may offer at least an
occasional alternative in general elections and thereby enhance the
bargaining power of the Negro vote.

In unintended support of that, the Republican Party is developing fairly rapidly in the South. Its leaders are generally rather young
—the average age of the Republican state chairmen in the region in
the 1968 Presidential campaign was just under forty. The party is
building a local base first of all in the region's rapidly growing
metropolitan areas, using a number of well-targeted Congressional
districts. It increased its hold every two years throughout the sixties. The GOP held only nine House seats in the South and border
states in 1960, and that was barely above the number held ten years
earlier. But the party was up to eighteen in 1964 and thirty-one in
1971. Republicans now hold a fourth of all the Southern and border
districts and could readily capture ten to twenty more during the
first half of the seventies. The GOP's share of the popular vote in

the South has also grown every two years for over a decade, doubling during that period.

The GOP is making headway more slowly at the state and local levels than in Congressional and Presidential races. But headway is apparent there, too. In the South and border states, the GOP held no governorships in 1950 but six at various times in the last half-decade. Similarly, it held 263 state legislative seats twenty years ago but 477 at the outset of the present decade. That trend has been buttressed by a host of already-active Democrats switching parties. Some GOP leaders, in fact, are already concerned over how to keep turncoat Democratic politicians from moving in on them.

Practically all students of Southern politics thus far have usually stressed the factors retarding the rise of the GOP at the state and local levels. They emphasize that Southern attitudes and loyalties alter only very slowly, and the 1970 off-year election results tended to confirm that. Political scientists point to the powerful and singular polarization that results from most segregationists being lower-income whites strongly attracted by the pocketbook appeals of the Democratic Party and hostile to the traditional economic conservatism of the GOP. They point out that the stale rhetoric against "the tycoons of high interest rates" and "Wall Street" has persisted far longer in the South than in the rest of the country. George Wallace, for example, delights in telling Southern audiences over and over: "The Republicans now, they havin' to meet in banks trying to figger what they gonna do about the Chase National and the Wall Street crowd. You know, they used to meet in little biddy banks to talk about us, but this time, we got 'em meetin' in the biggest bank in the world talkin' about you'n'me and what they gonna do. . . ."

The fact is, however, that the Republican Party is building a solid base in more and more communities, developing a lengthening roster of regional figures, and proving its "Southernness" on a broad range of issues. It is not reaching out just to ex-Wallaceites but is also seeking to synthesize a spectrum as inclusive as South Carolina's ultraconservative Strom Thurmond and Virginia's moderately liberal Republican Governor Linwood Holton. More important, the economics of the area are raising up an ambitious, new white middle-class which is Republican in outlook. The region's per capita income in 1950 was only two-thirds that of the national average; by 1960 it had climbed to three-fourths and by 1970 to about 80 percent. The average family income jumped almost 50 percent during the last decade in the South, compared to just under 40 percent for the nation. Even among lower-middle-income whites, improving economic levels are beginning to provide better take-off points for GOP converts; and the longer the race issue remains agitated, as it likely will for the foreseeable future, the less compelling are that group's Democratic ties. In a region that has always been acutely status-conscious and is now almost desperately looking for fresh badges of special standing, the Republican party offers a refurbished respectability quite the opposite of its old carpet-bagging image in the South.

The overwhelming majority of white Southerners continue to call themselves Democrats. But a big difference has opened up between their almost automatic party identification and their actual political attitudes. There have been substantial defections in the South from Democratic Presidential candidates ever since 1948. Southern support for the national Democratic ticket hovered around 70 to 85 percent during the Roosevelt period. It dropped to 50 percent in the 1950s, then to just over 30 percent in 1968. Now that fraying of party ties over the course of many years is beginning to tell farther down the ballot.

A number of supposedly safely entrenched, old-style Democratic senators and congressmen in the South could come tumbling down over the course of the seventies under the challenge of Republicans and newer-style Democrats. Many old-timers are lost in the new television era, and age is working against some of the more influential ones. Most, even while posing as Populists, have been propped up again and again by the area's vested economic interests, and the Republicans could soon be prying the latter away, for a whole new economic complex particularly sympathetic to Southern Republicans is emerging. The new GOP in the South can be a very conservative influence on the nation's Presidential politics. But in its probable loosening of some of the hold of Southern seniority on the Congress, the development could also have a mildly liberalizing effect over the course of the seventies.

What is happening in the South, state by state, is suggested by a closer look at Virginia. Once the capital of the Confederacy, it has long been at the center of Southern politics, not as flexible as the border states but not as rigid as Alabama and Mississippi. Virginia was the chief instigator of "massive resistance" against the Supreme Court's 1954 school desegregation order. The changing polity there was signaled, however, in the middle sixties by the defeat of the state's ranking Congressman, "Judge" Howard Smith, the elderly, conservative, longtime chairman of the powerful Rules Committee of the U.S. House of Representatives. He was beaten by a liberal Democrat in the primary. But the district then elected an arch-conservative Republican in November. Of Virginia's ten Congressional seats, Republicans won six for the Congress sitting in 1971–1972. It is the first Republican-dominated Southern Congressional delegation since Reconstruction days. And to take office with the start of this decade, the Commonwealth elected its first Republican governor since Reconstruction. The GOP began the seventies with only seven of forty seats in the state senate and twenty-four of one hundred seats in the state house of delegates. But those totals are the highest in this century and indicate a developing and usually moderate Republican Party taking root.

The segregationist Byrd organization, which long ran the Commonwealth, lost one of the two Senate seats it had controlled to a moderate Democrat, William B. Spong, in 1966. He even topped the separate vote that year for Senator Harry Byrd, Jr., who won the other Senate seat on the same ballot but had to run independent of the two major parties in 1970 to gain a full six-year term. Spong has been called the first representative of an emerging "eastern," urbanized Virginia. Spong's moderates, however, must contend with a rapidly growing, even more liberal wing of the party, especially in the populous northern and eastern tiers of the state. This liberal wing is broadening the range of Virginia politics still further.

Vast changes in the state itself underlie those political upheavals. The suburbs are growing at four times the rate of the rest of the Commonwealth. Three-fourths of the state's population will probably be living in just ten metropolitan areas by the end of the decade, thereby further vastly reducing the power of the rural whites. At the same time, the Negro vote is increasing rapidly in both size and sophistication. In the seventies nearly one in five Vir-

....

"Talking soul does not change the problem."

....

ginia voters is black. The flexibility of this group is suggested by the fact that over 70 percent of the black voters split their ticket in one fairly recent election, according to Louis Harris.

Even in Mississippi, a key redoubt of the Old South, signs of political change are unmistakable. Not until the middle sixties did the number of people engaged in industry finally exceed the number in agriculture. Yet the switchover is occurring so fast that the proportion employed in manufacturing could be double that of the rural areas by the middle seventies. By the end of this decade, half the state's populace may live around Jackson and in a booming strip along the Gulf coast. City residents, younger voters, and white-collar groups are gaining influence at the expense of hard-shelled rural whites. A small sign of the time is the fact that liquor sales were finally legalized in over forty Mississippi counties by the start of the seventies, though that still was well over a third of a century after the Prohibitionists had been routed in practically all the rest of the country.

Over half of the Mississippi Legislature's 174 seats were filled at the outset of this decade by newcomers, one of them the first Negro legislator since Reconstruction. In the same election twenty-one other blacks won public office, six of them after campaigning against white opponents; twenty-six other blacks lost to whites. The election of Charles Evers as mayor of Fayette near the end of the sixties—the first black mayor in Mississippi since Reconstruction—was another sign of black participation starting in the state's public life. Equally significant, the two-party system is beginning to stir, though it will come more slowly than in Virginia. Of a dozen mayorality elections in the state at the threshold of this decade, five were won by Republicans.

The label "moderate" is still given a white official in the state just for remaining silent on the racial issue; and the characterization, when it comes from whites, is not apt to be friendly. But Negro registration in Mississippi climbed from less than 25,000 in the early 1960s to over 200,000 at the outset of the 1970s, and more and more white candidates are openly seeking Negro votes at the local level and defending themselves as best they can. Often such a candidate will proclaim that he is not a moderate at all, but simply an old-fashioned Mississippi conservative running against a "demagogue." And even the crude appeals of unregenerate white supremacists are gradually giving way to a glossy right-wing line.

The principal prod for change in the state is a spreading recognition of the high economic price being paid for clinging to the past —a recognition put into focus in this remark of a prominent business consultant: "I'd say one of the towns along the Mississippi Gulf Coast here would be a great place to invest some money if you could afford to wait a while. Right now, the racial environment in these towns makes them not very attractive to many skillful people—particularly those in the glamour industries."

Even with the fairly rapid political changes taking place in the South, the chasm between Northern and Southern Democrats over Presidential politics perhaps could widen in the decade ahead. The Northern Democratic Party will probably be seeking to attract the restive blacks, the new wave of young people, and the growing support for social change in the middle class more overtly than the GOP can be expected to do. That appalls much of the white South. But when Northern Democrats are forced to choose between the expanding tendencies in the big urban states and catering to long-gone Southern segregationists, it is not hard to guess which way most of them will go. Actually the region is incubating a whole new cadre of bright, newer political figures who may just possibly be able to bridge the North-South differences. This crop is most easily indicated by South Carolina's polished and pragmatic Senator Ernest ("Fritz") Hollings. But even when brokered to a precarious common denominator, the differences between the South and the Democratic Presidential party are formidable.

The Northern Democratic Party probably must either largely write off the region in Presidential elections for some years to come or quickly help build a new foundation there. The development of a more liberal Democratic Party in the area would almost certainly accelerate the emergence of the GOP at the state and local level, but it would also hurry the region along to the full-blown two-party division discernible by the latter 1970s. Developing a Southern base for Presidential Democrats would require raising the proportion of moderate and liberal Democrats in the South from their present 15 to 20 percent share of the electorate, plus increasing the black vote from its likely 15 to 18 percent slice of the actual vote. If there is a three-way split in Presidential elections in 1972 and 1976, the Democrats would have a fighting chance if they could attract 40 to 42 percent of the vote. But getting up to that strength will require far more effort than the Democratic National Committee or other national Democratic groups have yet been willing even to attempt.

"I don't want love, baby, I want respect."

In contrast to that prospect, the South can look ahead to expanding influence within the national GOP. The 1964 and 1968 GOP national conventions and Presidential campaigns made clear that the region has already gained a major foothold in the Republican Party. The Southern states were allocated over 25 percent of all the votes in the 1968 convention and constituted the party's largest single regional bloc. In that redistribution of power, six Southern states gained additional votes and four Northern states lost. That is in keeping with the fact that the 1970 Census shows, in what amounts to a historic turning point, more people moved into the South than moved out of it during the preceding ten years.

The new Republican Party in the region will almost inevitably join forces with the more conservative elements in the North—primarily in the Western and Midwestern GOP—to mount a continuing bid for control of the national party. And that will exert an unmistakable pull to the right, and toward the South, on Republican Presidential candidates and national politics in general. The recurring temptation for Republican Presidential candidates to "go South" in their strategy, however, will be in tension with the possibility of the party attracting a larger share of the growing Negro bloc and moderate whites in the North. The growing dissidence of liberal Northern Republicans will also work against that thrust. The choice between the two bases will become increasingly difficult as the generation of young whites, with its racially more progressive and active nucleus, comes onto the election rolls. Influential GOP tacticians argue that with a more conservative national constituency than the Democrats, the Republican Party

"So here is a Cracker teacher standing in front of my child making him listen to 'Little Black Sambo.' See, that's the image the school gives him when he's young, to teach him his 'place.'"

can generally remain less explicit on the racial issue. But the regional and ideological tug-of-war could quickly become a critical struggle within the GOP. The underlying political reality, nevertheless, is that the Republican Party is moving into a position to put together a North-South coalition such as the Democrats maintained for over a century and a half, though with rapidly declining effectiveness during the last thirty years. In a historical sense, however, it must also be noted that while trying to maintain such a coalition, the Democrats helped bring on the debacle of the Civil War, and their party was in the minority most of the time that it tried riding a regional tandem after that.

In the Presidential politics of the early and middle 1970s, the principal alternative to Republicanism for some of the South will be provided not by the Democrats but by George Wallace's third way. Diehard segregationists cannot be placated by national candidates of either major party without these candidates probably losing vastly more votes in the North and West than might be picked up in the South. That might become a less valid premise for Republicans if racial tensions in the nation are seriously aggravated in the years ahead. But even if that comes to pass, the over-all public climate likely would strengthen a George Wallace more than the GOP. Even without that, however, the appeal of Wallace, or of some other Southern prototype, will almost surely persist, for it responds far more directly than the two mainstream parties probably can to those many "barbers and beauticians, steel workers and clerks, farmers, and other little people," as Wallace describes them, who feel frustrated or fearful about being left out, or left behind, by big government, the new education, the mass media, a sophisticated economy, the activist new and younger elements, and the whole complex emerging society which is displacing so much of the old and known. The nation is likely to continue changing rapidly in technological and social terms in the coming years, and this group is consequently also likely to continue to be agitated into political significance. It will be strongest in those states and social strata most resistant to change, and it will therefore hold out longest in the traditionalist enclaves of the Deep South.

At the same time, the limits of Wallaceism need to be noted. His 1968 campaign carried only one more state than did Strom Thurmond's far more hurriedly put-together Dixiecrat effort twenty years earlier, and the pluralities in those states were nearly the same both times. More relevant prospectively, the Wallace movement in the South further splinters the segregationist white sector already split between the new Southern GOP and the Democrats loyal to their national party, and that enhances the incremental possibilities of the growing black electorate. Wallace's net impact on history will probably be the not insubstantial one of keeping the most laggard of the South from bringing some of its key public premises into a closer relationship with those of the rest of the country for a while longer and helping to create a more racist and rightest political environment to which the major national candidates then almost automatically adjust.

Yet perhaps even more fundamentally, Wallace is important as a symbol of the elemental—and malevolent—forces infecting the body politic. In a very personal way he is a reminder, as Marshall Frady has written, "that the demonic is still at work in human affairs, even in this age of computers and slide rules and public relations task forces; that life and politics, after all, are simply larger than arithmetic." Wallace himself has been more explicit as to what he is about: "Hell, we got too much dignity in government now, what we need is some *meanness*. You elect one of those steelworkers guvnuh, you talk about a revolution—damn, ther'd be shootin' and tearin' down and burnin' up and killin' and bloodlettin', sho nuff. Steelworker wouldn't have to think about it—he'd just go ahead and do it. Anyway, I been tellin' folks for years, you ask if I hadn't, that there'll be fighting in the streets one day between rightists and leftists, between whites and blacks. Hell, all we'd have to do right now is march on the federal courthouse there in Montgomery, take over the post office and lock up a few of those judges and by sunset there'd be a revolution from one corner of this nation to the other. We could turn this country right around."

Over-all, the "South" as a political way of life once held sway well north and west of its present reach. In the 1870s, the real dividing line between the North and the Confederacy extended from Maryland across most of West Virginia, through the southern half of Ohio, Indiana, Illinois, and Missouri, then down over Texas. In more recent decades, however, Texas has affiliated more and more with the West. Kentucky, Tennessee, and Maryland are now far along in developing a two-party system facing north as much as south. Virginia and Florida are similarly moving out of a sectional orbit and into national patterns. Even Arkansas twice elected a Republican governor in the last half of the 1960s, though he lost a bid in 1970 for a third term. The new decade is almost certain to see a hastening of the continuing change in the region. The two Carolinas and Georgia could be as far along by the last half of the decade as the border states of Kentucky and Tennessee were at the outset of the seventies.

Much of the once "solid South" will undoubtedly try to resist for years to come the partisan and racial changes going on. But a relentless and now hurrying historical process is at work. It will provoke heightened tensions in this decade, and it will probably bring more political than social integration. But "somewhere," as James Vander Zanden has written, "between the white South's idealized white supremacist patterns and the Negroes' utopia of equality will be the outcome, itself transitory and subject to change. . . ."

CHAPTER 6

The Hardening Impasse: North

The South is in Montgomery, Alabama. But
the South is also in Cicero, Illinois. The South
is in Great Neck, Long Island. The South is in
Orange County, California. It's everywhere.
—LEW ALCINDOR, BLACK ALL-AMERICAN
BASKETBALL PLAYER

Sometime in the early 1970s, for the first time in the nation's
history, the majority of blacks will be living in the South no longer
—a historic consequence of the great black migration north and
west which began in earnest with World War I and reached flood
tide in the 1950s. That migration is not over, though it slackened
through the 1960s. Around 150,000 blacks still are leaving the
South each year; and the prospect is the exodus will continue,
especially among the younger, more ambitious Southern blacks.
Only about 5 percent of the Negroes—a little over a million—still
live on Southern farms, the basic source of the racial migration,
and they should mostly have left there during this decade. But
that will only lessen the trek out of the region, for even the Southern cities are often now only way stations for many blacks.

The critical focus of the racial politics of the seventies is no
large geographic area so much as the American city, wherever it

is. While the birth rate among Southern blacks about makes up for those who leave the region, the Northern ghettoes, in addition to the arrivals from the South, now generate almost a half-million annual increase in population on their own. The Negro population in the country's larger cities jumped between 1960 and the early 1970s from less than ten million to nearly fourteen million. By the middle seventies nearly one in every three residents of America's principal cities may be black. In 1980 a third of the nation's thirty largest cities could have black majorities.

The map of racial politics is still not indicated, though, just by shading some of the cities black or gray. While Negroes have been jamming into the urban ghettoes, building a potential to dominate the country's historic crossroads, the whites have been moving out to suburbia in record numbers and encircling them. The white population in the suburbs climbed from fifty-two million in 1960 to over seventy million in the early seventies and will probably reach nearly eighty million in the last half of this decade. The proportion of Negroes living in the nation's suburbs is hardly increasing at all despite a slight spurt in the number of blacks moving to suburbia around the outset of this decade. Negroes still constitute less than 5 percent of all suburbanites.

A long-range prospect was suggested by the National Commission on Urban Problems, headed by former Senator Paul Douglas. In the schools of the central cities, an important incubator for the America which will rise early in the next century, the Commission projected that the proportion of white youngsters probably will drop by 10 percent and that of nonwhite children likely will rise by over 100 percent between the late 1960s and 1985. The greatest geographic separation of the races is expected to occur not in the East or South but in the Midwest, where in 1985 90 percent of the nonwhites will likely be living in the central cities, but less than 30 percent of the whites. The national prospect is one of suburbia awash with whites and the cities crammed with young job-age blacks. The projections, the Commission concluded, "vividly portray the geographic fulfillment of the fears expressed

by the President's Commission on Civil Disorders—America is becoming an apartheid society."

Already, of course, a substantial part of practically every
metropolitan area in the country is, or is fast becoming, a black
enclave. As increasing incomes give outward mobility to lower-
middle-class white families, they have been moving out and leaving
the central areas in economic default to low-income blacks. But
there is irony here. For political purposes, a minority group could
hardly be distributing itself more strategically than are the Negroes
in this country. The massing badly aggravates de facto segregation
and poverty. But it also facilitates the face-to-face cohesiveness and
communication which help an undereducated minority achieve
political effectiveness. Nothing, in contrast, would subvert the
black community's approaching power more quickly than the
diffusion which so much of it wants through integration in the
suburbs.

Even a seriously discriminated-against, little-educated, poverty-
stricken minority usually develops into the chief power bloc in a
community well before its share of the population reaches 40 percent, especially when it appears headed toward becoming a majority. The polarization of whites and blacks has retarded that development for blacks, but over fifty communities of varying size
already have black mayors. Gary, Cleveland, and Newark, among
the larger communities, have elected Negro chief executives. The
necessary threshold may similarly be reached city-wide by the
black populations of Atlanta, Baltimore, Detroit, Oakland, St.
Louis, and Trenton in the middle seventies. By the very latter
1970s the threshold may have been reached in Chicago, Cincinnati, Columbus, Memphis, New Orleans, Philadelphia, and a number of other cities. Out of all this the country could see a sweeping
Negro political takeover rivaling the earlier rise to power by the
Irish in the cities.

The political ritual through which each succeeding immigrant
group has moved into American society has been about the same
during the last century and a half. The established elements have

first tried to ignore the intruders, then bribe the leaders of the new group with money and minor recognition, then buy off the rank and file with bread and services while increasingly trying to repress the more restive elements. Finally, however, there has been a tumultuous turning of the tables, with the insurgents taking power unto themselves district by district, city by city. Negroes, as the most recent social and political immigrants, are now fighting their way into the climactic phase of that progression, as the Germans, Irish, Italians, Poles, and so many others have done before them.

The analogy to earlier immigrant groups is limited, of course. For Negroes have to contend with not only economic and social barriers but also the complication of color. Yet black power is still but the latest manifestation of some very old American politics. As Gary's Mayor Richard Hatcher commented, "What's so unusual about people saying, 'We're going to control our own turf?' That's not separatism—that's good old Americanism." Like the earlier groups at the same stage, the blacks now seek not just to be absorbed into the existing electorate but also to assert their own identity, community, pride, hopes, numbers, and power. That stage, however, is likely to last longer for the blacks than it did for the old ethnic groups, for the black ghetto is vastly harder to rise up and out of than the old ethnic ghetto ever was. Many blacks, in fact, have come to believe that not only they but their children and their children's children as well are trapped there. By the second generation a considerable portion of those in the earlier ethnic groups could and did disappear into the established society, but the Negro finds he is almost always blocked off from that. For him, getting heard from right in the ghetto, rather than anonymity and escape, is virtually the only way to equality, or at least self-assertion.

Black organizing to work for social and political power was complicated for a number of years, as Oscar Handlin has noted, by "a confusion of goals and purposes created by the drive for integration. Nobody demanded of the Irish, Italians, or Jews who turned up in New York that they become a vanishing element.

Yet for a few years, that created among blacks and whites the impression that any kind of separatism was segregation and therefore undesirable." Now there is much less of this feeling in the ghetto, and the thrusting dynamic of Negro politics is black goals and black leadership—for blacks.

"They never let you forget you were black. We decided to remember we were black."

This unavoidably alienates many whites, but for some years to come the primary objective of the more assertive blacks will be to mobilize the black community, not placate the white majority. The latter can perhaps be negotiated with later, the newer black leaders have concluded, from a stronger, more independent position. Stokely Carmichael, an influential theoretician as well as sometime activist, has argued that Negroes now have turned to politics "because black Americans are a propertyless people in a country where property is valued above all. We have to work for power because this country does not function by morality, love and nonviolence but by power." At the same time, he has made clear that "black people do not want to 'take over' this country. They do not want to 'get whitey,' they just want to get him off their back, as the saying goes." The almost inevitable prospect is substantially more, not less, friction: more self-assertion and demands from the excluded, restive blacks, and more clashes with those who would slow or keep them down.

The strength of the country's two major parties over the years has been developed in great part by their ability to recognize emergent groups in time, then provide the political vehicle in those areas where there is most likely to be a breakthrough. A crucial test of both parties in the 1970s will be whether they can adapt more fully to the racial shift in the cities and make room there.

Unfortunately, in the 1968 Presidential race and 1970 off-year elections, most white party politicians were still generally attempting to "broker" the Negro vote through ministers, black office-holders, minority papers (where the buying of political ads too often also gains editorial support and news columns), and similarly available channels. And black "spokesmen" were often still willing to play their traditional role behind a façade of tougher rhetoric. An outmoded system of petty favors and pie-in-the-sky promises has kept the arrangement going. But it is eroding, and the surging impulse of millions of Negro citizens to be free and equal as well as black cannot be thus contained much longer.

A prerequisite to the major parties assuredly becoming better mechanisms for helping to resolve the racial impasse will be for the blacks themselves to raise their frequently indifferent levels of registration and voter turnout into a substantially larger force in the North as well as the South. While Negroes constitute about 12 percent of the populace, they usually make up only around 5 percent of the electorate. The black community thus has a very substantial reserve of potential voters. It will be augmented in this decade by the coming of age of the new generation of blacks, who make up an even larger proportion of the Negro population than young whites do of the white. Marshaling the additional vote will test the motivational effect of the black militants and the organizational effort of Negro moderates.

In some areas almost as large a proportion of registered blacks as of registered whites has been voting. Thus in the twelve north-central states, 70 percent of the nonwhites voted fairly consistently in the last half-decade, compared to barely over 75 percent of the whites. When a Negro runs for major office, the black turnout sometimes is even better. Similarly, Robert F. Kennedy, in the 1968 Presidential primaries, attracted a black turnout which proportionally exceeded that of the eligible whites in a number of areas. Experience shows again and again, however, that when Negro voters feel no real choice is offered to them, their participation drops sharply. It also seems apparent, in terms of the stylistic nuances of the present politics, that so-called low-profile white candidates, however well-meaning, do not turn on Negro voting groups at all well.

The rate of progress by Negroes in moving into the political mainstream over the years is suggested by the number of blacks elected to the Congress. In 1920 there were no Negro Congressmen. In 1930 and 1940 there was one. In 1950 there were two. In 1960 there were four. At the end of the sixties there were nine, including the first Negro woman, Mrs. Shirley Chisholm of New York City, plus Senator Edward Brooke, Republican of Massachusetts. For the 1971–1972 Congress, twelve blacks were elected. Prospectively, progress should accelerate. By the middle seventies there are likely to be at least twenty Negro members of the Congress, based on the presently projected concentration of the black population and its increasing political mobilization. By the end of the decade there could be around thirty. If Negro representation were to become equal to the group's proportion of the total populace, however, blacks would have over fifty seats in the House of Representatives. The actual size of the bloc indicates the continuing political restrictions on this racial and social minority and its abiding need for legislative support from the white majority.

The difference between some of the older and the more recent Negro members of the Congress suggests the less tangible political changes beginning to take place for black America. Chicago's William Dawson was the senior Negro in the House of Representatives from 1943 to 1970. He was originally sent to Washington far more by that city's white political machine than by the crowded, put-upon majority of Negroes in his district, and he became an old-style boss within his own district. Over the decades he gained important congressional seniority, including finally the chairmanship of the Committee on Government Operations. But he almost always followed Speaker Sam Rayburn's frequently cited dictum that you have to go along to get along. As a result he did not become one of the more outspoken leaders of the country's Negro community when it finally stirred politically. He was, in fact, a model of the Negro politician of the old school.

Harlem's brilliant, freewheeling, erratic Adam Clayton Powell was the next Negro to take a seat in the Congress—in 1945—representing New York's Harlem. Through seniority he rose to become Chairman of the House Education and Labor Committee. He used that power to push through historic legislation for civil rights, the poor, organized labor, and elementary, intermediate, and higher education. But long before he ran into trouble in 1967 over being seated by the House and lost his chairmanship, he took to absenting himself from his district for long stretches of time. A further source of trouble was that, like a number of Congressmen, both white and black, Powell was generally more interested in keeping the political lid on his base, and precluding the rise of young Turks who might someday challenge him, than in encouraging blacks to assert their full effect in Presidential, gubernatorial, and other elections. As a result, and even though accepted back into the House after being chastised there, he then was turned out by the overwhelmingly black voters of his district in 1970.

Detroit's John Conyers, Jr., first elected in 1964, exemplifies the newer Negro officeholder in both the Congress and a number of state legislatures and city councils around the country. Hardworking, informed, independent, Conyers repeatedly stresses the need for better political organization among blacks. He won the respect of the House of Representatives even while seeking to reduce its punishment of Powell. And he led the successful fight against Congressional scuttling of the Supreme Court's "one man, one vote" ruling. More militant blacks criticize him for working within the white political system at all, but Conyers is an ardent advocate of Negro power.

The harbinger of a still newer model of black leadership is Ronald Dellums, who took his seat in the Congress for the first time in 1971. Tough, disciplined, and polished, Dellums made explicit to his constituents that they had elected a "radical." His previous record in local government shows that he is as effective in institutional intricacies as on the stump. But his philosophy probably includes more of the Black Revolution and New Left stirrings of the sixties than any other member of his race yet to sit in the

House. Like New York's Congresswoman Shirley Chisholm, he indicates a new bluntness, even an abrasiveness on occasion, as well as sophistication among black politicians in the over-all political processes.

Senator Edward Brooke has emerged as still another kind of Negro politician: an able, wary loner who looks largely to white rather than black voters. But he is a case study not of what the evolving Negro leadership will likely be but of the wavering reach of white political attitudes. If Dawson was an Uncle Tom in the view of many young blacks, Brooke is Eliza crossing the ice—or, perhaps more accurately, the ivy.

The new decade will undoubtedly produce a few more Dawsons and some Powells and perhaps a very occasional Brooke. But the most frequent molds will probably be close to Conyers and Dellums. It is also likely that the Congress will be confronted

----

"What does the black man want? Everything you got and hope to get."

----

fairly soon by the election of a devastating black satirist on the order of Dick Gregory and the South's first black Congressman in this century.

In the overwhelmingly white political institutions, the critical dilemma for Negro activists at both local and national levels is how much to work within those arrangements and how much to go a separate way, how militant and abrasive to be in order to motivate the blacks and prod the whites, and how much to submit to the inevitable compromises of coalition politics. The Congress of Racial Equality, SNCC, the Black Panthers, and disparate other forces of black militancy have gone on record in support of a generally independent course, even a black political party, where Negroes are concentrated. SNCC indeed announced the establishment of such a party, though its purpose will not necessarily be to win elections. It may present candidates from time to time, but it will primarily be a pressure group to "help black people live better."

The hard-learned practicality of most Negroes, on the other hand, makes it unlikely that the heavy majority will long isolate themselves outside the main political currents despite the rhetoric of their more passionate leaders. Hard political bargaining, not isolation in a largely black party, is seen as the quickest and most direct apparent way to gain the additional resources and recognition blacks seek in most areas. The spreading influence of the militants almost guarantees increasing discord and assertiveness in Negro political relationships, but hardly mass separatism. The coldly realistic view of the coalitionists has perhaps been most succinctly put by Whitney Young, Jr., ever the practicalist and almost a "whitey" to some young blacks: "You can make quite a case for the moral decadence of white America, but you can't make a program based on its collapse by 1975." What actually seems to lie ahead in Negro politics, then, is a combination of coalitional compromises and thrust-and-cut militancy.

This duality may be self-defeating to a considerable extent. But it will also allow the militants to make breakthroughs which the moderates would be unable to achieve in anything like a comparable time period, yet which only the moderates will then be able to consolidate. The more demanding activists also insist on gains for far more of the black populace than the moderate, middle-class Negro groups usually do except in rhetoric. That extra effort is crucial in a period when the next substantial increase in Negro political and social power depends heavily on activating the great mass of still-isolated low-income blacks.

To the extent that Negro politics do operate "within the system," the key question is: With whom might Negroes combine to get more than the "too little, too late" which the younger group and newer leaders conclude they are getting out of their prevailing tie with the Democratic Party? It has been suggested that a Republican Presidential candidate like Senator Charles Mathias of Maryland could draw a substantially larger portion of the black vote than the 5 to 10 percent that Goldwater attracted in 1964 and the slightly larger share that Nixon got in 1968; a special alliance could then develop out of that. According to this argument, such a candidate would at least force the two parties to bid against each other more aggressively for Negro support. The likelihood, however, is that the Republican Party is going to be pulled too strongly in this decade by its own burgeoning conservative wing and Southern prospects in Presidential elections, not to mention traditional fiscal restraint, to provide the follow-through necessary to convert any initial flirtation with Negro voters into meaningful substance and continuing plausibility, much less achieve the kind of basic realignment which Franklin Roosevelt brought about with this constituency for the Democrats.

Coalition politics for Negroes will more likely than not finally come down at the national level to trying to develop a closer concert of interest with one or more of the other major elements in the Democratic Party and then to exert greater leverage on that loose and lumbering confederacy. A special possibility would be substantial black support for a potential independent candidate like John Lindsay or some other figure with appeal in the socially more progressive enclaves of the general white electorate. Blacks have shown increasing political independence and a capacity for exploiting such situations. But there would still likely be some fall-off through this alternative. Many of the established black politicians have close ties with the older forces in the Democratic Party, and moving much of a less-educated, party-conscious constituency like the Negro rank and file away from the Democratic Presidential nominee to an independent party candidate might be possible but would still be difficult.

Building an alliance between the black community and other social groups with similar social interests, however, would also not be easy at all soon. Martin Luther King, in his book *Where Do We Go From Here?*, wrote of the large number of poor whites who share similar economic and social grievances with Negroes, but Martin Duberman has pointed out in response that "reality, as we all know it, is only one, and probably one of the weaker, well-springs of human behavior"; and many poor whites have long "put race before all other considerations—including self-interest." Organized labor, despite the frequent testimonials of its national leaders, is increasingly conservative, racially torn, and hardly reliable in any really hard squeeze on the Democratic base in behalf of blacks. Similarly, the traditional liberal elements in the Democratic Party have been increasingly detached and even disturbed about their tie with the stirring black community, though they still mouth the same old platitudes. If Negroes have a broad-based potential ally, it is the active vanguard of better-educated, young white Northerners coming of age. For both Negro moderates and traditional liberals, however, such an alliance could turn out to be a mixed blessing. First, it would be a sharply disruptive factor within the Democratic Party, for it would draw from essential elements of that normally embattled party base. Second, neither the black militants nor the more active young whites will likely be content just to demand more economic, educational, and other governmental programs and appropriations. Instead, they will be seeking a much more democratic power system. Even the most tenuous explicit alliance of Negroes and any considerable portion of the younger white activists will provoke sharp countertensions in other parts of the electorate, but such a coalition still constitutes an important prospective group on the racial problem and on many other issues well beyond that.

Of special prospective relevance, an unmistakable radical shift in attitude has taken place within much of the Negro community in the last half-decade. Thus Louis Harris found 54 percent of the blacks convinced in 1966 that whites were hostile or indifferent to them, but the figure had swollen to about 70 percent by the outset of the 1970s. A fourth of all Negroes thought the draft laws were unfair to them in 1966; almost half felt that way at the start of the decade. Just over 40 percent thought their rate of progress was too slow in 1966, almost 60 percent by 1970. Even before Martin Luther King's assassination in April 1968, a

Harris poll concluded that about 15 percent of the Negro population joined or would have been willing to join in the riots that
had already struck about a score of cities. Fifteen percent does not
seem like a very large proportion; but, as Harris pointed out, it
adds up to over three million people—a sizable enough group for
serious trouble and possible insurrection in any society in history.
Almost as important, he found an additional 35 percent of the
Negro population have been "sympathetic spectators" of the riots
and that support was as great among relatively well-educated and
economically advantaged individuals as among less-trained, poorer,
transient blacks.

At both the national and local levels, there has been a considerable dilution of the support for the mediating methods of Roy
Wilkins and the older Negro leaders. A younger, more independent
and insistent breed of blacks has seized the initiative. The number
of really militant blacks is still fairly small, as their critics constantly like to reassure themselves. But groups like the Black
Panthers became more respectable among Negroes even as that
organization was harassed by white police. Of more importance,
the black militants are giving voice to the feelings of so many
other blacks that to wait longer for equality is intolerable. Most
critical for the future, they are connecting with the young people
of the ghettoes. Harris found that by the outset of this decade 58
percent of the ghetto young were convinced police brutality is a
fact of life, and 70 percent think the police do more harm than
good. Almost half think ghetto riots have been "justified," while
less than a third of the group conclude the contrary. Half believe the
riots were "helpful," and only 20 percent conclude the opposite.
Almost half think blacks can still win their way peaceably, but
over a third do not. In short, as Senator Edward Brooke has
warned, "A disgruntled and potentially revolutionary class is growing at a record pace."

The serious purpose of the militants is perhaps best attested to
by the fact that they have been introducing a stronger sense of
self-discipline into black communities. Many of them have con-

cluded that even while asserting the independence of their race, they cannot let their people squander themselves in the kind of formless riots which followed King's assassination. A number of them now seek to keep the lid on the ghettoes as much as possible in order to protect the inhabitants there and husband their resources for more effectively resisting the domination of black

> "They killed Malcolm X and produced Stokely and Rap. You kill Stokely, he will multiply. You kill Rap; he will multiply. Now you don't know me, so maybe you don't want to kill me. You might just want me in jail. But you get me off the scene, and I'll multiply."

neighborhoods by white institutions. Some have undertaken demonstrations not only to help educate and unite the ghetto but also to drain "community energy" so that it will not explode in violent disorders. In this sense, the black ghettoes have become vastly more organized than ever before.

This group does not rule out the possibility of selective uprisings if needed to defend itself and its values, and to advance its cause. And some other militants—actually a very small number—may seek to channel some of the stirring energy into deliberate "incidents," a kind of guerrilla warfare where the risk is less and organization takes precedence over spontaneity. In both groups, however, the real objective is self-rule. They are trying to draw a line not to be crossed by white police, white educators, white welfare workers, and the rest of the white community in neighborhoods where blacks are in the majority and have a culture and value system which the intruding whites have been unwilling to respect. The underlying objective has been expressed by Stokely Carmichael: "The love we seek to encourage is within the black community, the only community where men call each other 'brother' when they meet. We can build a community of love only where we have the ability to do so among blacks."

Fundamental to the new self-assertion among not only blacks but also among Mexican-Americans, Indians, Puerto Ricans, and other groups is the conclusion that the white majority has rarely done much to help lift a minority group up from poverty and discrimination except under duress. The new emphasis on black history has prominently noted, for instance, that black volunteers were not allowed to serve in the Revolutionary Army until after the British had begun to admit freed slaves into their ranks and the colonists had to match the move or default a large potential man-power pool to the Redcoats. The Founding Fathers embraced the institution of slavery in the Constitution even though providing for an eventual end to the importation of slaves, a gesture benefiting the domestic slave breeders more than the American conscience. Abraham Lincoln, it has been pointed out over and over, signed the Emancipation Proclamation primarily to undermine the South rather than for any humane or moral reason. A century later the other major party, under John Kennedy and Lyndon Johnson, "became reluctantly involved, then slowly veered toward com-mitment" to better conditions for Negroes, as Yale historian C. Vann Woodward has put it, but only under the relentless prod-ding of the Negro protest movement. Little in the country's recent experience suggests that the white majority will be much more solicitous of Negro needs in the future than in the past unless it costs money, power, and stability to be otherwise.

A striking change in the temper of the white sector has taken place on racial matters over the course of the last ten years, just as in the black community. In the early part of that decade, public opinion surveys showed that only about a fourth of the white population thought Negroes were moving ahead too fast—a pro-portion perhaps composed mainly of the intractable hard core opposed to any black progress at more than a snail's pace. By the middle sixties, however, half of the white populace had decided Negroes were making headway too rapidly. And by the end of 1970, Gallup found almost two-thirds were opposed to speeding up integration. In all, a massive reaction by any standard. Similarly, opinion surveys early in the last decade found that most whites believed Negro children were being provided an inferior education. But not too many years later, with hardly any change in Negro schooling and more black children in segregated classes than ever before, a heavy majority of whites thought that the education black youngsters were getting was as good as that being given white children, despite repeated professional studies showing just the opposite.

Comparable shifts in supposedly objective observations have been taking place across a wide spectrum, obscuring, distorting, and recasting the country's political realities. But perhaps most revealing is the gap between white and black reaction to the rallying cry of "Black power!" One study found nearly 40 percent of the whites interpreting the slogan as representing a move by Negroes to rule whites. Less than 10 percent of the blacks defined it that way. For the overwhelming majority of Negroes who actually advocate black power, it simply symbolizes their dignity. "To most whites," Stokely Carmichael has commented, "black power seems to mean that the Mau Mau are coming to the suburbs at night. . . . Once again responsibility is shifted from the oppressor to the oppressed."

What distinguishes the new racial politics from those of the past is not just the vastly greater concentration of Negroes and changing tone of black demands, but the spread of white antagonisms and fears beyond the immediate neighborhoods where the Negro buildup is occurring. During almost the entire first two-thirds of this century, with a few exceptions such as the Ku Klux Klan's role in a handful of state elections in the North during the 1920s, the unconscious racist attitudes which pervade so many of the country's social relationships did not play an explicit political role above the Mason-Dixon line. The issue was too far down the list of most people's concerns, and Northern politicians were content to "leave well enough alone." Recently, however, race has become an active and sometimes primary issue in a considerable number of Northern states. It is a classic example of a dire problem long in the country's midst but without cutting political effect until it moves from the dim awareness of most people to seemingly being an active threat to them.

In-depth opinion studies have again and again found that since the middle 1960s millions of whites have consciously come to fear that physical violence may be done them, especially by Negroes.

....

"We steal sometimes to get even. Nobody asks us what we want, they just make decisions for us."

....

Yet the hard truth is that the overwhelming bulk of all crime is committed by whites against whites and blacks against blacks, not across racial lines. Indeed, over two-thirds of all aggravated assaults and the great preponderance of murders are committed not by strangers, but by members of the victim's own family or circle of acquaintances. Even in riots Negroes have been the chief victims —victims of overkill by the police, as pointed out by practically every major study made of ghetto outbreaks thus far, and of the chaotic use of weapons by the rioters. More fundamental, the incidence of crime is not a racial matter but a factor of economics and of social and individual pathology. As James Q. Wilson has written, "Unsurprisingly the odds in favor of being the victim of a violent crime decline very quickly with increases in neighborhood income—the chances are nearly six per thousand population of being a victim of violent crime in an area with a median income of under $8,000 per year, but less than one in a thousand in areas with incomes over $8,000 a year." Despite such facts, the flare of violence, particularly as projected by the mass media, has stirred primordial fears which politicians have been quick to exploit over and over under the guise of condemning it.

In that context, even the relatively unhostile voter has been under conflicting pressures, a fact reflected in polling done during the '68 Presidential campaign. In the early autumn, the electorate was overwhelmingly concerned about all the disorder in American society. But as the autumn progressed, more and more people became disturbed by signs of racism and brutishness in the Wallace campaign. As a result, as the Harris poll reported, "An 80–20 split against disorders turned into a 60–40 split opposed to condoning racism." In effect, the country pulled back from the racial pit. But the uneasy balance makes it almost certain that the tensions will continue.

Actually, the average white American, insulated as he or she is from the ghetto, has vastly more to be afraid of from the family automobile and medicine cabinet or from slipping in the bathtub than from dark strangers. Automobile drivers under the influence of alcohol kill 25,000 Americans annually. Commenting on the attitude of some Americans toward ghetto rioters and looters, former Attorney General Ramsey Clark has asked, "Why not shoot drunken drivers? What is it that causes some to call for shooting looters when no one is heard to suggest the same treatment for a far deadlier and less controllable crime?"

Burgeoning crime statistics do not necessarily reflect the actual crime situation. Crime reporting in recent years has become far more comprehensive than in the past, and what appears to be skyrocketing crime is in part fuller reporting, with bigger crime reports often used to justify bigger law-enforcement budget requests. Rising standards of living are also contributing to the swelling figures—there are simply more bikes and cars, for instance, left around. And we are more mobile and accessible to each other than ever before. The wide-open branch bank is an inviting parody of the situation. Most important, the population has increased most sharply in the age group—fourteen to twenty-nine—which has always produced most of the serious crime. "What appears to be a crime explosion," James Q. Wilson noted, "may in fact be a [younger] population explosion." A report of the Presidential Commission on Violence came to much the same conclusion. The fourteen-to-twenty-nine age group will continue to expand in the seventies, and so will population density, mobility, and material temptations. The numerical crime rate is consequently also likely to thrive despite temporary fluctuations. Sociologist Albert Reiss has said: "I think we are going to have to learn to live with a high urban crime rate." The crime issue is consequently also almost certain to be disturbing the country's populace and therefore its politics for some time to come, even with passing downturns.

The most tangible political consequence of the racial controversy must still be looked for, however, not in the general citizenry but in the immediate neighborhoods toward and into which the expanding ghettoes are moving. Throughout American history, restless, destitute, new immigrant groups moving into run-down neighborhoods have clashed with the hard-luck trailings of the prior groups that have begun to move out and up in society. The early Germans were put upon by the original English stock. Then the Irish were persecuted by the nativists and fought with the recent German arrivals in a series of exceptionally bloody riots. Later the Irish fought with the Italians—and so on, immigrant wave on immigrant wave. Now the volatile ingredient of race has come to the fore. Increasingly the collisions have been between whites and blacks—plus Puerto Ricans in New York, and Mexican-Americans in the Southwest. In the early 1970s, about thirty-eight million Americans—nearly one-fifth of the nation—are living in neighborhoods where both whites and nonwhites can move and are moving. The overwhelming bulk of them have income levels at which the daily living is not easily scratched out even before the contentious color factor is added.

Cleveland provides a fairly typical case history. The sharpest hostilities in that city during the last ten years have been in neighborhoods like Collinwood, a white area next to the Negro Glenville sector. Collinwood residents can readily be found who boast that "when the civil rights groups said they were going to march in this neighborhood, a bunch of the guys at the club decided to form vigilante groups." Members of Cleveland's Welfare Federation recurringly report "We keep hearing there's a build-up of guns in the Collinwood area." In a white sector on the western fringe of Hough, the main Negro section of Cleveland, signs have been nailed on telephone poles and painted on buildings warning *Nigger, this is Alley Rat Territory. Keep out.* Anti-Negro agitators from

....

"Would Americans systematically destroy 22 million blacks? My answer: Look at the record. More specifically, I believe they can. I believe they will."

....

the North American Alliance of White People, the White Citizens Council of Ohio, and the Cleveland-based National Christian Conservative Society have concentrated most of their efforts in the neighborhoods segregated along ethnic lines such as Murray Hill, which is primarily Italian, and Dowinski Park, which is mostly Polish. When black militant Fred (Ahmed) Evans was sentenced to death in 1969 for a gunfight in which several Cleveland policemen were shot, the white judge sternly declared there had been no trouble, no guns until Evans and his separatists came along. But the facts of the community have been quite to the contrary.

In the 1930s Franklin Roosevelt diverted much of the racial tension of that difficult time by stressing the overriding needs and common aspirations of the lower and lower-middle economic groups. In effect, he polarized politics around class. The uneasy racial truce he forged, however, finally came unstuck in considerable part as the Negro concentration in the North mounted and blacks started to assert their equality more demandingly. The re-emergence of race as more influential than class had been predicted by political commentators ever since the late thirties. It was staved off again and again—until the last half-decade.

What has been happening can most readily be traced through the Northern, urban so-called "Catholic vote." It includes those of Irish descent and the southern- and eastern-European immigrant stock that F.D.R. rallied to help overthrow the long-prevailing

Anglo-Saxon-Protestant-Republican hold on this country. During the 1930s and 1940s "the Catholic vote" was overwhelmingly Democratic. Then, in 1952 and 1956, under the spell of Eisenhower's popularity, the Cold War, and a rising standard of living, it split almost evenly between the two major parties. In 1960 it rallied to John F. Kennedy by better than a two-to-one margin, and in 1964 the ratio rose still higher in the Johnson landslide. But in 1966, with inflamed racial tensions breaking into the open, the Democratic vote in this group dropped precipitously in state after state. In California, for example, it fell from over 70 percent in 1964 to barely above 50 percent in 1966. In Michigan it plummeted from 75 percent to just over 40 percent, in New Jersey from almost 70 percent to less than 40 percent. Those are massive swings by any political standard. In 1968, nationwide, this group of voters divided almost evenly between the two parties as its historic tie to the Democratic Party in Presidential elections again reasserted itself to some extent. But the group also contributed significantly to the Wallace vote in the industrial Northern states. The Harris poll reported that Wallace got over 20 percent of the so-called Italian vote and almost the same portion of the "Slavic-American vote." In New Jersey and Ohio, as two examples, the defection to Wallace among these two blocs more than provided the margin by which Nixon beat Humphrey there. In the 1970 off-year elections, Gallup reported Catholics shifted to Republican candidates and the right.

The particular relevance of the racial issue to the ethnic groups embraced in "the Catholic vote" is reflected in public opinion surveys. The proportion of those groups disturbed over racial violence and opposed to Negroes moving into their neighborhoods has been measurably higher than in the rest of the population. For instance, while a bare majority of the total white populace in the last half of the 1960s said they were against blacks moving into their part of town, 60 percent of the Irish and Italian-Americans felt that way and almost 80 percent of the Polish-Americans. These ethnic clusters contain large numbers of the people who are still scrambling for a full role in U.S. society and now find their neighborhoods and blue-collar jobs overlapped by the expanding black ghetto. These groups also, of course, contain substantial numbers who have disappeared into the middle class and suburbia. But even when this happens, the unity of the ethnic vote tends to persist to some extent.

The net effect of these groups in relation to the dynamics of social change has become vastly different from thirty or sixty years ago. Then they were a wellspring of cultural diversity and political change; now they constitute an important bastion of opposition. They have tended, in fact, to become a major redoubt of traditional Americanism and of the anti-Negro, anti-youth vote.

With the brunt of the backlash falling most heavily on Democratic candidates, it might be anticipated that political expediency would cause an increasing number of them to try to modify the party's historical strategy toward minority groups. Basic factors, however, are operating to keep the party's political self-interest more or less in tandem with its philosophical commitment, however uncomfortable that accommodation may be at times. A large Negro vote in the big Northern states is generally essential for the Democratic Party to carry them, and that vote is needed not just marginally but decisively. When a Republican candidate can win as much as a third of it, the Democrats are dealt a crippling blow. Republicans may occasionally take a large state with hardly any Negro support at all, as Ronald Reagan has done in winning the governorship of California twice. But Democrats can hardly succeed in the more populous states without strong black support, and that leverage could become even more important as Negroes raise their registration and voter-turnout levels.

Richard Scammon and Ben Wattenberg have argued that the strong hold economic concerns have had on American politics since at least the 1930s is being challenged to a considerable extent by the so-called Social Issue. They group within that term race, crime, student unrest, political protest, permissiveness, and much more. There are, of course, strong crosscurrents within that large and very mixed bag, and it should not be forgotten that the last forty years have been deeply stirred by a number of social as well as economic controversies. Nevertheless, even after the impact of the Social Issue in the off-year 1970 elections is discounted in part, it undeniably indicates a vigorous public ferment at work, and it must be taken into account. How much U.S. politics may shift under this pressure only the coming elections will demonstrate. But experience suggests a moderating effect seeks to break through a little while after any new political surge like this one, and that could further blunt or channel this development.

There is a widespread assumption that the recent social discord is abating. Republicans ambivalently want to claim credit for that and still hand-hold any residual resentments. Democrats hope the heat is off, since they are blamed for the restive groups, which are usually part of their coalition. But the party also wants to encourage the further aspirations of such groups, if only to encourage an election-day turnout. Despite recurring claims of all quiet in the ghettoes, on the campuses, and in the fight against crime, the country will likely continue to experience social ferment throughout this decade. Equally important, however, politicians will not be able to exploit or pander to it as much as in the past.

"The only effective strategy is shock."

An apocalyptic of the racial issue is that during the approaching years the nation's cities could be wracked by black guerrilla insurgency like that mounted in recent decades against white colonialism in other parts of the world. And certainly that is not at all impossible, given the seething conditions in the ghettoes, the climate of violence in our times, and the precarious complexity of large communities. "The Negroes of this country may never be able to rise to power," James Baldwin wrote in *The Fire Next Time*, "but they are very well placed indeed to precipitate chaos and ring down the curtain on the American dream."

It has also been suggested that if more summers of violence again come, paramilitary forces will be patrolling the major U.S. cities for months at a time, as has already happened in Wilmington, Delaware; that "justified" bloody examples, even martyrs, will be made; and that the black enclaves will be both contained and continued. These events, too, are possible, given the grotesque fears and frustrations which have infected this society of late, the heavy reliance of the nation on military force to meet its most fundamental problems, the advanced police equipment now available, and the reluctance of the white majority to pay the high price of preparing millions of unskilled poor people for the increasing sophistication of the American labor arena. If such contingencies come to pass, moreover, they will be likely to be accompanied by restrictive laws and emergency proclamations heralding the gradual or sudden end of many present freedoms for everyone. And if that should happen, our national politics will consist largely of the edicts of patriotic authoritarians dedicated, like tyrants of earlier times, simply to "saving" us—and the weapons of the enforcers plus the answering guns of a nationwide resistance movement swiftly grown to include vastly more whites than blacks.

It is most probable of all, however, that the racial problem will be painfully worked out through the existing political and social processes, not happily or well but pragmatically. But if recent history suggests any fairly reasonable projection, it is that, *first*, the prevailing white power structure, without regard to either major party or any particular personality, will do the least possible about the problem unless relentlessly pressed, and, *second*, the younger, more active blacks are not going to lapse back for long into either subordination or the patience of their older recent leaders, regardless of all the fond wishes and repressive instincts among some of the white majority. The prospect may be most comparable to the struggles of the blue-collar white people who waged a series of bloody battles from the 1870s to the 1930s for the right to organize unions. The impending passage, however, will be vastly more difficult and dangerous than even that violence-pocked chapter in the history of American labor. The surge of America's blacks up from the base of this society is a long-delayed historical force that has now been deeply stirred. It could convulse the seventies and scar much of the rest of this century. But one way or another it is irrepressibly upon us.

CHAPTER 7

Shifting Sources of Power

"How do you really move all those people? How do you get inside them, and know and feel what genuinely moves them, and get them to know and feel what you're so concerned about—and then get them to go with you?"

Robert Kennedy gazed out of the airplane window, speaking mostly to himself as his chartered American Airlines campaign flight neared Los Angeles International Airport. Below him were hundreds of thousands of houses, apartments, stores and office buildings, and lines of traffic threading off in all directions. He had just lost the 1968 Oregon Presidential primary; as he headed into the California showdown to try to gain the support of "all those people," he was perplexed and frustrated, and reaching.

The staggering demands of a Presidential campaign come clear with the realization that the vast mosaic of metropolitan Los Angeles is but a token of the scores of millions of individuals who must be reached in some tentative, mysterious way in order to gain, and hold onto, the nation's highest office. But Robert Kennedy's query is the persisting dilemma of practically every candidate and elected officeholder—local, state, and national. After the reapportionment for the 1970 census, the average Congressman, for instance, will have nearly a half-million constituents to reach and represent—a far cry from the fairly simple role the Founding Fathers had in mind for the country's legislators. In actual fact, we are now trying to make a political system designed for a few million individuals in a largely agricultural economy and fairly static society work for over 200 million people in a post-industrial environment and a time of almost blinding social change.

How *do* you move all those people? The political technicians, usually seconded uncritically by the press, consider that it is done with a news name, an organizational following, eloquent or at least glib speech writers, expert campaign aides, a sense of the nation's needs and mood, personal presence, and the chimerical qualities of leadership which go into that—plus, increasingly of late, a right kind of face, a good voice teacher, a winning make-up man, a creative media agency, and, above all, money. But even with all that, neither the nature nor the ultimate locus of political power is so easy to pin down in a democratic society.

Pushing deeper, C. Wright Mills argued some years ago that a series of "power elites" controls America by holding the "command posts" among its various groups. Daniel Bell has taken a more cautious approach, urging that "power is a difficult subject. Its effects are more observable than its causes." He concludes that politics, and we, now work through "collectivities," not in the open market place of nearly unfettered individual choice proclaimed in political folklore.

In *The Federalist Papers* Madison and Hamilton made clear that the practical men who drafted the Constitution believed political power resides ultimately in self-interest and the uneasy equilibrium which politicians are constantly working out among many divergent groups. But J. Kenneth Galbraith has more recently argued that huge "technostructures" are now enveloping both government and the private economy, and they have an overpowering sense of *organizational* self-interest which often ignores or obscures the interests of both the individual and the larger society. Further, he contends, these technostructures are becoming so influential that they make a mockery of any equilibrium which might be struck among the small, individual units.

Another useful insight has been offered by social critic David Bazelon: "Modern power is, at the root, psychological. . . . [It] is an aspect of emotional organization; emotional organization is a result of culture, or at least results in culture.... Having, for our speculative purposes, thus connected politics and culture, we then notice the peculiar deficiencies in the American culture-power complex. The general proposition is that we are an *ad hoc* society. It is a major effort just to hold the situation together. Our first necessity is always accommodation according to the given circumstances. This puts brokerage up front." Old Boss Tweed would doubtless have grunted agreement with Bazelon's conclusion but sneered at the more abstract concern with how society operates. Tweed's approach was summed up in his comment "The way to have power is to take it." The practicing politician of the 1970s, however, needs to sift through the increasingly complex interest groups, equilibriums, and psychological organizations in which major changes are taking place, and perceive what they suggest about the shifting sources of power.

One reason the American voter is so hard to reach is that he moves around so much. James Reston has written: "Damn people won't stand still. One fifth of them [now over 40 million] move every year.... They are moving out of the rural South [and, he might have added, the rural Midwest] into the great cities of the North, and drifting westward and southward into the vast sunny crescent from San Francisco through Texas to Florida." In the coming decade, the northeast and north central regions will continue to hold about half the nation's populace, but the population center has finally gotten to the Mississippi River. That picture, moreover, does not take into account the movement within states. Nor does the net redeployment show those who are moving against the stream. For example, while over thirty thousand shifted from Nebraska to California in a single recent year, over twelve thousand made just the opposite move. Altogether, about the same percentage of Americans are in the process of moving across state lines today as a century ago.

Much of what all this twentieth-century "pioneering" may mean psychologically has been suggested from the detached perspective of the London *Observer* by Michael Frayn: "Humbert

Humbert, driving Lolita endlessly from motel to motel, lives one of the most fundamental of all American myths—the idea that *you can always move on.* The feeling is one which even the most skeptical Americans express in one form or another. They mean it figuratively—that you can change jobs and even careers comparatively easily, or get a college education in middle life. But they also mean it literally—that if you don't like it where you are, there's always somewhere else. . . . The faith in the potentialities of Moving On springs from the optimism which is such an attractive and humanistic attribute of the American character and nourishes the sense of liberty which Americans undoubtedly feel. Like the hope of heaven, it makes the shortcomings of the here and now endurable; but I suspect that it also helps to perpetuate the shortcomings —to encourage the impermanent, makeshift atmosphere which renders some places in America so ripe to be moved on from."

Politically, the result of all the moves during just the last ten years is more tangible: a far-reaching reshuffling of the nation's political power. This is best indicated by the gain and loss of seats in the Congress in 1973 as a result of the reapportionment based on the 1970 census. Nine states lose Congressional seats and five increase their strength. A seat is being lost in the House of Representatives by Alabama, Iowa, North Dakota, Ohio, Tennessee, West Virginia, and Wisconsin. Pennsylvania and New York both lose two.

The states gaining one Congressman are Arizona, Colorado, and Texas. Florida is adding three, and California gains five, moving from thirty-eight to forty-three, to have the largest delegation in the Congress for the first time. The Census Bureau anticipates that during the seventies California and Florida will continue to be the highest population gainers, with the Golden State up another 30 percent by the end of the decade and the Sunshine State up 40 percent. Each will then be entitled to another major increase in Congressional strength. More broadly, accompanying the nation's redeployment of population is a development of more autonomous economic power in the South and West, and that is fostering independent social, cultural, and governmental tendencies further challenging the power of the Northeast and Midwest.

Another political fallout from all the mobility has been the exclusion of up to twenty million adult citizens from eligibility to vote in any given election. Almost all election laws have a strong bias in favor of fairly rooted residents. That works especially against millions of young people in their twenties and early thirties, members of minority groups, and the poor, all of whom are among the more transient of our population. Recent Supreme Court decisions have sought to assure the right to vote for most of this transient group. And over the course of the decade the effect of those holdings may liberalize politics as much as the new generation may.

The immediate haven in which Americans are more and more coming to light, is the metropolitan area—more specifically, the suburbs. In 1940 the suburbs housed less than 20 percent of the total populace. By the early 1970s they have come to hold nearly 40 percent. By 1980 they may have almost a majority. But already they wield the kind of political influence once held by the rural culture symbolized by the log cabin, then by the small town and then, with Franklin Roosevelt, by the big city.

In 1975 three-fourths of the people will be living in population clusters containing one or more large cities and scores of loosely scrambled surrounding communities medium and small in size. Two-thirds of the populace will be concentrated in less than thirty such metropolitan areas, a convenient prospect for Presidential campaigners and their media time-buyers. Yet less than one-third of the populace will actually be living in cities with a population of 100,000 or more; only about one-tenth will be in cities of over a million, a smaller portion than in 1900. The Republican National Committee prepared a report for Nixon's 1968 Presidential campaign which concluded that the suburbs boasted more voters than the big cities in all but two (New York and Texas) of the ten most populous states. Over-all, during the 1960s all the central cities combined grew by less than a million people, while the suburbs gained about fourteen million more individuals.

The shifting balance of power is readily perceivable city by city. Chicago, for example, grew steadily during the 1960s, but the population of its suburbs grew twice as fast. Philadelphia expanded its populace by several percentage points, but its suburbs increased by nearly 15 percent. The city of Los Angeles experienced only a slightly slower rate of growth than its suburbs, but it too is losing Congressional and state legislative seats to suburbia, especially to arch-conservative Orange County. The populations of Boston, Cleveland, Cincinnati, Pittsburgh, St. Louis, San Francisco, and a number of other cities remained almost the same, but their surrounding communities soared by up to 20 percent. And what is happening reaches well beyond the better-known cities. Connecticut, New Jersey, and Alabama are illustrative. In the first state, four of the eleven largest cities had population losses during the last ten years. In New Jersey, nine of the thirteen largest cities lost population. In Alabama, every major city suffered a net population loss except Huntsville, a center for space-exploration work.

Industry and commerce have also been moving to the suburbs, ensuring that economic power is shifting, too. A study by Paul Davidoff and Neil Gold in the latter sixties concluded that 80 percent of the jobs created during the last twenty years in the large metropolitan areas of the country have been located in the suburbs, not the central cities. That trend has been picking up speed, and it is anticipated that almost all new plants built in the seventies will be located outside the central cities. In effect, even the Industrial Revolution is being suburbanized.

The larger cities are threatened by a vast mismatch of jobs and people. Traffic congestion, air pollution, and the many afflictions of sheer bulk have caught up with them. Witness after witness testifying before Senator Abraham Ribicoff's extensive Senate subcommittee hearings on urban problems agreed that even if the Congress promptly enacted the most farsighted city-rehabilitation legislation (a dubious prospect), it would be ten to fifteen years before major results could be achieved. To affect really sweeping changes, programs would have to aim toward transformations by the end of the century, since any basic rebuilding of the American cities in a social and human sense involves at least a thirty-year cycle.

New York City illustrates many of the big cities' problems and the causes, which are far more fundamental than the endless immediate crises wracking that city and occupying the attention of the daily press and most voters. The human changes taking place are suggested by the fact that since World War II New York City has taken in well over two million Negroes and Puerto Ricans, roughly as many people as flocked into the entire U.S. in the great Irish migration between 1845 and 1870. And yet during the 1960s the city's population remained almost static, while there was a 20 percent increase in the population of its fifteen hundred suburbs.

The related economic shifts are massive. Lower-income groups have been replacing outward-bound middle- and upper-income families. Similarly, lower-paying, lower-capitalized manufacturing concerns are replacing better-paying ones. During the last two decades, the city has lost over 250,000 manufacturing jobs—over one-fifth of its total. In the greater New York area, about 750,000 new jobs were created during the last ten years, but fewer than 100,000 of those were located in New York City. By the last half of the 1960s, for the first time, the city was producing less than half the personal income of New York State. The welfare load grew from an average of not quite 5 percent of the city's inhabitants during the 1950s to over 10 percent at the outset of the 1970s. Welfare lists in the rest of the state increased from only 2.5 percent to somewhat over 3 percent.

New York City's welfare population, now well over a million people, is larger than the whole populace of fifteen American states. And there are still several hundred thousand other New Yorkers eligible for relief but not yet applying for it, with large numbers of additional potential recipients pouring into the city every year. Worst of all, more than 600,000 of the city's children are dependent on welfare—over one child in five. The great bulk of the welfare recipients are mothers with dependent children, plus the aged and disabled. Only about 50,000 of the recipients are so-called "employables," and many of these are alcoholics, addicts, and others with physical and emotional infirmities.

In net effect, New York City's burdens have been increasing at the same time its revenue base is being seriously undermined. Equally important, the changes in the economy and population have been undercutting the city's leverage on the state government for assistance just when that help is needed most. At the start of this decade, New York City was providing the state with over $2.5 billion a year and getting back a little over $1.5 billion in state aid. Within the city, self-preoccupied, self-perpetuating public bureaucracies have taken over the police, education, welfare work, fire protection, and even garbage collecting. The city is serviced by 300,000 employees welded into bureaucracies concerned mostly with rewarding mediocrity. At another level of concern, over half of the students in the city's public schools are black or Puerto Rican, but nearly 90 percent of the teachers are white. Most fundamental of all, the city's sense of cohesiveness is eroding. "Oh rotten Gotham," Tom Wolfe exclaimed, "sliding down the behavioral sink!"

The political tendency is to blame this or that public official for all the trouble. New York City's cab drivers, for example, curse Mayor John Lindsay. But basic conditions are actually in charge. "It may be said that nobody 'runs' New York," Wallace Syre and Herbert Kaufman have written. "It runs by a process of negotiation and mutual accommodation." The process works, insofar as it does work at all, through shifting coalitions which may temporarily unite or divide City Hall, the various ethnic and religious groups, the blacks, the general commercial community, Wall Street, the Central Labor Council, the major public employee unions, special institutional forces like the Roman Catholic Archdiocese of New York, the media outlets, the city's intellectual establishment, and a host of other sources, some deliberate and overwhelming, some discontinuous and subtle. New York City has actually functioned less and less well ever since the old political organizations which serviced the individual neighborhoods were undermined by the reformers of fifty to eighty years ago. Basic and lasting improvements in the public life of the city are doubtful until some new social and public patterns for handling grass-roots needs are developed.

Mayor Lindsay told the Ribicoff subcommittee that New York City would require approximately $50 billion to be rehabilitated physically and governmentally during the 1970s. Ribicoff replied that if a comparable effort were to be made in other major cities, the total outlay would run to $1 trillion, nearly half of the revenue that the federal government expects to take in during the decade. Left to its own devices, however, New York City, like most other large cities, is bankrupt. At the outset of the seventies it was already receiving a billion dollars a year in assistance just from the federal government; Lindsay foresaw a future deficit of almost another billion dollars.

Los Angeles, though one of the newer cities, is rapidly devolving through the same life cycle. The population of Los Angeles increased less than 20 percent during the last ten years but its welfare rolls more than doubled, and their cost quadrupled. Property tax rates in most major cities generally are already well above the level which usually discourages new industries from moving in. By 1975, in desperation, cities holding more than half the nation's big-city population will probably have had to impose muncipal income taxes, commuter levies, or still other new exactions to gain more revenue. As a short-term measure, the additional funds can have a modest ameliorating effect. But in the long run the tax trend is almost certain to accelerate the middle- and upper-class evacuation of the central cities.

Against that background, the increasing leverage of the suburbs merits a closer look, though even they are sufficiently diverse in makeup and outlook to make generalizations only very broadly useful. Compared to the average American living elsewhere, suburban dwellers are younger, better-educated and more prosperous; they have more children, newer dwellings, and a larger ownership interest in where they live. "A keen sense of property rights and a sharp concern for tax rates," John Peters has noted, "comes with the key to a suburban home." Suburbanites are also, however, more heavily mortgaged. Life "under the fallout from the charcoal burner," as former suburban editor Richard Kluger concludes, is more stressful, more affected by isolation from meaningful social contact and more taken up with ceaseless striving and involuntary socializing than life elsewhere. One of Levittown's leading advocates and residents, sociologist Herbert Gans, concedes a considerable "inability to empathize with diversity" among the suburbanites he has studied. The President's Task Force on Suburban Problems warned that the "cultural dehydration" of suburbia is having alarming consequences in terms of both crime and a more general alienation, especially among the young.

A study of Levittowners found almost half were Democrats, a fourth Republicans, and little over a fourth independents. Not quite half were Protestant, over a third were Catholic, and about 15 percent were Jewish. Not quite half had some college education. Only in being overwhelmingly white is suburbia homogeneous. The racial polarization taking place in this country, in fact, is directly caught up with the growth of the suburbs. In the early sixties, fewer than 150,000 whites left the central cities each year. By the early seventies, over 500,000 were leaving annually, and the exodus is still accelerating.

The fact that blacks have not similarly been moving in wholesale numbers to suburbia (even after taking into account a small pickup in the rate at the outset of the 1970s) is rooted not only in overt racial prejudice and a political lag in enacting open housing laws, but in hard economics as well. Gans has written: "Barring miracles in the housing industry and in federal subsidies, the subdivisions of the seventies will be too expensive for any family earning less than about $7,500 in 1967 dollars. Even if suburbia were to be racially integrated, cost alone would exclude most nonwhites." Another frequent factor is suburban zoning, which favors middle- and upper-income families and usually works to exclude the poor. In wealthy Westchester County outside New York City, Davidoff and Gold found 60 percent of the land zoned for at least one-acre lots.

To the many Americans who can get there, the suburbs seem to promise a resolution of the conflict deep in the American make-up between a desire for both the advantages of an urban society and agrarian nostalgia. The massive shift of population from the countryside to metropolitan areas during the last century and a half was a triumph, in important part, of the drive to get ahead and a desire for convenience. But there is also a powerful lingering want for the wide-open spaces and elemental feel of "Marlboro country." The Gallup Poll has reported that just over a fifth of the American people want to live in cities, a little over a fourth prefer the suburbs, and almost half list small towns or farms as their first choice. "The middle landscape" of suburbia—trees, a patch of grass, greater separateness from neighbors, home ownership, local autonomy—has loomed as a workable compromise.

Instead, however, the clash between the rural longing and urban reality will almost certainly be sharply intensified during this decade. For the urbanizing of the suburbs—the filling in of space, the displacement of houses by high-rise apartments, the congesting of many institutions and processes of daily life—is picking up speed and will be rushed along as more and more people stream out of the core cities and the countryside, and as the over-all population growth is felt. Half of the new housing in the greater Los Angeles Area and in New York's Nassau County, two strongholds of the suburban dream, is already on the multi-family type. The President's Task Force on Suburban Problems has warned that slums are rapidly encroaching on the new suburbs of the last two decades; crime, decay, and pollution are growing at about the same rate in suburbia as in the central cities. The huge increase in the twenty-five-to-thirty-four-year-old group during the 1970s—the prime home-buying group—should both further crowd the present suburbs and set off a whole new wave of suburbanization—as well as a building boom and all the local and national political pressures that go with it.

President Nixon has noted that we must build the equivalent of a new city of 250,000—a city the size of Tulsa—*every month* between now and the end of the century just to stay abreast of the anticipated population growth. Most urban experts dream of rebuilding the cities on models of the great metropolises of Europe, or of starting huge chrome-and-plastic communities from scratch out in the great open areas still remaining. Most suburbanites, however, are anti-city to a considerable extent. They harbor the suspicion of congested, polyglot metropolises manifest throughout the country's history, from the Jeffersonians through the Populists to the new conservatives and hippies. Suburban voters have rallied time after time in recent decades in support of the old battle-cries of "home rule" and "local independence." And they have repeatedly rejected efforts to reduce the multiplicity of local governments which block metropolitan solutions to metropolitan problems. In fact, like many inner-city blacks, they insistently want more autonomy, neighborhood by neighborhood.

Reconciling the developing drive for decentralization with effective action on the over-all problems which burden metropolitan areas will be one of the challenges of the seventies for national as well as local leaders, and it will be an especially demanding one: the psychological distance between the cities and suburbs is profound. "I feel I'm a citizen where I live," commented the mayor of a small New Jersey town who commutes to Manhattan daily to design industrial power plants to be located all over the world. "The only reason I've been coming here [to New York] for twenty years is because of my occupation. I don't like the place—downtown is dirty, people are impolite. I don't see anything similar in our problems at all. The minute I get out of the city, I don't think of it at all." Herbert Gans comments: "The suburbs have nothing to gain by helping the cities. It's easier to turn their backs as long as they can get to their jobs. The only things they'll do, don't mean anything—take a few black kids for the summer or come into the city and paint a few slum houses."

The voting record of suburban Congressmen at the end of the 1960s and outset of the seventies has actually been closer to that of urban than of rural members of the House of Representatives, according to separate studies by Professor Richard Lehne and the Washington *Post*. But the underlying hostility of the suburbs toward the core cities still remains a major impediment to any massive assault on their interlocking maladies of poverty, racial inequality, and physical debilitation of the environment. In a more bitter vein, Joseph L. Lyford has commented: "The slum tells us something about the true extent of our commitment to the principles of equality expressed in the Declaration of Independence and our Bill of Rights. . . . Our matter of fact acceptance of the slum—that it is here to stay—and what it does to human life and aspiration is a sign of our ability to desensitize ourselves to human suffering, which is not unlike the complacency of the good Germans who would live near the concentration camp because they were able to convince themselves that it did not exist." In contrast to the United States, it should be noted, slumless cities already abound in Scandinavia, the Netherlands, Switzerland, and even West Germany.

Unless consciously diffused, the tug-of-war between the inner cities and suburbs of this country could erupt more fiercely in the coming years than did the struggles between the farmers and city-dwellers in earlier periods. The two present antagonists are joined together more closely by technology, geography, even the air they breathe, than the opposing forces in those earlier economic and political tugs-of-war; but the proximity only aggravates the rudeness of their rivalry. The balance of power already lies with the suburbs, lessened in effect somewhat by their decentralization and preoccupation with "privatism." Even with those limitations, however, the political styles, symbols, and substance of the seventies are likely to be heavily influenced by the neo-agrarianism, heavily gadgeted modernity, and personal strivings that are the essence of suburbanism, a way of life and outlook already more influential politically than either doctrinaire liberalism or conservatism.

At the same time, suburbia's effect on the shape of the future cannot be seen wholly in terms of traditional life styles and social struggles, for the suburban way of life itself is changing. That this is so and how it is developing were suggested by David Riesman with remarkable prescience over ten years ago in an essay called "The Suburban Dislocation." Besides foreseeing, well ahead of time, an unusually sharp break in the "track of generations" (a phrase borrowed from de Tocqueville), Riesman also noted in the suburbs "a growing homogenization of roles" as a result of women taking over some areas once the exclusive prerogative of men and husbands taking part in the work of the home, PTA, and other activities formerly pursued almost solely by women—in effect, the "transversal" and "unisex" tendencies now so evident in the younger generation. And he made the point that in the suburbs, as in the rest of society in less dramatic ways, "we are witnessing a tremendous but tacit revolt against industrialism" and the values of functional efficiency in which it disciplined people. Riesman found "many decisions to prefer companionship in the present to some distant goal. . . . For millions of people, work no longer provides a central focus for life; and the breadwinner is no longer the chief protagonist in the family saga." In a still deeper sense, as Riesman made clear in another essay several years later, what is widely being sought is an almost intuitive disorganization; in essence, a silent, inner rebellion against the organized society. "The reaction to organization and its beliefs," J. Kenneth Galbraith has added, "may well be one of the most rapidly developing political moods of our time."

The New Left has been singled out as the main locus of those trends and, closely related, as having no sense of the past or anything after now. The so-called silent majority, in contrast, has been considered of late to be the bulwark of stability and continuity, even tradition. Yet twenty years ago, in *White Collar*, C. Wright Mills noted about the same group: "The new Little Man seems to have no firm roots, no sure loyalties to sustain his life and give it a center. He is not aware of having any history. . . . Perhaps because he does not know where he is going, he is in a frenetic hurry." Most of the recent young activists are but the offspring of the very time and class about which Mills was writing; and what the older society now so strenuously condemns in them pertains first of all to itself.

In net effect, and as in most of history, the young have been shaped much more by what they have sensed and seen than what has been preached at them. Equally relevant, the most ardent of the New Left and the squarest of the self-professed squares of suburbia end up much closer in what they are like inside and want of this world than either group would ever care to admit. For the future, their mutually reinforcing tendencies suggest important changes in what may be sought in both the private and the public sectors of American society. The pervading shift in emphasis is implicit in a collection of signs sketched as a *New Yorker* cover by social satirist Jim Stevenson: PICK THE FLOWERS . . . WALK ON THE GRASS . . . GO.

The shifts of political power taking place in some of the main segments of the U.S. economy are at least as far-reaching as those occurring from city to suburb. The clearest example is the continuing decline of the farm bloc. There are already more people in America's urban slums than on all of its farms, and by the end of the seventies the farm vote may have almost faded out as a major constituency. When Franklin Roosevelt was elected President in 1932, the agricultural sector included over 25 percent of the American people. That base of the Jeffersonian Republic now constitutes only 5 percent and is still slipping fast.

More people have left the farms just since 1950, in fact, than still remain on them—just under 10 million. By 1980 the farm sector may have less than 3 percent of the populace. The over-all trend, moreover, tells only part of the story. The average farmdweller is poorer, less educated, in worse health, and socially less integrated than the average person living elsewhere. Half the nation's poor live in small towns or rural areas. Television and other technological developments have brought the back country closer to the rest of the nation than ever before, and there were substantial economic improvements in a majority of the farm counties during the 1960s. But the agricultural sector is still not keeping up with the main part of American society in economic, educational, and other upgrading. Perhaps the most fateful warning is the fact that only one out of ten of the young people reared on farms expects to seek permanent employment there.

For a long time the movement from rural areas occurred in

response to the attraction of the cities. But more recently it has primarily been the forced result of the mechanization of farms. Agriculture is being rapidly displaced by agribusiness. Between 1950 and 1970 the total number of farms still operating was cut almost in half (a million farms disappeared during the 1960s alone) and the size of the average farm doubled. In the early fifties the average farmer supplied less than fifteen consumers. In the early seventies he should be able to do that for about forty-five. The per capita output in agriculture has increased three times the per capita output of industry during the last three decades. At the same time, the increased use of fertilizer has allowed fifty million acres of farmland to be retired. By 1980, it is anticipated the average farm will require two to three times as much capital to operate on as in the late sixties. A Department of Agriculture publication describes the American farmer of the not too distant future as working "in an air conditioned farm office . . . scanning a printout from a computer center . . . typing out an inquiry on a keyboard which relays the question to the computer." He will specialize in virus-free plants developed to make use even of the stalks and, to accommodate all the equipment being used, and he will use "automated [field] machinery directed by tape controlled programs and supervised by television scanners mounted on towers."

Agriculture continues to exercise influence in national politics well beyond its voting numbers, partly because of its historic momentum, partly because the family-run farm is making a last desperate stand, and partly because large manufacturing and financial interests with concentrated economic power have an economic and political stake in the farm sector, though only very secondarily in the small farmer and rural poor. An analysis by Richard Lehne shows the number of "rural" Congressional districts (those where a majority of the population lives outside the Census Bureau's standard metropolitan areas, which embrace the suburbs and central cities) declining by about thirty-seven—or 20 percent—between 1966 and 1973. That still understates the real drop forthcoming in agricultural representation, but even then the sector will remain substantially over-represented on the basis of the proportion of its populace in the nation's total population. It should be noted that Lehne projects that the representation of the cities after reapportionment will drop only slightly (from 106 seats in 1966 to 100 in 1973), while the number of suburban Congressmen climbs from 92 to 129 in the same period and the "rural" bloc falls from 181 to 144, with the remainder being "mixed" districts. In any event, the farm bloc is about to shrink very markedly again; voting patterns in the House consequently will change, too, on a wide range of domestic and especially urban issues. The ideological shift will probably be gradual, but it should still be clearly discernible by the mid-seventies. At a minimum, agribusiness interests will have to look more and more to a quite different political base for leverage than has been relied on in the past. Conservative suburban representatives are the readiest at hand, but divergent outlooks on many matters will increasingly impede such an alliance, particularly as the developing congestion and consumer consciousness are felt in the suburbs.

During the 1960s, the federal government paid out about $25 billion for clearly defined public assistance purposes throughout the nation but over $45 billion merely in farm support. Many of the billions paid through the agricultural programs helped in net effect to idle acreage and buy the machinery which displaced poor white farmers and poor blacks, especially in the South. That, in turn, added to the ultimate welfare costs incurred to maintain many of those pushed off the land—and also to the urban tensions now rampant. "The agrarian myth," that ideal of the rural way of life, has long tended to deny the existence of poverty or tried to explain it away and insulate the countryside from any connection with the problems of the rest of the society. But in many rural areas an aggressive war on poverty would now be more relevant for most of the people still there (and to whether they leave their farms and add to the congestion of the cities) than all the commodity supports and other agricultural subsidies built up over the years. The latter programs, however, have been able to maintain strong bipartisan backing—a classic example of political lag and of the readiness of politicians to ladle out tax funds along already-established lines while resisting newer and smaller programs based more directly on human need. The National Food and Fibre Commission has called for future agricultural policies based on free markets rather than governmental supports, but a majority of that group also insisted that present programs be continued "until the problem of excess capacity in farming is alleviated and farmers are able to earn incomes from the market that are comparable to nonfarm incomes." The snag is that the country is hardly closer to solving the excess-capacity problem today than it has been during the last fifty years.

A Parkinson-like rule of government and politics is that as a nation grows and moves from one period into another, it uncritically continues high-cost programs for a smaller and smaller group of recipients and persists to do so long after the original reasons for the effort have faded. Many of the subsidies and a considerable part of the vast bureaucracy of the Department of Agriculture are now prime examples of that. That Department, for example, is thirty-four times larger than it was in 1900, though there are now far fewer farms and farmers to serve. A point to watch in the politics of the coming period is whether special-interest rhetoric and influence will be able to continue the costly public maintenance of even the more prosperous of an agricultural economy which, whether we like it or not, technology is relentlessly reshaping.

If the farm bloc is in the elderly stage of the political life cycle, organized labor, that lion in the streets in the 1930s, is now deep into middle age as a movement, weighted down, occasionally bothered by flickering images of a younger, more vigorous time of life, but now only infrequently able to do—or interested in doing—much about its once youthful ardor besides talk about it. Samuel Lubell, as a firsthand observer, described the mood of union locals in the New Deal period as that "of street barricades and sit-down strikes." In the early 1950s he sized up the mood as being about like that of a lodge hall. Today, however, it is often closer to that of a business bureaucracy, with computers and batteries of clerical employees organized in their own bargaining units and a well-padded self-seriousness such as is generally found in a corporate accounting office or governmental personnel section.

Behind that settled exterior, however, a considerable generational split is developing. "The young guy wants money, the middle-aged guy wants security, the older guy wants pensions" is the way an official of the International Longshoremen's and Warehousemen's Union summed it up. Lubell could write in the early 1950s that "the inner dynamics of the Roosevelt coalition have shifted from those of getting to those of keeping." But many of the present rank and file have come to maturity just in the last decade and are stepping up the pressure for getting again. The new group has substantially more education and a much stronger sense of personal independence than the older union men, plus all the wants of the affluent society. In the seventies the new generation will be putting a vastly increased number of young people into the nation's work force and thus into the unions—young people who have little feeling and less regard for the great, maturing struggle through which the labor movement has passed since the 1930s. They will almost inevitably further intensify the pressure for getting, and getting *now*.

This will increasingly disturb both organized labor and the nation's economy. Most of the current union leaders at the national and intermediate levels are products of the New Deal period and the subsequent aging process—"government-made men [wanting] status within the national power elite" C. Wright Mills called them some time ago. A substantial turnover in the top ranks of labor is almost certain to occur before too long if only because of the actuarial odds. But quite without regard to those openings, a major conflict is brewing between the older and newer forces over both priorities and styles.

Half of all union members are now less than forty years of age, and a quarter are under thirty; over half will probably be under thirty-five within a few years. About half of all union members live in the suburbs, but three-fourths of those under forty years old live there. Around a third of all union members have been making $7000 to $9000 a year, another third over $12,000 a year. In more subjective terms, a "union man" not long ago connoted a craftsman or factory worker who lived in a crowded section of an industrial town, worked long hours, had little free time, and could generally claim only elementary school training. The union member of the 1970s must far more often be thought of as a leisure-seeking suburbanite with a high school education and a strong concern about his own identity and status.

A closer look at the rank and file's opinions has been provided by a study made in 1966–1967 by the Kraft polling organization for the political arm of the national AFL-CIO. The report was not supposed to be made public, but parts of it were leaked to *The Wall Street Journal*, and much of the rest was then released. It showed younger union members more preoccupied with their own lives—their homes, taxes, recreation, and neighborhood problems—than with the broad public issues on which the national AFL-CIO and United Auto Workers have long tended to concentrate. An overwhelming majority (from 70 to 95 percent) supported the traditional union position on such matters as Medicare, minimum wages, workmen's compensation, federal aid to education, and much more. But only a little over half backed organized labor's opposition to a compulsory open shop or so-called right to work laws. Less than half favored open-housing legislation, but significantly, the number of younger members concerned about racial matters had grown to triple that of older workers and twice as many of the younger ones supported civil rights efforts. Members under thirty were more emphatic than the older group in believing their union should take a stand on important issues, but at the same time they declared their freedom to assert their own position. Thus on the Vietnam war, to which national AFL-CIO leaders gave unstinting support from the very start of the U.S. military buildup there, the Gallup Poll has consistently found rank-and-file members usually divided almost the same as the rest of the country.

The so-called organized-labor vote—roughly just over a fourth of the voting electorate, including family members—has been receding as a cohesive bloc in American politics for many years, though with occasional temporary upsurges. Its deliverability was generally overestimated, however, even in its heyday—by both the friends and foes of labor. In 1968, in the Democratic Presidential primaries and the general election, the labor vote splintered badly despite the biggest, most expensive drive in history by the national AFL-CIO, including the distribution of over fifty million pieces of literature and labor contributions and services at the local and national levels estimated to total $18 million. The Gallup and Harris polls reported a large portion of the labor vote "came home" to the Democratic Party in the closing weeks of the 1968 Presidential race. But even then a smaller proportion voted Democratic than since before the New Deal. Labor officials subsequently boasted of the effectiveness of their 1968 drive. But the final figure (56 percent), and the fact that another 15 percent seriously considered defecting up until almost the last minute, suggest the longer-term erosion at work. In the 1970 off-year elections, blue-collar workers were under the pressure of the economic downturn and a last-minute crash effort by most union leaders to persuade their rank and file to vote Democratic. A majority did, but the recent defection continues, even though at a slower pace, and the most important point that can be made about this once relatively cohesive political group is that it is now scattering its votes almost like the over-all electorate.

Union members, like practically everyone else, will have to be appealed to in terms of substantive issues, social styles, and specific attitudes rather than on the basis of "union solidarity" or which candidate has "labor's endorsement." The discontented workers of the 1930s are now well along in years, usually far better fixed financially, tired of the old battle-cries and arguments and, as one old-timer put it, "unwilling to fight to get what we already have." The younger union members have practically no tie at all to the old shibboleths and slogans. What is happening is not a return to Samuel Gompers' advice that organized labor should be an independent bloc which swings between the two major parties and holds the balance of power. Instead, the labor vote is simply splintering and responds most readily to calls based on personal, neighborhood, and other considerations to which the unions are only incidental. A national AFL-CIO publication conceded after the Kraft study that property taxes and sewer lines have bumped many of the traditional issues of concern to organized labor even among its own rank and file. "From now on," one experienced combatant in labor politics has commented, "there will be an enormous drifting vote not committed to any party or faction. Included in that number are millions of 'young marrieds' and first voters."

The attempt of the national AFL-CIO to adapt to the new conditions is reflected in a pamphlet put out for the first time during the 1968 Presidential election, setting forth "general guidelines for the development of political action in the suburbs." When the pamphlet was first distributed to union locals, a labor spokesman noted: "The key to winning elections is working where people live—we have tended to work where people are affiliated." The statement contains much of the essence of the new politics and, in fact, of our entire emerging society. So long as the economy is not doing too badly, the shift is from where people work to where they dwell—from the economic to the social to a very considerable extent.

It is nevertheless probable that even while finally beginning to face up to the new realities in the suburbs, labor will achieve highly uneven results there over the long run. In structure and temperament, the unions and the suburbs are quite different kinds of social and psychological systems. The two have much in common, including a concern with status and crime in the streets, a reflexive anticommunism, old-fashioned nationalism, and the identification of their middle third of the economic scale with the upper rather than the lower third. But the unions are more preoccupied with protecting and perfecting the programs of the last third of this century than with mounting breakthroughs into this last third. Suburbanites, in contrast, especially the younger ones, tend to be future-oriented. The labor movement is a bastion of the organized society of the industrial revolution. The impulses stirring in the suburbs are toward a rising inner disorganization which seeks to be "different" and "free" in some subjective and still largely inarticulate sense.

The suburban and "younger" trends are further increasing the built-in diversity within "labor." Another but different dynamic doing the same thing is the large influx of blacks into blue-collar jobs long held by whites and organized by the unions. These developments are wrenching the labor movement in sharply differing ways. But they all are contributing to the potential anti-establishment stirrings there.

Organized labor still represents almost 30 percent of the nation's main work force, but even that is down since the 1950s. Total union membership remained close to eighteen million during the fifties and sixties, but the number of jobs in nonfarm categories rose by over twelve million. Both automation and the upgrading of the labor market will prospectively take over a number of areas where the unions have been strong in the past. Growth of "the service economy" and the drive to organize more white-collar workers, as illustrated by intensive recruiting of teachers and computer programmers, offer additional opportunities for unions. But the labor movement will be lucky to hold close to its present share of the total work group during this decade.

Organized labor is actually now much stronger as a lobbying bloc than as an electioneering force, but it will inevitably be hard-pressed there, too. If it cannot persuade and marshal its own people as a broad-based movement, it will hardly be able to maintain its influence with the Congress or any other political institution indefinitely. Labor's main influence currently comes from the substantial campaign contributions it makes. In the off-year 1970 elections, for instance, the unions reportedly provided over $700,000 in the state of California alone. If campaigns for federal offices are eventually publicly funded even in part, however, such union leverage would be undermined. It is no coincidence that the AFL-CIO has been a major opponent of that kind of legislation, as well as of proposals to establish a Federal Elections Commission which would audit and supervise campaign funds for candidates for federal office.

In the economy and politics of the coming period, organized labor will unquestionably continue to be a major factor, particularly within the Democratic Party. But it faces substantial internal stresses, including increasing diffusion. More fundamental, the movement still must recognize and come to grips with a time and setting evolving in a way quite distinct from its own institutional outlook. Over-all, organized labor is like a great steam generator, still producing a lot of power but less and less efficient in its lumbering massiveness while, all around it, compact nuclear generators are starting up with a capability potentially well beyond the limits of any social, political, and economic machine last redesigned and rebuilt *circa* 1936.

The great power bloc loosely alluded to as business has also gone through a considerable evolution since the 1930s. It is now substantially less separate, less narrow in defining its self-interest, less self-conscious in its public outlook than it was then. In fact, after first bitterly resisting (and fairly frequent ideological protests still are heard), business has for all practical purposes accepted the prevailing "managed economy" and "welfare state." Indeed, it has become both the biggest single recipient of governmental exemptions, contracts, preferences, and other paternalistic handouts and a primary source of public revenues, both a powerful influence for the further bureaucratizing of government and the subject of endless regulation.

In the coming decade, the business sector will be able to rely on many channels of political influence, especially as a result of the attitudes and interests it shares with much of the communications industry, the broad-based middle- and upper-income sector of society, and the middle-aged and older electorate. But its principal direct leverage will come from paying the television pipers for the campaigns of the vast majority of candidates. The favors expected in return in such relationships are rarely any longer as direct and explicit as in earlier periods. Yet the words of so many large contributors are still unmistakable: "All I want is the right to be heard when I have a real problem," "We'd just like a reasonable understanding of our situation," and inevitably if unconsciously, "A sympathetic hearing is all I ask."

It is commonplace and accurate to emphasize the concentration of wealth in this country and the staggering political power that flows from it. The fact is often cited that over two-thirds of all privately owned corporate stock is in the hands of 2 percent of the American families. And there is impressive evidence, as a Congressional staff committee report documented in 1968, that the increased concentration of power which has taken place during the last ten to twenty years in the larger banks, especially in their trust departments, is awesome and potentially dangerous. In the manufacturing field alone, half of all the assets twenty years ago were controlled by 200 corporations; now only 100 corporations hold that power. The buildup is in fact one of those silent developments in one decade quite capable of politically exploding unexpectedly in the next, just as the elimination of over half of the nonwhite Southern farms with an income of less than $2500 a year during the 1950s exploded in the 1960s in the urban ghettoes.

An analysis of U.S. politics primarily in terms of business and financial concentrations, however, is not sufficient. That does not really explain many underlying things which are happening. Great public leverage unquestionably results from massed financial resources. That is made clear just by looking at a list of the several thousand large contributors who raise most of the money for the two major parties. But a wider-ranging inquiry is needed in seeking to identify sources of power. A look must be taken at the developments taking place throughout the economic system to find which key parts are expanding, which are contracting, what counterbalancing centers are flourishing, and what concentrations are altering.

One of the more significant economic changes coming about and having widespread political consequences is what *Fortune* has called "the reversing [of the] pyramid of income." Historically, American society has been built on a very broad base of breadwinners with low incomes, with the groups above sharply tapering off in numbers. This situation existed as recently as 1950 and, somewhat moderated, in 1960. But now, for the first time in history in any major society, the percentage of families making over $10,000 exceeds the percentage of families earning less than $5000.

In between, at the center of the economy, in 1950 the total number of families in the $5000-to-$7000 bracket was almost double the number in the $7000-to-$10,000 bracket; by 1970 nearly the reverse relationship prevailed. In one sense, almost the entire structure of American society is rising; in another it is quite literally being turned upside down. The rise taking place at the center powerfully reinforces the educational and other upgrading.

The income rises are not, however, an undiluted blessing. A fairly typical American middle-income family moved toward doubling its income in the last dozen years, climbing to around $10,000 a year. But higher taxes have eaten up about 10 percent of the increase, and higher prices over another 40 percent. Expanding wants are taking most of the rest of the increased income and often also putting the family further into debt. "Psychologically," a report of the U.S. Bureau of Labor Statistics has noted, "they're under as much pressure as ever."

Looking ahead, it is quite possible that the average family will have an income of around $14,000 by 1980, and the average consumer will probably have at least a third more to spend by the end of this decade in terms of 1969 buying power. The effect of that in a more tangible way is indicated by industry estimates that two-car households will be up from seventeen million at the end of the sixties to twenty-six million in the latter 1970s; the number of homes with color TV will climb from nineteen million to fifty-five million. Concurrently, affluence will almost surely work its will on a mass basis as a powerful equalizing, destabilizing, goading force in American society and politics. Once prosperity was a major ally of the *status quo*. Now it is the opposite.

Without regard to Nixon's erratic economic policies, which require 8 percent economic growth in 1971–72 just to correct unemployment, *Fortune* magazine projects an average growth of 4 percent annually for this decade. That contrasts with the almost-zero rate that the Nixon administration brought about in its first several years in office and the annual average growth of 3 percent during the first half of this century and 3.6 percent since World War II. *Fortune*'s target rate takes into account a decline in working hours consistent with the economy's long-term trend and includes no more than the average annual gain in productivity attained in the recent past—an average of 3.2 percent during the 1960s. The projected rate of growth is below that achieved during the booming sixties. But *Fortune* contends that the economy was operating then beyond its long-range potential, for it was working up from the doldrums of the latter fifties and had unsatisfied demand and a substantial group of unemployed who could be brought back into the labor force.

There still remains, however, a huge unmet demand and, more important, need in this country. Further, the lowest level of unemployment reached in the sixties remains worse than that generally achieved by the industrial economies of western Europe and Japan. The U.S. has not even come close to fulfilling its own commitment to full employment adopted as national policy in 1946. Instead, it has generally kept the lid on inflation more than any other major country in the free world, at a substantial cost in unemployment and lost productivity. Economist Arthur Okun, the youngest man ever to be appointed to the Council of Economic Advisers, has shown that an extra point in the unemployment rate means a 3 percent loss in the gross national product. Even a very conservative application of "Okun's law" suggests the high cost of the unemployment and underemployment of the middle and latter 1960s—a period of very low unemployment by historical U.S. standards. Between $30 billion and $40 billion in additional goods and services could have been turned out each year if the unused but available labor group had been put to work. That would have paid for most of the federal government's entire annual appropriations for other than military purposes during that period. The significance of the unemployment rate in human terms is reflected in the fact that a hike of one-tenth of 1 percent in unemployment means a loss of jobs, and thus of most of the family income, for about 100,000 breadwinners.

A staff study prepared for the Joint Economic Committee of the Congress in the latter 1960s concluded that "the U.S. economy has a potential rate of economic growth of between 4 and 4½ percent per year" through 1975. But it warned of substantial unemployment concurrent with that, particularly in the younger age brackets, which already suffer the highest unemployment and where the long-term human and social costs of no work are the most devastating. Certainly the nation's employment will have to expand very rapidly in the period ahead just to accommodate the unprecedented wave of young people born in the post-World War II baby boom and now settling down into their working years. The labor pool has grown at an average annual rate of 1.3 percent during the last two decades, but through almost all of the 1970s the rise will likely be around 2 percent a year.

Economist Joseph Froomkin contends that the heavy influx of young people into the job pool in the early seventies requires a real economic growth rate of 4 to 6 percent a year if a condition approaching full employment is to be achieved. But, as he recognizes, that growth rate is rarely achieved without inflation, and the pressure of the expanding labor pool toward inflation will be reinforced by the continuing high rate of technological change and any further decrease in the size of the armed forces. Judd Polk, director of the U.S. Council of the International Chamber of Commerce, has suggested that even a 4 to 6 percent rate of real economic growth will not be enough to provide for the changing population profile and help meet strong public expectations in the period ahead. Looking at what some other industrial countries have attained in the last ten years, he suggests a target of 10 percent. Whatever goal is sought, however, an important measure of any President is not only how well he copes with inflation and curbs unemployment but how fully he brings to fruition the nation's economic potential, for his responsibilities encompass not only short-term problems but also the country's longer-run fulfillment.

An indication of the muscular development of the American economy during the sixties is the fact that its annual output at the end of the decade was about equal to its output in 1960 plus the entire output of the Soviet Union in 1969. The U.S. was adding the equivalent of a Canada to its economic base annually and a West Germany every five years. Even with the recent economic difficulties, it is expected that electric-power use in the U.S. will double between the late 1960s and late 1970s; industrial output is expected to climb (using a 1960 base of 100) from just under 170 in 1969 to over 275 by the late 1970s. In essence, "a third industrial revolution" could impend, especially through more electronics, atomic energy, the miniaturizing of equipment, and individualized production and services.

Still another development with profound consequences is that some of the most elemental sources of our daily experience are changing. The soil gave the nation its roots and values, but now few of us work the soil. Fewer and fewer people even work rough machines. More and more we work with paper, plastics, and panels of buttons. The nerve ends of our daily life are yielding a different feel. And we are now commodity-minded, not raw-material or property-dominated. "What must be grasped," C. Wright Mills quite accurately urged, "is the picture of society as a great salesroom, an enormous file, an incorporated brain, and a new universe of management and manipulation."

The typical American breadwinner was for a long time the farmer, then with the spread of industrialization he became a factory hand. But the proportion of the total work force made up of unskilled blue-collar workers, like that of the farmers, has dropped precipitously since the 1930s. In 1957, for the first time, the number of white-collar workers exceeded that of the whole blue-collar group. Now the white-collar group is by far the largest segment of the labor pool (over half), followed by blue-collar workers (a third), the service sector (not quite an eighth), and farm people (a fast-fading twentieth).

A still further critical change in relative numbers and public strength is building up among white-collar workers. In the early to middle seventies, also for the first time, professional, managerial, and technical "knowledge workers" will be more numerous than all the rest of the white-collar group—the clerical, sales, and administrative workers. The ranks of the knowledge workers will also be larger than the whole group of blue-collar workers, excluding foremen and special craftsmen, who more and more relate to the managers above them rather than the employee group below.

The service and clerical-administrative groups have been growing rapidly of late, too, but their rates of increase may slow as the difficult automating of service and administrative functions picks up speed. No such slowdown appears to be in the offing yet for the knowledge workers. The number of professional and technical workers, for instance, will double just during the first half of the seventies: four and a half million individuals will be added to those categories. Most important, since relative rates of change rather than total size tells where the greatest social and political influence tends to be developing, it should be noted that the technical-professional group is currently growing more than twice as fast as the work force as a whole.

It can be argued that what is emerging in the professional-managerial-technical group is a new class with the numbers, knowledge, and money required to assert itself and dominate society. And it could develop into that on some matters. Certainly there will be more and more political appeals to this newly prosperous, increasingly political, and rapidly expanding sector. But the interests, views, and drives within the group are too diverse for it to be cohesive on many issues. And the continuing rise in the educational attainment, affluence, and independence of those who make up this element is accentuating, not narrowing, their diffusion. The so-called propertied class of the past had highly traditional, fairly simple interests around which to rally. The new group is badly split between public and private interests, tangible property holdings and intangible status incentives, even competing economic, social, and other values. It increasingly lacks "coherence as an historical force."

A group that, by contrast, is losing its proportional position yet at the same time is becoming even more explosive politically consists of those who work for themselves. In the early 1800s over

80 percent of the working populace were self-employed. By the 1930s, however, over 60 percent were working for private employers for fixed wages or salaries; in the early 1970s close to 80 percent will be so employed. With another 10 percent working at the various levels of government—up from 5 percent since the start of the era of liberal dominance in the 1930s—only about 10 percent will be left working for themselves. The old-fashioned, much-touted ideal of rugged individualism and an economy of small entrepreneurs is a hardy one, and between 20 and 30 percent of the present U.S. working populace have been self-employed at one time or another during their working lives—the economic equivalent perhaps of what the young acclaim when they urge "Do your own thing." But as made clear by the long downward trend of that portion of the work force which is self-employed, the traditional entrepreneurial attitude is relentlessly being frustrated and pinched off.

Small businessmen are still numerous and politically influential, but over the longer course they are being crowded out onto the fringes of power; the widespread awareness of this is already making millions of individuals who identify with small business, like many farmers, anxious and antagonistic. In the 1960s, these feelings germinated much of the sense of social impotence on the Far Right and in the Wallace vote. Bigness is both dominant and deeply disturbing in the country's present politics.

At the same time, the rapidly expanding professional, managerial, and technical group is taking over from the old-fashioned, fairly primitive economic individualists the function of sustaining the ethos of independence, though in subtler and more sophisticated forms. The emergent base of enterprise and liberty is thus now educational more than economic. There is possibly a greater fragility to freedom as a result of that shift. But it could perhaps also lead over the long run to a less materialistic, more sensitive society.

Still another development of political as well as economic and social consequence is that more and more American women are going out to work and in other ways gaining greater independence and influence. The much-publicized women's liberation movement is only the grossly exaggerated tip of a more fundamental and solidly based development. Almost 45 percent of all American females over seventeen years of age are expected to have at least part-time paid jobs outside their homes in the early 1970s. If the present trend continues, nearly 50 percent could be so employed by the end of the decade, and they would make up a third of the paid labor force.

More than one out of three women now works *full time* outside of her home. About the same percentage of married women work as single women, though there is a measurable drop during the years when small children are at home. Surprisingly, the higher the family income, well up into the upper-middle class, the greater the likelihood that the wife will do some paid-for work away from home. Women exert even greater influence on society as family-budget spenders than as outside workers, but the latter role is increasingly influential. Perhaps most significant in an underlying sense, women tend to take jobs not as much for income reasons as men do, but for "the opportunity for a fuller life," "contact with more people," "a desire for experience outside the home," and the like. Those motivational underpinnings are reaching deep into American society and politics, and they are almost sure to have vast public effect.

The peace issue, "the population bomb," consumerism, and a growing list of other matters could draw a considerable sector of women together as a loose special-interest group over the course of this decade. At the outset of the sixties there was little public awareness of the volcanic potential of either the Negro stirrings of that time or the then still-dormant student community. At the threshold into the seventies the political restiveness of an increasing number of younger women could have similar implications. And by the middle to latter 1970s it is quite likely that feminism will have attracted, activated, and loosely coalesced more women, especially upper-middle-class and younger women, than at any time in the last half-century. The deeper psychological layers into which that leads is suggested by questions now being raised by new feminists like Joanne Cooke: "Why do we look to men for our definition, direction and strategy? ... Why do we spend all our time worrying about men when they spend most of theirs worrying about their work? ... What ever happened to *our* history?"

Another development affecting the basic distribution of power is resulting from what Charles Reich of the Yale Law School has called "the new property." New kinds of "wealth" are crystallizing within the private sector, such as job-secured status in private organizations and changed relationships and balances of power inside corporations and other structures. In areas like these, the independence and influence of some of the most active parts of society are being fought out. Concurrently property, as it has traditionally been identified, has been subjected to more and more regulation and, in effect, reconstituted with a "public interest." Government itself has become a vast source of new largess—of jobs, contracts, subsidies, benefits, franchises, occupational and business licenses, and the use of public resources and services. These, Reich points out, "are steadily taking the place of traditional forms of wealth—forms which are held as private property. Social insurance substitutes for savings; a government contract replaces a businessman's customers and good will. The wealth of more and more Americans depends on a relationship with government." The federal government alone now spends close to one-seventh of the entire national outlay each year and is responsible for the allocation of even more of it. During the last two decades nine out of every ten new jobs have been created in response to the activities of the public and not-for-profit sectors rather than the private-profit economy.

Not just the independence from government long enjoyed by owners of traditional private property is being affected. So are Bill of Rights freedoms. Regulations are administered and public funds are given or withheld for a wide range of reasons, some of which are spelled out and some of which are left unstated. Government now often grants or withholds jobs, contracts, and other benefits only after investigating a person's personal life and political activity

—including whether he has ever invoked the protection of the Fourth Amendment or might assert the guarantes of the Fifth Amendment—and a number of other matters. And in the background, supposedly legitimate contacts and not so legitimate special influences spin their webs.

Reich's analysis is not a buildup to an old-fashioned championing of "property rights." He believes further erosion of these is "the inevitable outgrowth of an interdependent world." But he urges that how government regulates the old property and dispenses its largess of the new kind of property must be made subject to more definite guidelines so as to keep public officials from imposing what are really unconstitutional conditions, delegating governmental powers to private groups, turning administrative discretion into bureaucratic delay and arbitrariness, and using authority beyond its initially authorized purpose or without regard to any rule of relevance or reasonableness. In short, thoughtfully distinguishing *the public's interest* from *the government's interest* is one of the most important and complex value and institutional challenges of the coming politics.

While developments like those are considered, however, care is needed not to lose sight of the fact that the national economy is actually a vast ocean with many crosscurrents, shoals, and storms, not just a warming Gulf Stream. The poverty among us still stands out grimly. And the poor, as history shows, are a potential well of power—or antipower—just as surely as are the wealthy, especially in restive times such as these in which the nation is caught up.

Michael Harrington, in his now-classic tract *The Other America*, noted that the basic material for his inquiry was the same as that *Fortune* used about the same time for a major statement of its own on the U.S. economy. *Fortune* saw a cornucopia for most Americans; Harrington saw the human misery and hopelessness beneath all the plenty. Both observers were right. The presence of poverty in the midst of all the surging economic growth is a poignant reminder that the forces shaping the future do not work equally on all parts of society. Most people are making fairly steady headway, and some are achieving spectacular progress. But a considerable number are barely moving and some are being left behind, sucked under by the other propulsive forces.

How many Americans are considered "poor" depends on what level of income or need is used to define poverty. The criteria of the Bureau of Labor Statistics and Census Bureau claims less than one person out of seven now lives in poverty. The proportion of the poverty-stricken unquestionably is down substantially from the one out of three Americans whom Franklin Roosevelt found "ill-housed, ill-clad, ill-nourished." But it is still a significant sector of America—more than twenty-eight million individuals. And even if a much larger effort than has been made thus far is mounted to combat the problem, one out of ten Americans will probably still be mired deep in poverty in 1980—twenty-three million individuals. Currently, by the government's own admission, almost 25 percent of the country's children live in families that are poverty-stricken or nearly so. In the present social climate, those young people constitute a huge source of human deprivation and potential social unrest. A 1970 report of the business-oriented Committee on Economic Development concludes there has been no decline in the poverty group's size or overall redistribution of wealth in the U.S. in the last twenty years.

During the Depression so many people suddenly found themselves jobless and in poverty that the political process could not long have ignored them even if it had wanted to. Equally important, millions of those then without work had previously been productive and socially involved. Now a different situation prevails. The poor are not only a substantially smaller segment of the over-all society but also the latest generation of the historically isolated, alienated, and discriminated-against in this country—economic, social and political left-outs. But nothing has provoked fiercer opposition by many mayors, city councils, and congressmen of both major parties than attempts to arouse the poor to organize and participate politically. The objection of those sources has been to poor people declaring their independence and asserting their views while receiving public funds. Yet business, agribusiness, and many other subsidized and specially protected groups have long done exactly that while receiving huge handouts. This difference in attitude toward the haves and the have-nots suggests how much the basic social struggle is over power, not principles or programs. Lyndon Johnson expected the war on poverty to breathe new life into the old Roosevelt coalition. Instead, in dozens of cities, it quickly sharpened the hostilities between the slums and city hall, between black activists and white unions, between the socially aroused on one hand and the politicians and public administrators on the other. The situation is but another example of the restive elements in American society being told to work within the system, yet finding firm barriers put up to prevent them from gaining a real role in it—and then being put upon by the police when they go outside of it.

It is anticipated that around a third of the present poor will slowly climb out of poverty during this decade as a result of the nation's economic growth. Perhaps up to another third may sooner or later leave poverty as a result of special governmental and private programs. The remaining third, however, require meaningful and permanent assistance: this group consists largely of the aged, disabled and otherwise unemployable. Yet as the ranks of the poor, hopefully, shrink in the years ahead, the difficulty of exerting political muscle on behalf of those still trapped will continue to rise right along with the success of the over-all effort. The predicament points up the inadequacy of the nation relying on simply the political capacity of each group or interest to protect itself and assuming that a decent and tranquil society will then automatically result.

The greatest shift in power taking place in American politics is not across the geography or in the economy or social arrangements of the country, but simply within most individual voters. It is the current tipping of the balance of political power from the economic to the psychological to a certain extent—from the stomach and pocketbook to the psyche, and perhaps sooner or later even to the soul.

The want for food, shelter, and material goods has been the

principal sovereign for most of history, dictating expansion into the lands of others, demanding the fruits of trade and thus determining the strongest cultural contacts, provoking and justifying wars, and providing the impetus for the overwhelming majority of man's political attainments, much of his social evolution, and even some of his esthetic achievements. The human creature will unavoidably always be caught up in the web of satisfying his hungers, physical comforts, acquisitive desires, and economic security. Enough of the basic economic drives of most Americans, however, are now being satisfied readily that other aspects of their nature are coming into stronger and stronger play. Affluence, the electronic and other heightened bombardment of the senses, and a whole phalanx of very ancient fears and dreams enlarged by science, psychiatry, and the rest of our modern culture are both liberating us from our digestive tracts and enthralling us to other parts of our being to a greater extent than has ever before occurred for most of a large society. The 1970 elections, held amid an economic slowdown, showed that pocketbook appeals still carry some political clout. But these now must contend with other themes far more than in the past.

Even in traditional economic terms, the great struggles of the past for decent working conditions, workmen's compensation, unemployment benefits, minimum wages, the right to organize and similar economic legislation have lost much of their pulling power. Most voters would adamantly resist attempts to cut back those gains, but most people are barely stirred any longer by proposals to strengthen such legislation for themselves, much less extend it to others. Millions of Americans are still not covered by the present guarantees and work in filth or danger, receive hardly enough pay from long hours of work to buy the bare necessities, are unemployed much of the time, and endure an existence which most of us would not tolerate for ourselves for a day, much less a lifetime. The majority of citizens, however, have now been provided for, take the safeguards for granted, and may be willing to give their sympathy in passing but not their active support to those still unprotected. In effect, the main forces in the political battle have moved on, leaving behind the socially and often physically maimed.

Even for the majority, it is important to note that neither job security nor social security, as Andrew Kopkind has noted, "has brought workers the satisfaction which is supposed to be rightfully theirs as smokers of mentholated cigarettes or as weekend bowlers." The resulting frustration has increasingly pervaded the political right and left, the old and young, white and black. As a result, more and more the dominating thrust of public controversy is becoming a search for individual meaning, relevance, status, and even self-fulfillment. The nuances of that search may come close to providing a continuing thread for the politics of the seventies. The overriding needs of the citizens of the thirties were economic, and Roosevelt responded to those. The pervading wants of the new mass society are more inward-looking. Sometimes explicitly, sometimes almost unknowingly, people are asking "What is happening to me?" and "What do I stand for, believe in, feel?" Anyone who would be the new Roosevelt of the period will have to be keenly attuned to that growing concern over individual worth and purpose. And he will probably have to be able to provide—*project* is the word of the media—a sense of assurance and achievement for all those who are sorely troubled and searching.

But the psyche is being disturbed not only from within but from all around us, too. Crime, war, the nuclear holocaust, environmental dangers. Race, status, stability, unrest. The changes going on in people and in their relationships, the congestion of a mass society. Anarchy, repression, revolution. Rather than dwelling just on Scammon's "Social Issue," it would seem to be more useful to consider what might be vaguely termed a broader, deeper Psychological Issue. What is gnawing at so many people was summed up by British psychiatrist R. D. Laing in *The Politics of Experience:* "We do not live in a world of unambiguous identities and definitions, needs and fears, hopes, disillusions. The tremendous social realities of our time are ghosts, specters of murdered gods and our own humanity returned to haunt and destroy us. The Negroes, the Jews, the Reds. Them. Only you and I dressed differently. The texture of the fabric of these socially shared hallucinations is what we call reality, and our collusive madness is what we call sanity."

Most politicians and most practitioners of present-day psychiatry, along with our own "older" selves, still tell us to accept reality as defined by society. But evidence accumulates that much of the world and many of the ideas and pieties of twenty, thirty, and fifty or more years ago are grossly inadequate, even dangerous, for the times we are living in and the still-different era we are entering. Much of the public world, as Theodore Solotaroff has commented, "is quite literally driving more and more of us crazy in the effort to adjust to it," though it has been dismembering and redrawing "the lines of sanity in an age that has seen 'normal' men destroy nearly one hundred million of their fellow men." What society increasingly offers, as Solotaroff contends, is not a reality principle, but a "steady barrage of pseudo-reality [which] alienates us from our senses and sense."

As viewed by Jefferson, John Adams, and others in the generation that founded the Republic, man was a rational, optimistic, fairly uncomplicated creature quite capable of governing himself. But the image of man which is increasingly seen is closer to that of the ancient Greeks: creatures torn between reason and madness, obsessed with visions of death and violence, and more and more seeking abandonment in Dionysian disregard of old taboos. That is the imagery not just of the more independent and creative modern writers and artists but also of the actual war-making, domestic conflicts, and much of the rest of the daily scene conveyed to the mass audience by television and the movies. As McLuhan has said, literature and art at their most significant really are mostly "a Distant Early Warning System that can always be relied on to tell the old culture [and, he might have added, the old politics] what is beginning to happen to it."

For good or bad, politicians have also now turned intently to the sciences and arts of the psyche. The old-time ward heelers and political bosses, like primitive tribal leaders, maintained close contact with their people and usually understood them intuitively. But with the advent of the electronic media, a more self-conscious effort has taken over, initiated on a large scale first by Madison Avenue on Eisenhower's behalf. Then John F. Kennedy brought a little-discussed but brilliant understanding of modern communications to politics. Now talk of "behaviorism" and "psych-warfare" pervades even the grubbiest of political headquarters. Social psychologists, communications specialists, and "in depth" public relations firms have taken over from old-fashioned campaign managers not only at election time but also in the subsequent practice of governing, as the Nixon White House staff and executive offices amply show.

The common reaction is to decry the newer techniques and increasing concern of politics with the subconscious. Certainly the new skills can and unfortunately will be abused. Yet the emerging recognition of the psyche as the critical center of political and other power only faces up to the fact that every man is already a battleground of his various faculties and functions, and the old rationalism was hypocritical in its refusal to recognize the whole man. In fact, psychiatry and, more directly, much of our behavior have shown that man is considerably less rational than the Fo ading Fathers who charted our political system during the last days of the Age of Reason believed him to be. One of the major tasks of political thinking and action in the coming period must be to try to develop a more realistic foundation for democratic politics than the riddled eighteenth-century theories still be.   uncritically invoked.

The hard truth of the matter is that the prevailing political system is not solving or defusing the really searing problems confronting the nation either at home or in its relations with other societies. With inexorable rationality hundreds of millions of lives are imperiled by international crises again and again, and the disaffection in the domestic environment continues to grow. Perhaps any different political premises would only aggravate the underlying problems. But secular and spiritual salvation might be approached through a more forthright concern with all the greed, hate, terror, alienation, and self-righteousness building up. The

still-budding tendencies of the politics of love—of human reconciliation and community—at least offer an alternative viewpoint
from which to consider the established values and society. At a
minimum, more humane sources of political and moral power
have to be found than those on which we are presently too often
relying.

CHAPTER 8

On the Domestic Side of Foreign Policy

Southeast Asia, the Middle East, the Soviet Union, the world now enter the living room and the bedroom of the average American family almost daily with the televised evening news. Far-off events flicker across the faces of family breadwinners, housewives, and children enthralled by the electronic replay of death and destruction, pomp and people half a globe away—a modern parody of prehistoric nights when shadows from life-protecting fires both fascinated and terrified families huddled in caves.

"We live in a world tending to unify," Milovan Djilas has noted, ". . . this is one of the greatest events of our time." The ease of intercontinental transportation, the growth of world markets, the intertwining of international monetary systems, the spreading use of communications satellites, the tie-line of our car radios to practically everywhere—these only begin to suggest what is coming to pass barely noticed, or is taken for granted, but with profound, almost daily effect on just about everyone. The world may not yet quite be Marshall McLuhan's "global village." But at a minimum, military and aerospace developments are steadily curtailing the extent to which any major society, especially a rich and powerful one like the United States, can withdraw into itself for very long. There are intercontinental missiles, nuclear submarines, camouflaged "fishing trawlers," and satellites ready to carry hydrogen bombs and unleash their power at the touch of a button, with the metropolitan areas of this country now among the principal targets of the nuclear age and even an American first-strike incapable of protecting us from devastation.

Foreign policy not long ago was the private prerogative and charade of the highest circles of government; now it is more and more the real godhead of much of the national mood and fortunes, even of the continued existence of many millions of rank-and-file citizens. Simply in the most tangible terms, the country's relations with the rest of the world fuel a key incremental sector of the economy. The primacy of international matters for the electorate is mirrored in public opinion polls. Since 1950 (about the time the general public came to realize the implications of the Soviet Union's then newly acquired nuclear capability) questions of war and peace have topped all other public issues a heavy majority of the time. At the outset of the 1968 Presidential election, as one recent example, more than 55 percent of those interviewed said the Vietnam war was their principal concern, compared to only half that percentage being most uptight over the highly touted law-and-order issue.

The activists of the coming generation have been considered of late to be signaling a historic attempted retreat from the world because of their insistence on further reducing substantially the nation's military involvement abroad and their lead in stressing domestic reforms instead. Yet that group is also more aware of, educated about, and psychologically involved with the rest of the globe than any previous generation of Americans. As a result of jet travel, there is also an unprecedented and little-noticed intermingling of the young activists of the world. Most of the present young people are considerably more likely than their elders to develop a conscious relationship with other cultures and societies —based, however, as much on their sense of the human species as on the present reality of the nation-states. Power politics and the grosser aspects of the human race will almost certainly checkmate some of these more humane inclinations sooner or later. But in being more concerned with people than with nations this group portends sharpened conflicts and the need for new rationales for American foreign policy. It is also yet another sign of "a world tending to unify" and of the evolution of attitudes and values going on throughout U.S. society, though generally in less pronounced and provocative ways in the older sector.

Of this country's many public maxims, none has been extolled more over the years than the patriotic piety that "politics stops at the water's edge" and "foreign policy must be bipartisan"; Kenneth Crawford has called them the "Jehovah of our political tradition." Yet few homilies have been violated more frequently in the past. And none is more likely to be disregarded in the future as American foreign policy reaches deep into the nation's odds for destruction, pocketbooks, conscience, and—consequently—its politics.

George Washington, in his Farewell Address, decried the "baneful effects of the spirit of party" on the nation's international relations. Practically every succeeding President and Secretary of State have also invoked that warning—and ignored it, when that served their self-interest. Such contradictory behavior, however, merely emulates Washington, for his Farewell Address was concerned with not only foreign policy but also with undercutting the anti-Federalist opposition politically. At Alexander Hamilton's urging, Washington even delayed publication of the address (he never delivered it) until closer to the time the electors were to choose his successor, so that it might affect that decision.

The extent to which international developments have more recently been implicated and exploited politically is reflected in the Presidential campaigns of the last thirty years:

1940. F.D.R. promised "Your boys are not going to be sent into any foreign wars." At the same time he undertook to make the American economy "the arsenal of democracy." He thus dispelled the Depression but only by tying U.S. prosperity to the war effort.

1944. Voters shied from changing horses in the middle of a bloody stream, and Roosevelt played his role of Commander-in-Chief that election year for all that it was politically worth.

1952. Eisenhower promised "I shall go to Korea," belabored the Democrats as "the war party," and offered himself largely on the basis of his international military stature, thereby assuring a huge victory.

1956. The eruption of the Suez crisis just before the election obscured practically all other issues and turned another sure win for Ike into an even greater victory.

1960. John F. Kennedy found a "missile gap" which disappeared after the election, decried the loss of Cuba to communism, and claimed that American prestige in the world had never sunk lower.

1964. L.B.J. declared "We don't want our American boys to do the fighting for Asian boys," warned of Goldwater's belligerent international views, and talked about leading a great crusade for peace.

1968. Nixon, Humphrey, and Wallace, each in his own way, pledged an end to the war in Southeast Asia and a sweeping reappraisal of America's priorities abroad and at home. Nixon claimed to have a plan (never revealed during the campaign) for an early end to the war. And, by coincidence or otherwise, the incumbent Democrats, after long refusing to de-escalate the Vietnam conflict, suddenly called a bombing halt five days before the election. A close Nixon friend just as quickly got the American-maintained South Vietnamese government to indicate some well publicized reservations about that move, all on the weekend before the U.S. balloting.

During the last decade, even the off-year Congressional elections have been heavily embroiled with international events. The Cuban missile crisis dominated the headlines during the last days of the 1962 campaign and the growing public discontent with the Vietnam conflict contributed substantially to the reaction against the incumbent Democrats in 1966. That year the President campaigned for his party not by stumping the country but by taking a highly publicized "nonpolitical" tour of the Pacific up to less than two weeks before the election. For the 1970 off-year elections,

Nixon took off on a similar junket barely more than a month before the election, beginning in Italy and ending in Ireland, thus identifying with two key voting groups in the present politics. In the last six weeks or so before the election, he also announced a speeded-up troop withdrawal from Vietnam, pledged further tangible aid to Israel (formerly held off), and both pressed peace overtures with the Soviets and stepped up the Cold War rhetoric, thereby offering something for just about everyone. Some old-timers in the Congress still contend that successful politics are built principally on post-office appointments, public works projects, seniority, and service to "the powers-that-be" back home. But more and more senators and congressmen have come to concede in recent years that "good politics" require an articulate view of international affairs, and that whether for good or bad, foreign policy will likely be deep in the middle of most future elections, explicitly or otherwise.

The politics of the early and middle seventies will almost inevitably be affected by the political aftereffects of the Vietnam war, despite the Nixon administration's de-escalation of the U.S. involvement there. Even if American spending and involvement in Vietnam rapidly fade as a campaign issue, the historical forces unleashed in U.S. society by that war will be felt for years to come. The conflict has provoked one of the two or three most sweeping re-evaluations of the country's basic assumptions in its entire history. It compounded a gathering discontent among many groups and, most basic of all, polarized long-simmering tensions between humanitarian and technological values in American society. First it stirred the left; that then aroused the right. But regardless of the immediate appearance of things, the record suggests that the net effect of every war in this century has been to move the nation to the right for a while. Woodrow Wilson's effort to "make the world safe for democracy" was thus followed by a dozen years of domestic retrenchment. The first Congressional election after World War II brought to Washington some of the most reactionary legislators in many decades, and they generally turned out to be the spear-carriers of the Joseph McCarthy era. Reaction against the Korean war moved the country to the right again and helped put a Republican in the White House for eight years. The reaction to the Vietnam war was quickly reflected in the 1966 and 1968 elections, and it could continue to be felt for some time.

The increasing complexity and danger in international affairs have generally been considered a prime cause of the growth of Presidential power in the last thirty years. Inseparable from that, the various occupants of the White House, whether wittingly or otherwise, have been using foreign policy for their own domestic purposes, such as more readily to assert their image upon the nation and history, keep at bay fundamental economic imbalances, placate powerful constituencies like the military and its homefront allies, or cope with other strong internal pressures. Domestic "anticommunism," for instance, has been almost as much an influence on the White House, Congress, and State Department at times during the last twenty years as have the actual events of the Cold War elsewhere in the world. The supposed need of Presidents to prove to some people in this country that they can maintain "stability" in areas abroad claimed to be of special importance (no matter how oppressive or unreliable a particular oligarchy allied to the U.S. may be there) could now prove to be as significant an influence as domestic anticommunism has been in recent decades.

A number of senators and scholars have expressed growing concern over the White House practice of deciding the nation's international course, and thereby dominating the country without first obtaining much advice or almost any consent from the Senate, much less from the House of Representatives. But it seems unlikely that Congressional complaints about unfettered Presidential power justified in the name of foreign policy will come to much so long as they are mostly an intragovernmental tug-of-war. Commanders-in-Chief are too powerful and independent to be deterred for long or in a supposed crunch merely by Congressional resolutions, appropriations limitations, and hearings or other investigations concerning foreign affairs. Perhaps more to the point, too many key members of the Congress are tied to the White House by party considerations, defense contracts, and other means for a sustained legislative strategy to prevail on international issues.

A formidable challenge to the Presidency may be developing, however, from a more hardy source than the Congress. An influential sector of the public is now giving fairly regular attention to the handling of international developments. This was hurried by public confrontations over the Vietnam war, but it is being fed for longer-run purposes by rising educational levels and closer communications with the rest of the globe. The challenge will be reinforced by the political arrival of the new generation of voters and especially by its cadre of activists, whose views are seriously at variance with the premises of U.S. foreign policy during the last third of a century. For most of American history, Presidential power and popular power have been ascendant and have usually been mutually reinforcing. Now the growing popular and critical concern with foreign affairs could put them on a collision course over the long run.

The intellectual community is producing an articulate group of international specialists often at least as able as those in government. Highly competitive world-wide newsgathering agencies are now frequently faster and more incisive in reporting what is happening in the world than are official channels. The almost nightly television coverage of the Vietnam war, for instance, facilitated a synthesizing of domestic attitudes—if not knowledge—independent of governmental leadership or propaganda, and usually well ahead of them. In net effect, the resources for public consideration of events abroad, apart from what the government says, are now much greater than ever before.

These checks and balances have their limits, of course. James Reston has called the influence of the press, for example, "usually exaggerated," and he cites the much vaster resources of the White House through the endless flow of information across the President's desk, his ability to move quickly, the enormous powers of persuasion open to him, the Polaris fleet at his command, and the credibility gap of the press itself. But Presidential power is also limited, easily flawed, and erratic. In fact, a new emphasis on the limitation of the Presidency is a noteworthy feature of the writings and other public commentary by a number of those who have worked in the White House during the last decade.

In one critical area of foreign policy, however, the Presidency now has much vaster power than any Caesar ever commanded: by a single quick decision he can start the short sequence to nuclear holocaust. Once a President takes the oath of office and demonstrates such minimal qualities of sanity as satisfy his own immediate subordinates, the decision whether to opt for catastrophe is virtually his alone. Without any serious scrutiny of the institutional arrangements into which the development of nuclear weapons intruded, the American political system during the last quarter of a century has come to place in one individual a kind of divine right over the life or death of hundreds of millions of people. It is an even more absolute authority than that existing in the Soviet power structure, where at least two leaders and usually a committee of a dozen or more are now responsible for the really major actions. When President Johnson conferred with Premier Kosygin at Glassboro a few years ago, the press reported the American proposed the two make a "deal," man to man, to roll back the Vietnam war and other festering problems. "But I can't, Mr. President," Kosygin replied, reportedly somewhat taken aback. "I'll have to consult the Politburo."

Any attempt to build into the American governmental edifice a decision-stage safeguard—such as possibly a Supreme Council of State that would include representatives of the legislative as well as executive branch and become the sole authority for the first-strike use of nuclear weapons—would almost certainly be met by cries that making more than a single individual responsible could result in a fatal delay for the country at a moment of mortal peril. But dependence on a single individual's judgment may be even more dangerous. For, like the U.S., the Soviet Union has designed its defense system so as to be able to absorb any initial attack and still get off a nuclear counterstrike which would lay waste this country, making the unfortunate ones not those who perish but those who might survive. But an important distinction must be made between the latitude a President has as keeper of the nuclear firing code and the increasing challenges to which he is subject on other international ventures. The elective process and popular pressures operate only in a very preliminary and glancing way on that first prerogative, but more and more in the treacherous and expanding latter area.

GREATER KANSAS CITY *
Kill first day   — 500,000
Succumb later   — 400,000
Survive injured — 200,000
Others   — 200,000

The main domestic semantics of foreign policy during recent decades have been great avenging abstractions, as they had to be in order to invoke a righteously martial spirit—"the *protection* of

* Conservatively estimated casualties in the event of a nuclear strike in the middle 1970s, using the basic study prepared for the Joint Atomic Energy Committee in 1959, adjusted to the 1975 population projections of the National Planning Association, plus density changes and other recent data. Premises as to megatonnage, wind conditions, accuracy, and the extent of damage vary from area to area in order realistically to approximate an over-all attack.

The Soviets rely on larger-megatonnage weapons, the U.S. on more precise, smaller-megatonnage weapons. Twenty-megaton devices might be used on large, settled areas here. A single such weapon could shower fallout on cities as far apart as New York and Washington, with contamination from a heavy attack persisting for years. Medium-sized cities like Akron, Peoria, San Diego, and over sixty other logical targets of roughly the same classification could be devastated with much less megatonnage. One megaton equals five-hundred times the chemical explosive tonnage of the bombs dropped on Hiroshima (78,000 killed, 84,000 injured) and Nagasaki (21,000 killed, 41,000 injured). Beyond those fairly immediate casualties, leukemia among the survivors at Hiroshima and Nagasaki

freedom" ... "the *threat* of communism" ... "*Red* China" ... "*Communist* Russia" ... "aggression" ... "duty" ... "peril" ... "commitment" ... "deterrence" ... "enemies" ... "allies" ... "subversion" ... "survival" ... "The Flag" ... "strength" ... "weakness" ... "a great crusade" ... "national honor" ... "peace with honor." What such language actually invokes are elemental aspects of our national make-up. The domestic side of foreign policy provides as penetrating and disturbing a glimpse into the American subconscious as the racial pit—the specters often are not unlike apparitions of Dante's *Inferno.*

The usual arguments over international affairs, whether carried on in the hushed, wood-paneled, seventh-floor suite of the Secretary of State or the bedlam of a press room, are conducted almost entirely in terms of what "Moscow" or "Bonn," or somebody in "Owagadougou," is doing or thinking, or the latest arms and economic data, or abrupt events abroad. But there is also need to take into account more explicitly the underlying national attitudes and

GREATER CINCINNATI	
Kill first day	— 700,000
Succumb later	— 300,000
Survive injured	— 100,000
Others	— 200,000

emotional distortions which also go into the making of foreign policy as surely as do secret cables. Among these are what D. W. Brogan years ago called the American "illusion of omnipotence and omniscience" ... the insistence by many people on decisive results in an often intractable world ... the endless conflict between

---

did not reach a peak until five to seven years later. Continuing studies also indicate a long-term increase in other kinds of malignant cancer. It is expected that genetic disabilities will continue to show up for generations. All this is quite separate from the number of initial casualties and their disposal, the destruction of hospitals and sewage-disposal facilities, and the like.

the nation's generosity and its occasional apparent contempt for much of the rest of the world ... our "live-and-let-live" self-image, yet the messianic ardor deep in our national makeup ... the compulsion to prove our strength and determination and national virility abroad, then afterward the quick and fickle forgetfulness ... the reliance on crisis upon crisis to motivate the nation, and the tawdry exploitation of those even for personal excitement ... the inflammatory ideas of equality and self-determination engendered by the U.S., yet the growing rigidity of American policy in the face of a restive and increasingly change-driven world ... the historic commitment to international idealism, yet the reliance on militarism and materialism in making our way wtih other people ... the sweeping simplicity of so many of our national declarations, from Wilson's Fourteen Points to the recent hyperbole over Vietnam, yet the pragmatic backing and filling in carrying out those promises or, more often than not, finally getting out of them.

Other nations suffer from similar or worse distortions. But if America cannot handle its own hangups, it can hardly expect to be able to cope with them in other cultures. The intended deceptions so common in international relations are actually most often self-deceptions. Thus the Soviet Union rationalized for its domestic audience that it invaded Czechoslovakia in the fall of 1968 in order "to protect the people" there and forestall "outside aggression." And the U.S. persists in its efforts to pacify, protect, contain, stabilize, and influence (the old-fashioned word was *rule*) much of the rest of the globe.

The most critical international relationship throughout the seventies will continue to be that between the United States and the Soviet Union. But how they get on with each other will depend not only on the other's conduct but also, in large part, on the extent to which the naïveté and neuroses of each society distort or preclude a realistic understanding by itself of what is really happening. The Cold War has already persisted with greater tenacity in American and Russian minds than in the actual world. To a very considerable extent, local conflicts and interests have superseded the polarized clash of Communist and anti-Communist forces; and nationalistic pretentions have generally proved able to motivate people more strongly than such abstract ideologies as Marxism and capitalism.

A crucial and continuing challenge for this country is not to panic recurrently over the endless dangers, crises, rivalries, and revolutions elsewhere, some of them before too many years likely in countries with a nuclear capacity. Already the post-Cold War setting has overstrained America's poise and restraint. But the situation threatens a long drawn-out domestic as well as foreign ordeal for a people who have almost always sought to simplify their international relationships into a single good and bad, then compulsively try to have their own way. Frustration over a tumultuous world could have a deeply disturbing effect on the country's mood in the decade ahead.

Another kind of potential tieup can be illustrated with Red China, home of one-fifth of the human race and already possessed of a modest but developing nuclear capacity. Historically, American attitudes toward China have been fairly ambivalent, ranging from John Hay's widely admired Open Door Policy (which posed as protecting China from other Western nations while actually seeking in considerable part to advance U.S. trading interests there) to the subsequent frenzy in the Western states of this country over "the yellow peril." A classic example of the use of foreign policy for domestic purposes was Senator Joseph McCarthy's repeated charges just two decades ago that the "loss" of mainland China was a Democratic-liberal-internationalist-State Department-intellectual-homosexual-softheaded-Communist sellout. That series of attacks was launched and widely supported, or condoned, without regard to the fact the Chinese revolution was successful primarily because of conditions there, not here: the corruption of the old war-lord regime which the U.S. had been propping up and still harbors in a moderated version in Taiwan; Mao Tse-tung's deft and ruthless blending of Chinese nationalism, peasant perseverance, and militant communism; and an ancient Chinese hostility toward foreigners, whether Europeans, Japanese, or Americans.

The coming years will almost inevitably reverberate from time to time with variations on Dean Rusk's now famous statement in support of Lyndon Johnson's course in Southeast Asia: "Within the next decade or two there will be a billion Chinese on the mainland, armed with nuclear weapons, with no certainty about what their attitude toward the rest of Asia will be." More recently, Secretary of Defense Melvin Laird has also found it useful to play ominously on that same theme to get Congressional appropriations for

SAN FRANCISCO BAY AREA
Kill first day	— 1 million
Succumb later	— 1 million
Survive injured	— 500,000
Others	— 500,000

the Pentagon: "I believe that we do not want to become hostages of the Chinese at any time in the future." In the decade ahead, as mainland China grows into a still greater power a key question for this country will be whether that emergence shall be recognized as a historical fact, perhaps to be influenced with patience and maturity—or is American society sooner or later to be deliberately inflamed against that looming giant? China combines two characteristics which readily excite our national subconscious (communism and a different race) plus two traits which many people find easiest to take on: technological backwardness and public belligerence, as millions of Americans perceive the "Middle Kingdom." It thus offers a convenient specter against which this country's anxieties might be let loose by elements anxious to mobilize America in a far-off "mission" while they engineer "national unity," extoll our "responsibility" in the world, render more and more power unto themselves—and mount a staggering sacrifice of blood and treasure.

There is no intention here to minimize the difficulties and possible peril which China could present. The point is simply that U.S. policy toward that ancient civilization will, for better or worse, emerge out of our own national temper as much as from developments on the other side of the earth. The dynamics of foreign policy occur *here* as well as *there*. Though we may be able to affect to some degree what happens elsewhere, we have much more leverage over the extent of our own rationality—or, as too often seems to be the case, a lack of it.

Two powerful political bases are discernible for political purposes on the domestic side of foreign policy, and their rivalry could be central to the American future. One is the prevailing and muscular alliance of traditional interests and thinking organized around the latest and most costly technology and the banner of *national security*. The other loose, still largely subjective massing is the spreading desire for peace through some inchoate *human commu-*

METROPOLITAN WASHINGTON, D.C.

Kill first day	— 1 million
Succumb later	— 800,000
Survive injured	— 400,000
Others	— 400,000

---

nity. This latest gathering is at only an early stage of formulation, but it is already a profoundly unsettling force. In fact, it is generating the first real challenge to the nation's heavy reliance since World War II on armed deterrence, sporadic conflict from decade to decade, and a precarious overhanging "balance of terror." In its most explicit and narrowly based form, this is the growing "peace vote," but that is only the tip of the iceberg. Both of these basic groupings are grossly inadequate simplifications for either substantive or political purposes. But they are the principal public responses, however inadequate, to the convulsive events which have shaken the world during this century.

The convergence of interests which President Eisenhower, in his last and most provocative statement in the White House, labeled "the military-industrial complex" has since more accurately been identified as the industrial-military-organized labor-scientific-higher education coalition; and that is the real order of benefit in this tie-in. It is less than the conspiracy its critics claim, but its existence is still much more than a coincidence. The U.S. Treasury has been paying out close to $50 billion annually in each of the last half-dozen years to corporations and other institutions filling military and defense-related contracts, now by far the largest business in the nation. Roughly 10 percent of the entire labor force has come to owe its paychecks directly to defense spending, and practically all of that group is unionized. It provides a firm buttress for the AFL-CIO's hard-line foreign policy stance.

The country's largest employer is no longer the automobile industry but the aerospace companies, still true even with the recent cutbacks in aerospace. While the auto industry serves nine million or more customers each year, the aerospace companies cater to only one that really matters: the U.S. government. This industry has also cornered a disproportionate share of the "knowledge workers" who constitute such an influential sector of the emerging economy and over-all society. Thus the aerospace companies have been employing more than 20 percent of the nation's entire supply of scientists and engineers. And those companies are but one facet of the industrial-military coalition.

In 1929, before the Roosevelt era began, the war industries accounted for 1 percent of the gross national product. In the latter sixties they accounted for nearly 10 percent; and even after the Vietnam budget reductions, they still take 7 percent. During the last four decades, the portion of the GNP taken by agricultural production has been reduced significantly, but the resources thereby released have gone into military spending rather than housing, education, health, and other domestic uses. Robert Heilbroner has estimated that the defense and space effort has been blotting up over 10 percent of what might be called the nation's total growth effort and almost two-thirds of all the research and development

> **GREATER ATLANTA**
> Kill first day   — 400,000
> Succumb later   — 500,000
> Survive injured — 300,000
> Others   — 200,000

work. Nuclear scientist and defense critic Ralph Lapp has commented: "Our commitment to weapons-making has distorted the free-enterprise system of our economy into a kind of 'defense socialism'—a system in which the welfare of the country is permanently tied to the continued growth of military technology and the continued stock-piling of military hardware."

The tie-in between defense spending and national decision-making is not vague and elusive but can be, and has already often been, pinpointed with specific key senators, congressmen, multibillion-dollar-a-year defense contractors, campaign contribution lists, military base locations, high federal executive-branch positions, and retired generals, admirals, colonels, and captains who turn up by the thousands working for companies doing business with the Pentagon. But much more basic than that, the influence of the military-industrial coalition has resulted from its importance to a great many local and regional economies. Defense contracts in recent years have provided payrolls for workers with some twenty-two thousand of the country's larger manufacturing companies acting as prime contractors. And under them, more than a hundred thousand other concerns have been doing some kind of defense work, spread out in over five thousand cities and towns across the nation. Federal Reserve Board Chairman Arthur F. Burns, while head of the National Bureau of Economic Research several years ago, warned that "the scale of defense spending has, to a significant degree, become a self-reinforcing process. Its momentum derives not only from the energy of military planners, contractors, scientists and engineers; to some degree it is abetted also by the practical interests and anxieties of ordinary citizens." The Pentagon has estimated that for every defense worker, three to five other

METROPOLITAN CHICAGO

Kill first day	— 1½ million
Succumb later	— 1 million
Survive injured	— 2 million
Others	— 4 million

jobs are created—butchers, bakers, bartenders, and so on. As J. Kenneth Galbraith commented, the "enfranchisement of the military power was in a very real sense the result of a democratic decision."

Looking ahead to the middle and latter seventies, defense spokesmen argue that the nation needs to increase its armaments spending substantially. The so-called wish list of the Joint Chiefs of Staff at the outset of this decade included the following, which is only a small part of the new weaponry wanted:

- A new strategic bomber costing over $10 billion
- A much larger successor to the Minuteman Missile, at a cost of $10 to $12 billion
- A new sea-based successor to the Polaris, costing $10 to $12 billion for both the submarines and surface ships
- A new continental air defense system costing $15 billion
- An expanded missile defense costing $8 to $14 billion beyond the $5 billion already budgeted, and eventually increasing to around $40 billion.

The projected costs will almost certainly go way up. A Bureau of the Budget study made only a few years ago concluded that weapons systems with sophisticated electronic components end up costing two to three times more than anticipated, encounter delays averaging two years beyond their contracted-for completion date, and still usually have a performance reliability less than half of that promised. Defense Department witnesses have testified before Congressional committees that it is fairly standard practice for the larger defense contractors seriously to underestimate their projected prices, then obtain Pentagon permission to increase the charges levied against the government later on. One high Pentagon witness stated under Congressional questioning that he had "never heard a [Defense Department] program manager propose cost reduction for a funding problem."

One basic factor that keeps the whole business going was summed up in the late 1960s by James J. Ling, founder of one of the nation's ten largest military and aerospace contractors. "One must believe in the long term threat," he said. The financial vice-president for Ling's operation at that time, Samuel F. Downer, added the political dimension: "Its selling appeal is defense of the home. This is one of the greatest appeals the politicians have to adjusting the system. If you are President and you need a control factor, you can't sell Harlem and Watts; but you can sell self-preservation, a new environment. We're going to increase defense budgets as long as those bastards in Russia are ahead of us [a strategic disparity the U.S. Joint Chiefs of Staff and intelligence agencies conclude to the contrary]. The American people understand this."

A differing insight has been offered by New Left elder statesman Paul Goodman, speaking at a Washington, D.C., symposium of top government and military officials and defense contractors to consider research and development prospects for the 1970s. "You are," Goodman told them, "the most dangerous body of men at present in the world. . . . You have disrupted ancient social patterns, debauched their cultures, fomented tribal and other wars and in Viet Nam engaged yourself in genocide. It is because of you that there are riots.... Your weapons have killed hundreds of thousands in Viet Nam, and you will kill hundreds of thousands in other Viet Nams.... The best service that you could perform is rather rapidly to phase yourselves out."

The near certainty, however, is that even with temporary setbacks, the industrial-military coalition will continue to flourish over the long haul. It specializes in what the United States does best: a technological outpouring which seeks to overwhelm this country's friends and potential enemies, still the vagaries of the human spirit in both "them" and "us," dispel the unknown and command the future. The effort constitutes a major stimulant to America's striving for material achievement, mechanistic progress, governmental

---

METROPOLITAN BOSTON
Kill first day   — 1 million
Succumb later   — 1 million
Survive injured — 400,000
Others   — 400,000

---

largess, pre-emptive authority, and great private gain in the name of the public good. The industrial-military sector bears a striking similarity to the business tycoons who thrived in the last third of the nineteenth century. They justified their drive for bigness and dominance in the name of rugged individualism, capitalism, property, and manifest destiny. Today's drive is justified on the basis of anticommunism, patriotism, prosperity, stability, and survival in the nuclear age.

A wide-ranging study by Dow-Jones' *National Observer* concluded that the industrial-military coalition "is real. And it's powerful.... This complex cannot start wars, but its interests are clearly served when wars go on. It extends favors to those who can help it, withholds them from its critics. But there is no evidence that any of this involves widespread corruption." Yet what now constitutes corruption? The most blatant bribery is petty compared to the substantial campaign contributions given and the governmental influence exercised to obtain or retain billion-dollar defense contracts for particular companies, Congressional districts, and states. Old-fashioned political corruption is small-time compared to the hold military contractors and their senators or congressmen have come to have on the U.S. Treasury and much of the rest of the federal government, plus a vast portion of this country's most trained human resources. The over-all development has given a significant part of American society a vested interest in continuously perfecting the means of human slaughter. And, as a Nobel laureate in physics remarked, "It's amazing how easy it is to find new and efficient ways to kill people if you put good minds to work on the problem."

Many of the nation's young activists have not lost all of their reasoning power when they accuse the established order of having "a preoccupation with dollars and death," yet most older people claim that they are unable to understand young people who insist there are moral limits to what "society" can be allowed to do. The politics of the coming period involve, however, more than a David-and-Goliath confrontation between those two viewpoints. No look ahead at this decade would be realistic if it failed to take into account the greatly enhanced interest and influence which the military itself now has in the nation's public processes. Americans have long prided themselves on the circumspection of their armed forces and firm civilian control of the military, and the country has not yet suffered a *coup*. But during the last thirty years, the military structure has moved from the periphery to the center of U.S. society and especially of its main decision-making. The nation now has a huge armed force; and the elite of the officer corps is unabashedly attentive to the country's priorities, general political course, and the military's place in the total scheme of things. Quite apart from the military's own sensitivities and initiatives, there is now hardly a public cause or viewpoint, from the Far Right through the two major parties and on to the doves in the Vietnam controversy, that has not recruited former military figures to stand witness for it.

A more tangible development is that in the last half-decade precedents have been set and, more important, attitudes conditioned for the deployment of military forces in key U.S. cities. Since the mid-1960s, for the first time in this century and possibly in the history of the country, the military has quietly reconnoitered practically every metropolitan area for avenues of armed approach, bivouac sites, and communication controls. The designation and training of specific Regular Army and federalized National Guard units for potential domestic use were major steps in the same direction. One of the Pentagon's principal think-tanks, the Institute for Defense Analysis, has also been used to blueprint the suppression of domestic differences over fundamental social issues—a long leap into sensitive civilian matters. There has even been established in the underground structure of the Pentagon a multi-million-dollar, around-the-clock domestic war room just to oversee internal crises and direct the use of military forces within this country. Troops were used in some of the race riots during the last half of the sixties, then on widely scattered college campuses, then in primarily political contexts like Chicago in August 1968 and Washington, D.C., for the huge peace movement gatherings in 1969 and 1970. Military surveillance on the domestic front is now routine. Each step has been taken only with the approval of civilian authorities. But the fact remains that the plans and precedents for military control of social and political disputes, and potentially even a military takeover, are one of the unblinkable legacies of the nation's recent history. The military was used infrequently in earlier times to help cope with a national disaster or aggravated labor dispute, but never to the extent and with the detailed prospective planning fashioned of late.

A latent question for the coming period is: How active might the military become on its own if the young generation and its allies, influenced by New Left activists, happen to win a substantial share of power in a national election later on, then undertake to make significant changes in the federal budget and existing foreign policy, including a 50 percent reduction of defense spending? The almost simultaneous emergence of a politically more aware officer corps and a change-charged, priority-altering new generation of voters could lead to grave problems. Perspective should also be kept on the fact, however, that in a time when millions of Americans are unsettled and looking for firm, simple answers, it is less likely that the armed forces would take over than that civilian leaders themselves might finally resort to armed solutions to their problems—will fail to lead soon enough with civilian programs and political persuasion amid all the uncertain circumstances prevailing, then will desperately, or with cool calculation, fall back on "the judicious interdiction" of troops and tanks. It is ironic that the possibility of a military government, if only in selected parts of the country, is enhanced after a decade in which civilian control of the Defense Department became more comprehensive than at any time since World War II. Yet that is the point the country has reached.

Another relevant development has been the buildup in the last several decades of a huge intelligence apparatus essentially for foreign purposes but based largely here at home. The Central Intelligence Agency, merely one arm of this apparatus, has become an important domestic contractor and woven a network of contacts and influence throughout the most powerful institutions of American society. It now controls one of the larger departmental budgets in the federal government and operates with a minimum of advance Presidential or Congressional supervision, as events have repeatedly shown during the last dozen years. It has developed a body of specialists preoccupied with covertly influencing national governments; and, like its Soviet, French, and other counterparts, it has even spent substantial sums in foreign elections. The CIA, in fact, reportedly spent almost as much money in the mid-sixties in support of the campaign of a progressive-democratic Presidential candidate in a traditionally friendly Latin American country as either the Republican or Democratic National Committee reported putting out for the 1964 Presidential election in this country.

Most Americans would scoff at the possibility of such influence ever being applied to their own domestic politics. But if intelligence sources sensed a serious threat to their institutional interests and national "responsibilities," a wholesale transfer of skills and resources by key men is not inconceivable. The lurking danger is raised here to suggest the new set of circumstances which have been quietly developing on the domestic side of foreign policy. A modern Machiavelli would probably be less prone to try to "buy" votes on either an individual or mass basis than to use the kind of international incidents which inflame entire societies in patriotic and timely ways. "The potential for a disastrous rise in misplaced power," Eisenhower warned in his farewell message from the White House, "exists, and will persist."

Increasing numbers of people, however, appear to be unwilling to settle for the force-emphasizing policies, defense costs, and military influence of the last several decades. This development is building not through a primary economic class or major social institution, as history often works its will, or even just among some noisy students, as sometimes seems to be the case, but as an already widespread and still growing dissatisfaction of the spirit, an equally important historical wellspring. What is coming into issue is not just a particular set of national policies but, broadly and vaguely yet still more consciously than for a long time, what kind of a society and world people want to live in.

A very small minority is genuinely pacifist. A slightly larger group seeks almost complete disengagement from the world, many of them in order to attend to domestic problems. In contrast to those elements, the overwhelming majority unquestionably still holds that national military strength is essential. But even much of that group is demanding a greater public emphasis than has yet been placed on seeking international community and common denominators. Not simply "peace-through-strength" but also peace through reconciliation. At the same time, public support is declining for unilateral foreign aid, large-scale military assistance abroad, big and semipermanent American garrisons overseas, and recurring resort to expeditionary forces every decade. The most likely prospect is certainly not complete global military disengagement, as the rhetoric of some politicians on both sides of the recent foreign policy debate have asserted. Rather it is for more of an economic and political effort and less of a military emphasis.

A number of different strands are coming together to form a loose peace constituency. First and largest in the long run are a substantial portion (though still a minority) of the approaching generation of new voters. Another major source is the increasingly independent women's vote. Still another source is a decided minority of men, but many in this segment have had extra educational and economic advantages and exercise influence well beyond their numbers. Also relevant, though outside the structuring of those groups, are the more ardent peace advocates. They alienate almost as many as they convert, but their passionate commitment is playing upon the idealism, moral strain and frequent sense of guilt in the American character; they are important over the long haul far beyond their numbers or the backfire from their stridency. That backfire, in fact, may be essential in order to get through to more of the population. The explicit and potential peace groups have been found by public opinion surveys to come in about equal proportions from both liberal and conservative, Republican and Democratic backgrounds. Perhaps most important, the peace massing draws individuals strongly motivated around this particular issue— a prerequisite for a minority hoping to influence the nation's highly pluralistic politics.

Occasionally, a crisis like the Soviet invasion of Czechoslovakia in 1968 or a longer-term development like the reduction of the number of U.S. troops in South Vietnam chips away at the less committed of the peace grouping. But the base of this emerging constituency is being augmented fairly steadily by the long-range factors of rising educational levels, affluence, and broader general exposure to the world. In the late 1950s, few people foresaw the-

GREATER PHILADELPHIA
Kill first day   — 1¾ million
Succumb later   — 1¾ million
Survive injured — 1 million
Others   — 900,000

vigor and influence which the student movement and black militants were to develop in the United States within barely half a decade. The peace movement may now be hovering around an even more significant take-off point, perhaps put off only briefly by the de-escalation of the American involvement in Southeast Asia.

The more assertive peace advocates might be considered as now being at about the same stage as the Abolitionists were around 1850, when the hard core of that fervent crusade was turning more and more from advocacy to action—and then from being content to smuggle slaves out of the South to also running guns in there. Even Henry Thoreau, that gentle philosopher of nonviolence, admitted finally helping to move guns. The Abolitionists were thoroughly loathed by vast numbers of Americans and ignored by most of the rest. But the movement defined a direction and generated a momentum which eventually led to both a broadening of human freedom and incredible slaughter. A zealous minority, it helped set in motion events which long determined the nation's politics and history—and still have an effect.

The peace constituency, even as augmented by its more subdued adherents, will almost certainly not come to power on its own at all soon. But it may grow large enough to exert much greater influence later in this decade, and it will doubtless keep expanding over the long run. If the military-industrial grouping should suffer a setback in one of the next several Presidential elections, that would most probably be caused by a more conventional coalition of the peace gathering plus far larger numbers of people opposed to heavy taxes and the substantial amount which still goes for military purposes even after the recent cutbacks, the continued centralization of power in the federal government, and the diversion abroad of vast resources and energies that might otherwise be directed to education, the cities, cleaning up the environment, and other domestic needs. Such an alliance would cut across a number of different ideological strands, and it would therefore probably be unreliable in any continuing sense. But it is not at all inconceivable that an early Presidential campaign will hear some clarion campaign calls to "Cut the Pentagon Budget in Half," "No Military Budget over 50 Billion Dollars," and "Less Taxes, Less Government, Less Involvement Abroad."

At the heart of the peace movement stirring among many young people is a broadening, occasionally even a complete, shift of attachment from the nation-state to a more inclusive and less structured human society. Much of this movement is still more introspective and moralistic than political. But Martin Luther King, Jr., an early champion of the contemporary peace surge, pointed out not long before his assassination: "Already our best young workers in the United States are talking about the need to organize in international dimensions. They are beginning to form conscious connections with their opposite numbers in other countries. There is yet not even an outline in existence of what structure this growing world-consciousness might find itself. But . . . the spirit is awake now; structure will follow."

Thus far, the groping toward a larger loyalty has not been injected into domestic politics except in some shrill attacks from the extreme right. But the fact cannot be avoided that millions of

Americans, especially younger Americans, are loosening (though generally still not cutting) their traditional ties in favor of a more independent personal ethic and greater subjective identification with the rest of the human race. The slightest surfacing of this has

---

METROPOLITAN DETROIT
Kill first day   — 1⅓ million
Succumb later   — 1 million
Survive injured — 1 million
Others   — 1¾ million

---

already provoked a reaction in the recent emphasis by millions of more traditional Americans on showing the flag. The shift among many of the young people could sooner or later precipitate a really venomous public controversy because it agitates the emotional nerve ends of patriotism, re-examines and rearranges the role and responsibility of the individual in society, disputes the primacy of the nation and the sanctity of oaths of allegiance, and denies military obligations in favor of other personal contributions. The clash could provoke another bitter witch-hunt by avenging nationalists, who would probably then turn on even George Washington for his repeated reference to himself as "a citizen of the Great Republic of humanity at large." The pre-eminence of a person's loyalty to his country over that to his local and regional environment was resolved in this country, as in most others, only by a costly civil war. A long and turbulent passage may have to be suffered again before another expansion and reconciliation of competing loyalties is worked out.

In politics, practically everything eventually gets down, of course, to the oversimplification, even the lubricity, of labels. In the last half-dozen years, for example, there has been increasing argument over not only who are the real peace-seekers but who are now the authentic "internationalists" and "isolationists." The inadequacy of such descriptions does not lessen the fact that much of our public thinking and politics finally take place in just such shorthand.

Most so-called political conservatives have evolved through World War II and the Cold War to make up a large proportion of the present hard-liners in this country. Aggressively anti-Communist, they are now the ones generally most willing to "go it alone" to resist whatever is labeled communism. And they are usually much more ready to support military than economic, social, or political solutions to U.S. problems abroad. Some of this element resisted U.S. intervention in Europe at the outset of both world wars, but it has generally been ready more recently to rally in support of American involvement in Asia as necessary to contain China. In-depth opinion studies suggest that most in this over-all group also rank among those most conservative on domestic matters.

A fundamental conflict exists, however, between the group's foreign and domestic objectives. The steps necessary to carry out an assertive and sometimes almost unilateral foreign policy run counter to the group's domestic opposition to the continued amassing of power by the federal government, high public spending levels, and substantial governmental leverage over the private economy. Thus far, that dilemma has largely been ignored or rationalized by conservatives attacking welfare and other domestic spending as the real cause of the domestic drift. But neither that criticism nor all the lip-service to "the tried and true principles of the past" alters the fact that much of the federal tax dollar has gone for the huge military build-up in recent decades, and much of the governmental concentration of power has resulted from that. The historical record of the last two decades makes clear that the international thrust of American conservatism is easily winning out over its individualistic values and its hope of significantly downgrading government.

Traditional liberals became identified with idealistic internationalism under Woodrow Wilson, then became directly power-

inclined with Franklin Roosevelt. As reflected most recently in the public papers of Lyndon Johnson, this group is still relying largely on historical analogies and foreign policy concepts which evolved just before and after World War II to meet the circumstances of that time. Initially, traditional liberals limited themselves to supporting joint action with other major powers, but the record since the latter 1940s shows that they have been increasingly willing to settle for secondary client-allies. They have thus tended to follow a course closer and closer to that of the conservatives on foreign policy matters. At the same time, the global activism of the

---

METROPOLITAN LOS ANGELES

Kill first day	— 1½ million
Succumb later	— 4¼ million
Survive injured	— 1¾ million
Others	— 1 million

---

traditional liberals has been cutting deep into the allocation of resources they need to pursue their declared domestic objectives. Both liberals and conservatives are thus suffering from a serious conflict between their respective internal and international views.

A third major grouping on the domestic side of foreign policy is now concerned with the limits of American power in the world and the need for much more "selective commitments." This rapidly gaining group contends the United States must seek to be an influence in the world primarily by humane example, not as a proconsul. It has been accused by such divergent critics as Richard Nixon and Hubert Humphrey of being "neo-isolationist." Yet many of its leading spokesmen, such as J. William Fulbright and John Sherman Cooper, as well as much of the intellectual community, were among those attacked most sharply only a decade and a half ago for being "globalists." And despite the more recent charges against them, they are still closer than the other two groups to the views of most of the rest of the world concerning this country's course in Southeast Asia, a new American relationship with Red China, the present state of the Cold War, and a number of other basic international questions.

The shifts of position going on in each of the three groups makes clear that the old labels of "isolationist" and "internationalist" have become useless. More important, the over-all structuring of the major public constituencies on foreign policy is changing: a considerably broader diffusion is developing. This may be only a transitory phase en route to a new two-way polarization. Or more likely, we may be on the way to at least a four-way division, with a sizable radical group also beginning to take root. This latest element will not necessarily be just domestically focused because it identifies acutely with "the downtrodden of the earth" and signals eventually changing social relationships both at home and abroad, with the nation-state more and more incidental to the open-ended technological, economic, and social forces at work. The over-all splintering of domestic opinion concerning the proper approach for

----

It can be calculated that a hypothetical nuclear attack of 10,000 megatons in ground bursts could, in the course of sixty days, destroy 80% of the United States, if unprotected, while an attack of 20,000 megatons could cover the entire country with radioactive fall-out, killing 95% of the unprotected population.

> **—Task Force Report to the United Nations Secretary General**

----

this country to the rest of the world could contribute very substantially to the breakup and rearranging of the long-prevailing political balance in the United States over the longer stretch ahead.

The loose groupings touched on here do not, of course, even begin to fill out the full range of domestic viewpoints in the field of foreign affairs. The most important additional element, however, is probably that very small, broadly informed collection of individuals who cut across the groups already suggested and seek to sort out the country's international problems one at a time, in their full complexity, without very often "striking attitudes before the mirror of domestic opinion," as George Kennan wrote of his onetime superiors in the State Department. This elite is exemplified by Kennan, Edwin Reischauer, Jerome Wiesner, John Fairbank, Matthew Ridgway, Llewellyn Thompson, and a young revisionist element still developing. The cutting edge of most of the really critical prospective issues in the world is discernible not from the domestic political dialogue, and certainly not from vapid State Department publications, but from the commentary of members of this minute sector.

Thus, outside experts such as Wiesner have reminded us that "one of the most encouraging aspects of the disarmament picture is that there are so many alternative steps we can take." And while the Congress regularly cuts back the foreign assistance program and the last four Presidents have reluctantly but regularly given in, almost all of these international specialists warn that the widening gap between the underdeveloped and developed societies is one of the great menaces to the future peace of the world. It provides a breeding ground of social convulsion and conflict; and the great powers are then drawn in to exploit (supposedly to stabilize) the void and end up confronting each other there. An over-all warning of what could lie ahead was provided by political centrist John Gardner at the 1968 Republican and Democratic National Convention platform hearings: "We're not only in trouble as a nation; we're in trouble as a species. Man is in trouble. And if you are not filled with foreboding, you don't understand your time. You and I grew up believing that we were making the world a little better for our children. But our children and grandchildren may be in for terror and trouble such as few of us have ever experienced."

The contrast between the profound issues of the real world and the preoccupations on the domestic side of American foreign policy could hardly be greater. The United States has been criticized over the years by some of her best friends for lacking a sense of awe in the face of the larger forces at work in the world and in history. But never has there been a time when an awareness of those forces, even a sense of a deeply foreboding fate as the ancient Greeks contemplated theirs, could be more essential than now.

CHAPTER 9

Programming Politics

One of the last decade's more publicized and practical innovations for politicians was "O'Brien's Manual," which outlined the fundamentals of local political work for John F. Kennedy's Presidential campaign. It was later updated for Lyndon Johnson and Hubert Humphrey, admittedly plagiarized by the Republican National Committee, and adapted by both the Tories and the Labour Party in Britain, the principal factions in French politics, and the President of the Philippines. First compiled by Lawrence F. O'Brien many years before he became Democratic National Chairman, the manual brought an organization man's thoroughness to precinct work. It tailored campaigns to the patterns of the suburbs, showed how to mobilize women more effectively, and pinpointed shopping centers as the modern equivalent of the colonial commons for political purposes. As useful as O'Brien's contribution has been, however, it belongs more to the political era of James A. Farley, F.D.R.'s campaign architect, than to what lies ahead. A neo-Orwellian revolution is under way with the electronic programming of the political process, especially with computers and television. Yet that development is still at an early stage of its potential.

The comparative importance of political techniques needs to be kept in perspective, of course, with the role of the candidate and all the other factors which go into winning elections. O'Brien, for instance, estimates that the candidate generates 90 to 95 percent of whatever effect a campaign has on the course of events, and that organization and strategy account for most of the rest. Even in that allocation, however, it should be remembered what former

Republican National Chairman Ray Bliss has called "the nuts and bolts" of politics—can usually make the difference between a winning and a losing campaign. The nuts and bolts remain essential, of course, but the new technology and social conditions demand radically new kinds.

When the Republican National Committee, shortly after that party's impressive showing in the 1966 Congressional elections, called together its national leaders to map strategy for the 1968 Presidential election, it quickly rushed through the rhetoric and ideology to get down to a discussion of the new techniques. "It was the kind of meeting where ten times as much thought was devoted to electronic data processing as to whacking the opposition," reported Washington *Post* political writer David Broder. Similarly, when the Democratic National Committee about the same time moved into expanded headquarters to prepare for the '68 Presidential campaign, interest centered almost entirely on the party's new computer room. The equipment pulls names out of a nationwide memory bank for precinct workers, campaign contributors in various categories of generosity, local publicity, and a number of other purposes. The machinery turns out thousands of "personalized" letters a day, each with the addressee's name inserted not only in the salutation but also somewhere later on in the message itself in an informal, folksy way. The equipment also allows for optional references in each letter to issues of particular importance to the recipient's part of the country, economic class, race, or other "classification." Capable of split-second information retrieval, the machinery even sorts out married couples from registration lists and combines them in one letter if they are both found to be members of the same party and living at the same address. Then no status-losing duplicate mailing will show up in a household, which is one indication of what electronic politics thinks is important. When the computer cannot identify the sex and marital status of an addressee so as to include "Mr.," "Mrs.," or "Miss," only the proper name is put on the envelope and the salutation retreats to a safe "Dear Fellow American."

The Nixon campaign in 1968 sent out five million computer-written letters for the candidate, each with three "particularized" references in the text. It was probably the largest "private" correspondence in history. Yet it will likely be dwarfed by the "individualized" mass mailings the computers spew out for the 1972 and 1976 campaigns. Well over half the Republican state central committees across the country have already computerized much of their work. Their Democratic counterparts are trailing far behind, but the operations of practically all state organizations of both major parties should have gone electronic within a very few years.

As early as 1966, in California, Ronald Reagan's campaign managers, Spencer-Roberts, turned over to one of their subsidiaries, Datamatics, Inc., the task of programming computers to identify those local areas with the greatest potential for a candidate with Reagan's "input specifications." In effect, a start at cost-effectiveness was built into campaign planning. But the project was recognized at the time as only a test run for more advanced computerized electioneering. Zeroing in on the specific neighborhoods where a significant number of votes can probably be switched or a much larger turnout brought about becomes more and more important as the cost of campaigning soars. Hard-to-come-by resources can be concentrated by a computer analysis of each district's recent voting patterns and a profile of income, age, race, registration, opinion, and other components, then a mathematical quotient assigned and a comparison quickly made of the most probable election-day inclination of each area.

The commitment of politics to computers opens up a whole new chapter in polling, too. Present national opinion surveys are generally based on a sampling of from twelve hundred to thirty-five hundred carefully selected interviews. But much broader statistical foundations will become available as the political history and ongoing changes in many thousands of precincts are put on electronic tape and stored in data banks. The likelihood is that politicians and public officials will be able to read, if not lead, the public with much greater precision as this decade develops. That will inevitably have its effect, for good or bad, not only on campaigns but on broad areas of governmental policy between elections as well.

There are important limitations on the application of the new computer technology to campaigning. The new processes are costly. For politicians hard pressed for funds, a practical question arises whether scarce contributions can better be used for these sophisticated techniques or for television; even this choice presupposes an ability to pay for the bare essentials of carrying on the candidate's own activities and getting an adequate staff. Between the two major parties, the generally better-financed GOP could gain a considerable further advantage. But the development also provides a situation in which organized labor, with its network of local offices, many of them already electronically equipped, could step in fairly quickly and reassert its political effectiveness at least in part. A start on that was made in 1968 when data on roughly three and a half million AFL-CIO families were computerized to provide special lists for precinct workers and mailing purposes. Another limitation to the new technology is that American society is becoming ever more mobile and fast-changing, even discontinuous to some extent, especially in rapidly growing power centers like the suburbs and California. This cuts down on the reliability of past political patterns statistically discerned and tends to put those who rely on them on the back rather than the front of incoming waves.

Even with computers, politics is going to remain an art, not become a science. But the art is rapidly becoming a statistician's dream and an old-fashioned pol's nightmare. In Edwin O'Connor's *The Last Hurrah*, the long public career of Frank Skeffington, a gnarled Irish political boss of the old school, came to a broken-hearted end because he failed to take into account the early political impact of television. Yet how much more obsolete he would have been, with his warm attachment for the neighborhoods and intuitive regard for people's foibles, in the face of the coming computer campaigns.

The new technology, however, can be used constructively as well as negatively. It can give a candidate a better insight into his constituents and help him present his position within their "filter" of assumptions, interests and even word preferences. It thus opens the opportunity to influence and lead public opinion more effectively, if less spontaneously, than in the past. In that sense, the development facilitates a closer relationship between the active political system and the democratic base.

Besides the rapidly stepped-up use of television and the introduction of computers, there has also come onto the market a wide assortment of additional communications technology which politics have barely begun to tap, such as closed-circuit television tying together scores of storefront headquarters, banks of automatic telephones capable of making hundreds of thousands of "short, polite calls" just before an election, and tape-recording listening posts to receive citizen complaints and then answer them with electronically controlled typewriters directed by computers. It would seem easy to dismiss these and other innovations as extravagant frills, but they can be effective as well as expensive. If only in self-protection, major political campaigns can no longer ignore the latest developments. Just at the rather pedestrian level of information-gathering, new possibilities are opening up. Beginning in 1970, for instance, a New York agency offered candidates a detailed daily analysis of what news and even key words are being picked up and played heavily by the press throughout the country. It is an appealing service for politicians more interested in following than leading.

A development of the most fundamental importance is the fact that the cost of getting elected to public office—or, worse, of getting defeated for it—is rising sharply. After only gradually going up for a number of decades, the cost of politics is now climbing steeply. Conservatively estimated, the total outlay for statewide campaigning nearly doubled during the last ten years in the most populous states such as California, New York, and Pennsylvania. In the medium-sized and the less populous states, like Wisconsin, Arkansas, Oklahoma, and Hawaii, responsible elected officials privately indicate that the cost sometimes almost quadrupled. Most of the recent rise has been due to the greater use of television.

The financial impact of computers and other new equipment has hardly been felt yet.

The authoritative *Congressional Quarterly* reports a less rapid rise in campaign costs than those private estimates, based on a nationwide compilation of the financial statements which many jurisdictions require candidates and campaign committees to file, plus estimates by political observers for states without disclosure laws. The filed reports, however, are notoriously understated. Even with that deficiency, the *Quarterly* shows a total outlay in the off-year 1962 elections of $80 million and in 1966 of over $120 million. For 1970, a conservative estimate of the total probable outlay: $200 million.

The high cost of campaigning in the bigger states is dramatized by California. The price tag on each of the last two winning gubernatorial campaigns, including the primary and general election efforts, and hidden as well as reported costs, has been estimated at over $4 million. The primary and general election campaigns of the Democratic winner of the U.S. Senate contest in that state in 1970 cost roughly $2 million, of which almost half a million was a post-campaign deficit. The cost of seeking other offices in the state is comparably high. To run for the House of Representatives from California now usually costs from $50,000 to $200,000, depending on whether the seat is fairly safe or toughly contested—and that outlay recurs every two years. A candidate for one of the eighty seats in the lower house of the California State Legislature cannot expect to spend less than $35,000 if he wishes to put up a respectable race, and the price tag can soar to $120,000. Again, the cost repeats every two years. In the last Los Angeles mayoralty race, over $500,000 was reported to have been spent on behalf of the winner, Sam Yorty, and over $625,000 was put out for the loser, Tom Bradley. Campaigns for the City Council there cost as much as $50,000 each; board of education races run to over $25,000 apiece.

In a Presidential election year, the total for all the campaigns in the country reaches staggering proportions: conservatively estimated, $175 million in 1960, $200 million in 1964, and $300 million in 1968. At the rate at which campaign budgets are climbing because of the increased use of TV user, politics could cost half a billion dollars in 1976.

Senator Eugene McCarthy, in his unsuccessful bid for the Democratic Presidential nomination in 1968, seemed to find one antidote to the rising costs. Unpaid student volunteers were heavily relied on. They slept in church basements or campaign headquarters in sleeping bags and subsisted largely on sandwiches, Cokes, and camaraderie. But even then each student volunteer finally cost around $5 a day and sometimes up to $10 a day just to cover transportation, food, and minimum incidentals. McCarthy campaign coordinators reported having over six thousand students in the field for at least two successive weekends in both the Wisconsin and Indiana primaries. The cost of this "free" labor ran to well over $150,000. Even the politics of student volunteers do not come cheap.

Who pays for politicking? At present, all this supposed democracy is bankrolled by a very small portion of the total electorate. Only about 6 percent of the adult populace have given even a dollar for political purposes in recent Presidential election years. The intensive effort by the Democratic National Committee and its local counterparts in the past to raise money with a "Dollars for Democrats" drive backed up by mass-media appeals has faltered badly and ended up mainly as window-dressing. To the extent that small contributions are significant, they have not been harvested by the Democrats' self-proclaimed "party of the people" nearly as well as by the GOP, which has developed computerized mail solicitations of the middle class into a fine art. The Citizens' Research Foundation, which specializes in the analysis of campaign financing, found Democrats receive roughly 70 percent of the dollar value of their total individual contributions in amounts of $500 or higher; the Republicans receive less than 30 percent that way. The GOP nevertheless enjoyed better than a two-to-one over-all financial advantage over Democrats nationwide in 1968 and perhaps a three-to-one lead in the 1970 elections. Individual incumbents often have special access to funding regardless of party. Minority party candidates are usually at the greatest disadvantage of all.

Major political fund-raising is based not on "little people" but on large contributors—the "fat cats." The GOP has long had its "Boosters Club" and now has an "RN Associates" for contributors giving $1000 or more. The Democratic National Committee used a "President's Club" during the Kennedy and Johnson administrations and now has a beheaded version of that. Members of these groups are urged along by gifts of personally autographed Presidential and senatorial pictures and other mementos, invitations to the White House, Congressional dinners, and even off-the-record briefings on foreign and fiscal policy. In addition to such badges of status, special arrangements have been made, as the euphemism goes, to expedite inquiries which large contributors have about problems they or their companies run into in Washington.

Besides joining political "clubs," most large donors also generally give through regular fund-raising dinners, with tickets for the single meal more and more often priced at $500 to $1000 a person—or $5000 to $10,000 a table, which is what important contributors are actually expected to buy. In 1968 the Republican National Finance Committee scheduled one $500-a-plate affair in Washington in the spring and another in Miami just before the party's national convention. Each event raised close to a million dollars. During the autumn campaign, Nixon raised $5 million on a single evening at simultaneous closed-circuit-TV dinners held in twenty cities. More modest fund-raising events are arranged in the nation's capital at $50 or $100 a plate to help augment the campaign finances of individual senators and congressmen. Ticket-selling often starts with a list of the twenty-three hundred members of the American Society of (Trade) Association Executives, many of whom are primarily lobbyists.

Presidential campaign costs totaled 40 cents per vote in 1960, 77 cents in '68. About three thousand individuals probably now furnish close to half of the total raised for the Presidential campaigns. Many of those donors are recruited in "subgroups" out of the automobile, aerospace, insurance, liquor, utility, and other industries, plus the union leadership. In the larger states such subgroups sometimes also put together several hundred thousand dollars apiece for a single gubernatorial or U.S. Senate campaign. More of the "war chest" goes to the preferred side, but some almost always also is given to the opposition to make sure of a "fair hearing" in case the election happens to go the other way. Some subgroups even showed through on the Nixon-Agnew financial reports which were filed—late—after the '68 election; thus checks were listed together from six top executives of Bethlehem Steel, nine officers from Goodyear Tire and Rubber, five from Republic Steel Corporation, and so on. On the union side, forty-six labor committees reported spending $7.6 million on the '68 Presidential election alone. That was 120 percent over what the comparable groups did in the previous campaigns. Overall, 20,000 donors gave $500 or more in the '68 Presidential campaign.

For the '68 elections, the Republican National Committee organized a $12-million drive early in the year to cover the regular ongoing activities of the committee itself and to help supplement what Republican Congressional candidates could raise. Funds for the Presidential campaign had to be solicited in addition to that. The over-all cost of a major campaign for President of the United States is difficult to estimate since so many local, state, and national groups get into the act. But the Nixon campaign admitted spending $21 million, the Humphrey campaign $13 million, and the Wallace campaign $9 million. A detailed study of payrolls, television buying, and other activities under the direction of those three Presidential campaigns indicates, however, that well over $30 million was spent for Nixon, $15 million for Humphrey, and $12 million for Wallace. The campaigns of Robert F. Kennedy and Eugene McCarthy just in the '68 primaries cost over $6 million for each candidate. Thomas Jefferson, in contrast, reported spending only $50 to get elected President in 1800, though that too could have been the usual understatement on such a matter by a politician.

Not too many years ago Eastern financial circles, particularly those in New York City, dominated the funding of Presidential campaigns and were able to exert considerable influence on who could secure adequate backing for the crucial prenomination drive.

....

If you want to run for major public office in 1972, **here is about the amount that you and your key backers would probably have to raise in order to have a fighting chance if you otherwise are not too far off the pace:**

For President

As the Republican nominee	Over $35 million
As the Democratic nominee	" $25 "
As an independent	" $18 "

For U.S. Senator from a highly

populous state	$1.5 "
For governor of a medium-sized state	$1 "

....

That was especially true within the Republican Party, whose financial channels make it one of the most highly centralized quasi-public institutions in the country. But there is now alternative financing available in both parties from the Midwest, South, and Far West as well as the East. At the state level, however, at least in the more populous states, the range of popular choice in most major races is still often limited to the few men who can win substantial financial assurances well in advance.

The staggering sums required to carry on American politics are beginning to reinforce the formerly low-keyed and utopian proposal for public financing of some of the costs of campaigning, especially at the Presidential level. Support for at least some modest reform has come from some highly pragmatic sources. Senator Russell Long, Democrat of Louisiana, a rough-and-ready politician if ever there was one, has argued that "at a cost of less than twenty-five cents per taxpayer per year, we can lift the Presidency above the debasing necessity" of soliciting campaign funds and all that entails. But Republicans, with their considerably larger private financial resources, have generally opposed public funding of campaigns. The step is also resisted by major interest groups whose principal leverage comes from contributions, including both the national AFL-CIO and most industry lobbyists. In addition to that barrier, the question of which party officials would be authorized to distribute the money and for what purposes must be resolved before such financing is likely to become available. The allocation of funds could be used to enforce "party responsibility," as most political scientists like to call party discipline, or for what could also be termed a return to old-fashioned bossism. What would be at stake is nothing less than control of the country's political parties.

Unfortunately, most voters are little interested in questions of campaign financing. Efforts to make lavish spending a campaign issue, as in several major contests in 1970, have evoked almost no popular response despite considerable press coverage. Nixon's veto of a Congressionally passed bill to curtail campaign spending on television in 1972 and beyond similarly led to much press criticism but little public concern. The fact that big spending can have considerable influence on who is nominated (the easiest stage for money to have effect) and finally elected passes most people by. Still, the problem of diffusing the influence of money between the private and public sectors, then among various possibilities within each of those areas, is real and basic. There is no single simple way to do that. But a better mix of sources is needed. Alas, most pending "reform" proposals are smug sieves.

It is a truism that by far the most influential direct factor in American political campaigns now is television, and its influence is still growing rapidly with each succeeding election. TV is restructuring the political system itself, creating a whole new circuitry of political relationships and responses in this country. What is happening is not just a further technological development or the spread of an increasingly sophisticated political technique, but a fundamental rearranging of power.

Ninety-five percent of all dwelling units are now reached by

TV; in fact, there are more homes with television sets than telephones. The average set is "on" more than five hours out of every twenty-four, with that amount of time going up markedly in the winter. Young people watch the tube an average of twenty hours each week. Federal Communications Commissioner Nicholas Johnson has pointed out that those young people who will go on and graduate from college will have spent more time watching TV before they even get to the first grade than they will ever spend in college classrooms and outside study assignments. On the other side of the social scale, one survey has noted that "poorer children seem to have no real diversion but television."

The specific political impact of the medium has been well documented. Roughly 65 percent of all voters (up from close to 50 percent a decade ago) consider TV their most reliable source of information for national and international news, and especially in making up their minds how they are going to vote. A fourth of those interviewed rely primarily on newspapers, fewer than one in ten on weekly newsmagazines. One in twenty Americans relies on radio for political information and insights. For national elections, the three TV networks may be more influential than all the newspapers, magazines, and radio stations in the country combined. Television's dominance over newspapers is narrower in state elections and is reversed for local news. But the over-all preference for the tube is likely to climb sharply as the adult population of the seventies comes to include a larger proportion of young people who grew up only in the electronic era. Elmo Roper some years ago found that the proportion of people who consider television the most believable of the various sources of information was substantially higher among twenty- and thirty-year-olds than among the older populace. Opinion leaders, in contrast, make considerably more use of printed materials than of the other media. But that small group, without regard to ideology, is comparable to the New England Transcendentalists who were preoccupied with reading and philosophizing while the Jacksonian base was off grabbing up most of the frontier and political power of that time. The Jacksonian base of today is made up of the television watchers.

The medium has become a shaping force felt year round in the development of national viewpoints and policies. It ordinarily does not determine major results itself, but works through and among a convergence of mediating factors and forces. It functions primarily to "focus" opinion. But the tube's key role is indicated most specifically right in the White House. John F. Kennedy, despite all the worldwide channels of information which ultimately feed into the President's office, almost always interrupted his regular work to study, not just watch, the nightly TV news programs. Lyndon Johnson installed three-eyed monitoring units in the President's office and living quarters and in those of his key staff members so that he and they could simultaneously view the three commercial networks. Richard Nixon made a point of removing Johnson's consoles, then surrounded himself with a staff drawn heavily from the advertising and media fields. For quite practical reasons, most other leading politicians have also learned to keep a sharp eye on television, and thoroughly know and use its viewing patterns by the hour, day, and season to get the kind of "market" they particularly want.

The extent to which the potential of the Presidency has been amplified by television is still not known. No occupant of the office has yet brought its full influence to bear—not even John F. Kennedy with all his grace, wit, youthful good looks, and intelligence. Richard Nixon has pre-empted more prime viewing time than any previous President, but he has fallen far short personally in being able to marshal the medium's real possibilities. What Franklin Roosevelt did with radio still remains to be done on television. A highly attractive, dominating President who fully harnesses the medium could shake the foundations of democratic government. Yet, unfortunately, little serious thinking and few specific proposals have been offered thus far on how to cope with such a possibility.

A nation whose Chief Executive can rely on preferential use of the most powerful propaganda tool ever developed is sooner or later probably headed for still greater centralization of power. Effective checks and balances need to be raised to contend with such vast potential leverage. But the step will have to be initiated by other than TV executives who work within the purview of the Presidentially appointed Federal Communications Commission. At a minimum (Spiro Agnew's efforts to the contrary), equal time needs to be built into the communications system for fairly promptly broadcasting critiques and viewpoints differing from those of a President and just as earnest in presentation as he is. At the same time, attention should be given to the stream of private calls, personal contacts, and mutual back-scratching which has developed largely since the early sixties between the White House and top executive offices of the TV networks. That is a critical new power relationship in American society, but one which no Congressional, regulatory, or scholarly watchdog has yet probed or may ever be able to penetrate adequately.

At the level of state and local politics, hordes of previously only dimly perceived public figures are continually scrambling for television exposure. The medium is less influential at those levels than on the national scene, but even the briefest local television coverage of a community figure generally gives him a status out of all proportion to the news or interview time provided. Television has turned press conferences at every level of government into instant stages, though still usually artless ones at best. In several of the largest states, there have emerged special public relations firms which, for a retainer of several hundred thousand dollars a year, will undertake to plant film clips for a candidate or other public figure on nonnetwork news shows. Publicity-wise officials like Ronald Reagan have gone so far as to produce and distribute their own privately financed film clips for TV stations to use.

The demands and capabilities of television are fundamentally reshaping much of the democratic dialogue and who controls it. The head of Nixon's advertising agency, a firm with experience handling such clients as Alcoa and Heineken Beer, afterward said the 1968 Presidential campaign was "the biggest consumer media problem that an agency has ever had." And, as Joe McGinniss has superbly documented in his book on *The Selling of the Presi-*

dent 1968, TV technicians and public relations specialists are taking over the political roles once filled by old-fashioned power brokers like Mark Hanna and James Farley, braintrusters such as F.D.R. and John F. Kennedy assembled, or simply the candidate himself. The latter's own day-to-day role is being altered, too. The increasingly frequent question in scheduling a candidate's public activities is simply "How will it look on TV?" The press corps which loosely attaches itelf to the more important campaigns is still assiduously courted, but the priority is on getting good television situations.

One objective is to get on TV interview programs and entertainment specials, as Nixon on NBC's Martin and Rowan's *Laugh-In* in 1968. A more regular goal is to build a first-class "scene" into the daily political schedule for the news shows. That is consciously done in places that camera crews can get to fairly readily, in situations which come across attractively, even vividly, "but not strident," and at a time early enough in the day so that the film can still get on the evening news programs. Instead of an endless round of speeches, meetings, and traditional handshaking, this new art form seeks to project candidates *doing, going, participating, involved* in simple but stimulating environments that provide good viewing. Not crowds so much as cameos. Even when a candidate has to give a set speech (delivered by the hundreds in every campaign), his advance men are now supposed to make sure the immediate setting is "uncluttered" and has the right kind of background for television—preferably a plain, nonreflecting wall or curtain, the ever-present flag and perhaps a campaign poster with The Man's name in big bold letters to belabor the obvious for TV cameras and still shots.

Even after the election, the winner almost always keeps "TV-chasing," though perhaps less frenetically. An incumbent President jets around the world, appears personally before a joint session of the Congress, inspects scenes of disaster, suddenly breaks into prime TV time for an emergency heart-to-heart talk with the American people. At a less Olympian level, the mayors of the nation's bigger cities have generally switched from their former preoccupation with ribbon-cutting to bouncing around the town doing action-oriented things that will attract local TV crews for the evening news shows. In square, safe ways, politicians are "turning on" under the aegis of TV just like the kids.

Some candidates still plod through an exhausting twelve- to fourteen-hour campaign day including, for instance, an early-morning factory-gate appearance, a coffee klatsch, at least three frequently interrupted and rubbery meals digested while delivering speeches, endless handshaking, several drop-ins that inevitably involve a brief talk, a reception around cocktail time, one or two unannounced fund-raising efforts back at the hotel, and finally, late in the night, a groggy strategy session in his suite. The new-style candidate, in contrast, while trying to appear to be "on the move," increasingly conserves himself for just one or two key events each day and seeks to look fresh and crisp just in case he is filmed somewhere for a sixty-second exposure on an evening TV news program. The old-style candidate goes after votes on a retail, almost one-at-a-time basis, and he needs "the stamina of a canal horse" to do it, as California's Pat Brown used to say. The new-style candidate seeks support wholesale, through the media; for this purpose it is more important to try to appear relaxed and poised. The new approach actually allows more time for thinking, but it is also less spontaneous. The handshake is still essential, and practically all politicians genuinely like meeting people or they would not usually last long in such a compulsive pursuit. But in the picture era the handshake, unfortunately, is becoming more prop than passion. The "set" paid television time of Presidential candidates still includes a mix of big-crowd speeches and informal studio settings, but the balance long ago shifted very heavily to the latter. It is possible, though hardly to be cheered, that candidates may someday never even have to leave sterile, air-conditioned TV studios and face the spontaneity and danger of live audiences that have not been computer-selected.

The political consequences of television are overwhelming not only campaigning but the whole political process. TV has undermined the ponderous national conventions even while dominating them. The medium's firsthand exposé of the 1968 Democratic convention in Chicago and, to a lesser extent, the Republican assemblage in Miami may finally do more to revolutionize the Presidential nominating process than all the political-science tracts and newspaper editorials written during the last hundred years on the many flaws of such quadrennial gatherings. Indeed, television is tending to erode all party loyalty with its personalized imperative. More fundamentally, television is now in the forefront of the host of forces elevating the play of impressions, appetites, and impulses— all mercurial things, capable almost at the same moment of both soaring and simply being vacuous. They are in contrast to the animating process of reason which the Founding Fathers in the Age of Enlightenment intended to have rule the nation. "Reason requires a high degree of discipline, of concentration," a 1968 memorandum written for the Nixon campaign observed; "impressionism is easier."

American voters once flocked to hear political spellbinders orate for an hour or two at a time; they would drive for hours by horse and buggy just to listen to a real "stemwinder." Now most audiences will not listen attentively to a speech for more than thirty minutes, and even that long a talk has generally proved to be unable to attract or hold television's mass audience. Heavily advertised TV speeches even by Presidential nominees, as distinct from Presidents, cause scarcely a ripple in the ratings of competing shows on other channels, whether those are Westerns, situation comedies, mysteries, routine dramas, or even public affairs programs. As a result, campaigns have come to rely more and more on "spots." The total outlay for those has been doubling about every four years, while the amount of money spent on longer presentations has remained about the same even with inflated costs. In 1968 there were over five million airings of spots for candidates across the country. Crusading Harry Ashmore would have them outlawed as baneful, but the harsh demand of the electronic media, as John Chancellor has commented, is "Think Short."

What is being attempted more and more in politics, as in advertising and other contemporary forms of persuasion, is simply easy and instant revelation, with little chance for the bits and pieces cast upon the air to be considered at all critically before the candidate races on to other matters, or the voter-viewer is inundated with other commercials. Instead of those who compete for the same public office having to square off in a loose give-and-take, each side in most present-day campaigns goes off almost entirely on its own, attacking the other in a razzle-dazzle of press stories and TV commercials. These create an impression that an exchange is taking place, but actually little effort is made to speak seriously to the same problems at about the same time and thereby help the public make comparison of the candidates and whatever substance they offer. Political campaigns have rarely facilitated the side-by-side appraisal which independent voters must finally make in their own minds, but that is becoming even more difficult with almost every election.

One possible step toward helping voters make a more direct judgment of the main alternatives before them would be for competing candidates to be asked by the press and citizen groups to use at least twelve days out of the last month before an election to discuss the same major subjects for the same evening TV news shows and for reporting in the same newspaper editions, according to a schedule set by either the candidates' representatives or a neutral source like the League of Women Voters. The subsequent day or two might even be used for critiques and rebuttals before the candidates move on to yet another major subject. A related reform, long overdue, would be for the Federal Communications Commission to condition the renewal of television licenses on a requirement that stations give extensive prime time without charge during the last several weeks before a general election to discussions by all candidates who have qualified for the ballot for local, state, and national offices. That could encourage extensive public education as well as some rigorous political scrutiny. It would also lessen the cost of campaigns, especially the funds spent on TV in the last hectic weeks before the election. The windfall income return which goes with TV station licenses conferring the right to exclusive use of a part of the limited spectrum of public airwaves more than justifies the modest amount of time that would have to be given for this public affairs purpose. If the FCC required all stations to make available the same evening hours, possibly on every third day for the last two weeks before an election, it should maximize the viewing audience and largely avoid having to compete with entertainment shows.

In concert with several select citizens' committees, the networks have pushed a bobtailed version of this basic idea, with extra time to be given to nominees of the two major parties. But these parties already have practically all the campaign funds and other substantial advantages that go with established operations. It would seem to be more equitable and socially productive if each candidate qualifying for the ballot stood before the camera on his or her own merits and did not get a special preference simply because of a party label. More fundamental, the major parties, already encumbered and slow in responding to changing public issues, should hardly be given discriminatory TV benefits which would lessen the need for their nominees to be as vigorous and thoughtful as candidates outside the regular parties.

In the last few years, incumbents have taken a number of steps at both the national and state level to reinforce their already substantial advantage at election time. These moves have often been justified as strengthening the two-party system in a time of unsettlement, but the institution of incumbency is actually the main beneficiary. Yet in a period of swift social change, buttressing the existing arrangements in legalistic ways can only widen the gap between the older and newer forces and compound, not mediate, the conflicts which abound between those warring galaxies.

On the substantive side of politics, the two leading national problems of the last ten years—the racial controversy and the

Vietnam war—became significantly different public clashes and historical forces because of television. Thus the cumulative coverage of TV's first war, as University of Chicago sociologist Morris Janowitz pointed out, "hardened and polarized public sentiment. Those people who are skeptical of the war now have a vehemence in their skepticism. Those who are for the war see Americans being killed, and they don't want these sacrifices to be in vain." Although all three networks routinely edited out most of the gore, the nightly scenes and sense of actual battle projected into American homes greatly accelerated and deepened two of the critical trends of our time. One is the growing sense of social shock and violence. The other is a rejection of the dominant order by a considerable number of people, especially young people. Some of them have reacted simply by opting out of the mainstream. But many others have hardened their fight with it.

In the racial controversy, it is highly questionable whether the first Negro sit-ins and other civil rights demonstrations in scattered parts of the South at the outset of the 1960s would have gained the national momentum they did had not television cameras focused early on the cattle prods and police dogs used against people trying to exercise their constitutional rights nonviolently and sometimes religiously. TV almost immediately brought what was happening to tens of millions of Americans, including those in the White House. At the same time, the impact of the routine grist of the medium on black homes has been suggested by semanticist S. I. Hayakawa in testimony before a Senate subcommittee: "Now imagine that you are a Negro teenager, to whom the television set . . . has been his constant baby sitter ever since he can remember. All your life, the friendly television set has been saying to you, 'You are an American. You are entitled to eat and drink and wear what other Americans eat and drink and wear. You must think about the same political issues and world problems that other Americans think about. You are a member of the national community of Americans.' "

The medium also, of course, brought the ghetto riots into

millions of living rooms of white Americans who would probably have otherwise remained largely unaffected by what goes on in black slums. Here the reaction has frequently been one of fright or hostility rather than sympathy, much less of wanting to help solve the underlying social and human problems. Indeed, many white Northerners have been complaining, as white Southerners did earlier, about TV cameras as an important additional source of incitement—both at a scene of trouble and in the larger social setting. A number of law-enforcement agencies and other citadels of traditionalism have been seeking to prevent, delay, or inhibit visual coverage of historic social controversies, just as some authorities in earlier times sought to suppress, stall, or censor information in the name of what they considered a higher cause.

Unfortunately, as a result of this hue and cry, some television news programs have shown themselves less committed in recent years to tell it as and how it happens, and are now more concerned with presenting social clashes in conventional forms that traditionalists are most comfortable with. Space shots have been given exhausting live coverage, but the central domestic struggles are only occasionally considered in any depth and are sometimes deliberately "cooled"—ignored, delayed, or slanted. It is as though the networks would have been willing to report the Boston Tea Party, but only after the Tories had reasserted control over the harbor; and those Indian-dressed activists would have been described not as men with strongly held grievances but as looters and lawbreakers. In this and so many other ways television reveals itself as being not only an inciter of change but also an ally of the *status quo*.

Many critics of television charge it with benumbing, neutralizing, and helping to brutalize American society as preconditions to totalitarianism, reducing everything to the lowest common denominator, pandering to shallow escapism, commercializing mass dissatisfaction and encouraging not just anti-intellectualism but anti-rationalism. As one observer said of many viewers, "Munching cheese freakies. Turning on the apocalypse." Just at the quantitative informational level, someone has found that all the words used on an average half-hour evening TV news show would not fill six of the eight columns on just the front page of *The New York Times.*

But it is also true that television reduces moral vacuity, for it encourages a much wider awareness among the democratic rank and file than they have ever experienced before. It is not likely, as Arthur Schlesinger, Jr., has said, that "the great issues of politics or ethics will ever be solved by the impressionism of the subliminal drama." Still, by exposing a vastly greater sector of people to public events and thus, in a sense, involving them in such matters more than they have even been before, the medium brings closer—some scenes suggest tumultuously closer—at least a low-grade version of the New Left's participatory democracy.

In the future it is likely that TV will bend politics and public affairs to its own particular forms and filters even more than has already occurred, and that in turn politicians will be making more and more use of its programming of perception and persuasion. At the most routine level, spots and the other tools of political TV may generally start earlier in campaigns and become perceptibly more polished, entertaining, distracting, and subliminally effective. Often, less use will be made of the candidate himself, especially if he is not particularly photogenic. Unlike most past political spots, those in the coming period will not be plotted and sequential as often as impressionistic, sometimes even disorienting. Sometimes, of course, there will be deliberate throwbacks to the old techniques. Ronald Reagan has sometimes used a not very good documentary style in his television material in California so that he would come across less as an actor and more as a public figure. But the over-all trend will be toward greater and greater use of controlled excitement, mood setters, shock, and innuendo, conjured up in fifteen or thirty seconds or, less often, a whole minute. TV politics are generally still making appeals which involve the viewer only minimally. In the future there will be more effort to invoke the mass audience, as McLuhan has put it, "as a creative, *participat-*

ing force." The 1970 off-year campaigns also point to an increasing Populist effort to run against slick and expensive TV spots of the opposition. But the longer-term prospect is for the medium to dominate American politics to an even greater extent than at present.

CHAPTER 10

The Changing Mainstream

This country's counterpart of the long-reigning, now nearly bankrupt British truism about "muddling through" is "middling through." Even in the face of great change and turmoil, there has been an abiding, thus far usually correct, assumption that moderation *will* prevail and the middle *will* rule—and that in the last analysis this is a sufficient public philosophy. Especially if embellished with a little rhetoric about reasonableness, common sense, and "let's be practical." Before the historic dominance of the American Center is uncritically taken for granted for the future, however, there is need to look closer at what is happening in that broad part of the political spectrum. For, besides having to face sharpening external threats, it is being divided and reworked by some fundamental internal contradictions and alterations of its own.

The middle class has proved during the last decade or so to be the main spawning ground for both alienated activism on the left and status anxieties on the right. More important, a growing portion of the better-educated, more affluent and active members of the middle class are setting the pace for sweeping changes in the country's life-styles and social relationships and thus, sooner or later, its politics. At the same time, the small-town and lower-middle-class elements of the traditional Center—the first group as the principal vestige of a much older America and the latter as the hardy legatees of the New Deal and the culture which came out of the 1930s and 1940s—produced much of George Wallace's 1968 vote. Over-all, important segments of the broad and long-stable Center are dividing and groping in quite different directions.

The Center's rampant unsettlement cannot readily be televised or simplistically railed against like student protests and ghetto anger. But it nonetheless is a massive contributing factor to the contemporary derangement. In a sense, the spreading anxiety is the inner riot of the so-called majority—the flaring trouble within so many straight people who think that only somebody else is provoking all the turmoil. Their troubles are aggravated, but not caused primarily, by racial and campus disturbances. In fact, the anxieties of the Center are victimizing the young and the minorities vastly more than the reverse. The awful truth is that the square society is currently using "the beards and blacks" much as scapegoats have been used throughout history—viciously and indifferently at the same time.

The convulsions taking place in the so-called silent majority are often submerged and self-repressed to a considerable extent, particularly compared to the overtness on the fringes. But the student activists, hippies, Wallaceites, radical right, and other explicit developments are not isolated happenings on the social and political periphery but rather highly specific symptoms of conditions and fevers at work in less articulate ways throughout the body politic. What has been seen on the surface are but signals of contagions existing in less intense forms among vastly wider ranges of the public, and often as conflicts within the same individual. Now we are all hippies to an extent; we are all bigots, too.

In the years ahead, events and politicians will be playing on the various restive aspects of us, drawing out some and helping to dilute others. But the last ten years has been an exceptionally eclectic, divisive, and unmooring passage for much of the American Center, and the effects will be felt for years to come. What we have been going through is largely the loosening. What still lies ahead is the hard and hesitant redefining of relationships, attitudes, and directions.

Barely twenty years ago, C. Wright Mills could argue with considerable merit that the country's "white-collar class" was, as a group, politically passive, publicly uncreative, and lacking in any genuine historical initiative of its own. Lubell, writing at about the same time and more immediately about politics, noted: "Up to now, at least, in our history, moderation has never been an effective means for achieving basic changes in voting habits." Over the longer run of history, in fact, the middle elements have usually sought to go where the power was and function mostly as hard-working technicians for whatever system of prerogatives and punishment prevailed at the time. Now, however, many of the most basic impulses for change are coming to bear through the middle. In the 1930s, the blue-collar group was in the forefront. Now it is the white-collar sector. Education, affluence, social mobility, a heightened cultural sensitivity—these and other influences are having their greatest impact not among the blacks, poor whites, or blue-collar workers but in the white-shirted sector: sometimes activating it, sometimes dividing it from the others, but above all fundamentally reconstituting it.

The vanguard for the principal changes taking place in the Center is the college-educated group. It is a decided minority itself, but a highly influential one. Where it is headed compared to the less prosperous whites is reflected in a survey taken by Louis Harris during the 1968 Presidential election:

In favor of open housing:
 Low-income whites   35 percent
 College-educated whites   54 percent
Support paying more taxes to control air and water pollution:
 Low-income whites   41 percent
 College-educated whites   55 percent
Support giving cities more money to tear down the ghettoes:
 Low-income whites   40 percent
 College-educated whites   56 percent
In favor of keeping the foreign aid program:
 Low-income whites   38 percent
 College-educated whites   51 percent
"Anti-Vietnam demonstrators are a major cause of the breakdown of law and order in this country":
 Low-income whites   65 percent
 College-educated whites   35 percent

"Liberals, long-hairs, and intellectuals have been running the country too long":

Low-income whites	64 percent
College-educated whites	26 percent

Those differences actually are less economic than educational and cultural, but easier living standards are making possible much of the psychological release which leads to the quite different social and political outlook of the college-educated group. And all economic and educational projections point to the rapid enlargement of the more "liberated" sector.

The principal group arrayed against the forces of change is the huge lower-middle-income sector—"working America," made up of almost twenty-five million white families whose breadwinners are typically white-collar clerks and blue-collar workers. The left has long held as a testament of faith that "the workers" are the main historical agents of social progress, but an important portion of this group is now providing the most tenacious resistance to further broadening the country's social, economic, and political base. Having gained a larger share of power institutionally during the last third of a century, this sector generally opposes—more accurately, is anxious about and therefore against—much additional change.

The dynamics among the white-skinned blue-collar and clerical group can be adequately considered only by getting behind what the United Auto Workers' education director Brendon Saxton calls the liberal-radical myth of the well-off "middle-class workers." This group unquestionably is far more fortunate than the poor whites and most blacks. It is more than comfortable, for instance, compared to embattled women trying to raise children on welfare payments in tenements in Harlem, Cleveland, and Chicago. But such a contrast fails to consider the unrelenting pressures still felt by most of the blue-collar and clerical populace, or the envied advantages of prosperous people who call on working-class whites to be more humane and understanding of those at the bottom of the economic ladder. At the same time, most of the upper-middle class continues to resent almost any demand by working groups for better wages, whether by hospital workers asking for barely a minimum wage or teamsters seeking something better.

This sector of white America has larger-than-average families, and they generally live on $6000 to $12,000 a year. Almost 40 percent have no education beyond grammar school. Less than 12 percent have had any education beyond high school. Three-fourths own or are buying their own homes. But almost half of these families, like the heavy majority of black families, depend on two or more wage-earners, and in not quite half the man who heads the house also moonlights a second job.

"Some workers do, of course, share the fruits of plenty," Saxton concedes, "but black or white—most don't. They live in a twilight zone, not hungry, but not full of steak, either. Some comforts come to them through expanded consumer credit, but the high costs of that credit generate tension, anxiety, and insecurity." Taxes take a higher portion of their income than is true in the brackets above and, sometimes, below them; and they seemingly get relatively little in return since their lives are not directly touched by many of the institutions their tax dollars support. They receive neither welfare payments like the poor nor business subsidies and services like the more prosperous elements. "Their sons, brothers, friends [have been] off being shot at in Viet Nam, while 'the rich college kids' stay home," Saxton notes. "They know that their sons and daughters—the few budding geniuses excepted—aren't going to enter the state university, much less a fancy school. If they are lucky, they may enter a local or community college and some-times receive a second rate education." Finally, the U.S. is late and miserly in providing social insurance such as most Western Euro-pean working families have long had to assure their basic security. Even with high wages and all the fringe benefits, the American working class is still torn by many of the strains which have dominated it for over a century; added frustration is being experi-enced as a result of each new surge of the upper group, whose income is increasing perceptibly faster notwithstanding its grumbling about the hourly wage rates of plumbers, painters, repairmen, and most other working people.

Deeper reaches of the chasm between the working class and the more fortunate sector were indicated by Seymour Martin Lipset some years ago: "A comprehensive review of the many studies of child-rearing patterns in the United States completed during the last thirty years [since about 1930] reports that their 'most consistent finding' is the 'more frequent use of physical punishment by working class parents.' The middle class, in contrast, resorts to 'reasoning, isolation and ... love-oriented techniques of discipline.'" There could hardly be a more elemental source for the recent stresses between the working class on one hand and the "love generation" and its upper-middle-class allies on the other. The contrast in early conditioning underlies much of the antagonism, for instance, between the police, almost all of whom are products of the lower-middle class, and the college activists, most of whom are from fairly prosperous and liberated, or permissive, family backgrounds.

The cultural revolution since the mid-sixties has further aggravated the estrangement between the more prosperous sector on one side and the lower-middle class on the other. The middle- and lowbrow cultures have been losing key battles to the avant-garde strain formerly confined mostly to artists and the wealthy. That culture has unquestionably been prostituted as it gained broader influence, often turning quickly into commercial clichés, a factor that only indicates the extent of its acceptance. In the most fundamental sense, this spreading cultural upheaval has become a powerful long-term generator of experimentation, protest, freedom, individualism, and—the binding thread—change.

The Puritan ethic to which the lower-middle class is now so loyal continues to be a massive conservative and conforming factor in the American character and polity. It has, for instance, even helped assure that the $20-billion-a-year "leisure industry" (the two words make strange bedfellows) separates most work and play into quite different segments of our lives. Even so, Puritanism is under greater challenge than ever before among almost all groups, a critical development further dividing the Center and disturbing the country. The status-descent of the WASP ethos from being the hallmark of the upper-middle class, as was long true, to becoming a self-eulogizing characteristic of the lower-middle sector suggests the cultural cycle which is now well along. The decline also tends to hasten the loosening of Puritanism's hold on the pace-setting upper group.

Class warfare has historically been considered primarily in economic terms, but more and more, in an affluent and educated society, it is cultural in its cut and thrust. The 1970s will almost surely witness an intensifying struggle between the politics which are sustained by Puritanism and the new lines of force attuned to pleasure and liberation; that clash could easily become more rancorous as it calls into question some of the most fundamental assumptions and inner tensions of millions of people. The key political struggle of the decade could well turn out to be as much over the nature of our culture as the politics of the 1930s were over the nature of the economy. The underlying campaigns likely to go on are indicated by the contending slogans "Make the World Safe for Sex" and "Support Your Local Censor."

Optimists anticipate that much of the lower-middle class will rapidly take on the general outlook of the college-educated element and thus ease some of the strains within the political and social mainstream. In support of that hope there is cited the horizon-broadening pervasiveness of the mass media and the style-setting, opinion-leading role of the more sophisticated sector. That expectation, however, underestimates the unevenness with which the social and other cultural factors are coming to bear in different parts of the populace. Thus even while much of the working class is adapting to the newer tendencies, gaining numbers of the college-educated upper-middle class are pushing into still more experimental personal modes. In a similar way, the black community is experiencing substantial economic, educational, and other upgrading, but most of the white community is also rising rapidly and keeps far out in front. Political psychology is shaped not only by

whether one's own group is better off than in the past but also by
its present and prospective position relative to others. The divisions
tearing at the Center are due in great part to the different rates of
change among important groups there and what that is doing to
the sense of security and relative standing of those elements,
especially the older and long-established ones.

Louis Harris has commented that the principal division now
operating in American politics is that between the underlying
forces of change and anti-change. He concluded that in 1968 the
latter group was the larger by about 55 percent to 45 percent, but
he speculates that by 1972 the balance between the two could
be just about reversed. In politics, there is almost always a marked
lag between the formation of a new reality and the time people
recognize and act on it. Equally important, the shifting ratio between these loose groupings cannot be carried over directly into
partisan voting prospects. Many individuals in the college-educated
group supporting substantial social change have been conditioned
to vote Republican; that conditioning will prevail over all other
pulls except under acute circumstances. Similarly, many in the
working class group opposed to much change are Democrats and
will vote that way even though that party nationally is the more
change-included on most social and economic issues. Further,
particular public leaders may be able to sharpen or obscure basic
historical trends for a time, but the underlying factors still have
their own vitality and momentum. The seventies should witness
the steady growth of the social-change coalition even in the face
of the built-in delays and undeniable reaction currently being felt.

Those now most resistant to altering the country's prevailing
social and political arrangements could respond in a number of
different ways, depending on how they are reached out to. The
situation was perceptively summed up by Andrew Kopkind during
the '68 Presidential election in terms of the white working-class
neighborhoods of Cleveland: "What has happened in working
class Cleveland, as in almost every other sector of institutional life,
is that the liberal 'center' has crumbled and in the vortex produced

by that cataclysm, the social rubble is spinning. Wallace is available to pick up some of the pieces. In gathering them to his campaign, he gives them a framework of issues and a rough structure of ideology which for the most part is arbitrary. If another political campaign got there first, different forms could as easily be constructed." That, in fact, is just what Nixon is attempting to do from a slightly different approach and what Robert Kennedy sought to accomplish from a substantially different position. Still other ways, from fascism to a New Left kind of freedom, are available if would-be leaders have the willingness, or willfulness, to attempt them.

The diversely possible approaches point up the malleability of even some of the apparently most rigid elements at hand. Bigotry and racial reconciliation, extremism and moderation, backsliding and fresh breakthroughs can be implicit simultaneously in the same group, the same individual. Equally, the situation reminds us that democratic politics is not just a sorting out of how many voters believe and feel this way or that. At the same moment, alternative recesses and opportunities are involved. The ambience offers hope as well as danger at the present juncture. It will do the country no good, however, if either party or the principal public figures glorify only, or mostly, the slower elements or, by the same token, just the more forward forces. Leadership able to rally both sectors is needed in this decade; yet that will not be achieved simply by splitting their differences and straddling. That approach could leave both groups deeply dissatisfied and troublesome. A critical test of any major figure will be his capacity to minister to the diverse ills afflicting the Center.

For practical political purposes, the early future must eventually be considered through the filter of the major parties, however tarred those now may be. And a look at the political statistics of the last several decades suggests some important underlying trends. Those have been hurried by the social controversies which erupted in the last half-dozen years. But longer-term developments have been under way without regard to the recent turmoil, which may actually be only a stepped-up, second phase of an already well-set historical unfolding.

Conservatively stated, the Republican and Democratic parties now have much less of a hold on the American people than they did a decade or a third of a century and more ago. That portion of the adult population which describes itself as Republican has dropped fairly steadily from a majority of the eligible electorate during the first three decades of this century to under a third at the outset of the 1970s. The Democrats are down from a clear majority during the Roosevelt years to around 45 percent; and that overstates the Democratic strength, since a larger percentage of registered Democrats than Republicans usually defects in elections nation-wide. The proportion of voters who consider themselves independents is up from a fifth in the 1930s to over a fourth. Most of the very latest increase in the number of independents has come from Democratic ranks, particularly in the South. But the independents are now about as numerous as the Republicans. This is the first time that group has challenged one of the two major parties for well over a century.

Ticket-splitting has also grown more widespread—among not only independents but also many who are not yet quite willing to renounce their party tie. As recently as 1948, one out of every five voters split his ballot. Now over half do. David Broder and Haynes Johnson concluded, after a nation-wide sampling for the Washington *Post* in 1970, that "less than one-third of those interviewed have supported the same party's Presidential candidate each time they voted since 1960. It's not uncommon to find a voter who has voted for three different persons, from three different parties, in the last three Presidential elections. When their choices for governor and senator this year and their preference for President in 1972 are added to their voting history, it becomes rare indeed to find anyone who is a down-the-line Democrat or Republican. . . . It is almost a rarity to find a voter who thinks of politics in terms of parties. Not only are voters splitting their tickets and shifting back and forth from election to election, but their perception of party differences is growing visibly weaker." Most threatening of all for the parties over the long run, substantially more voters in their twenties and thirties are splitting their vote and becoming political independents than is true among older voters, and the anti-party trend is accelerating among young people. Yankowitch found in 1970 only 16 percent of the students think the major parties offer any alternative.

Both parties have proved again and again to be more hardy than their critics, outlasting prediction after prediction of an early demise; and studies of voting patterns over the years have repeatedly found partisan attachments to be remarkably tenacious despite the American habit of deprecating practically everything political. The Republicans, for instance, seemed to rebound in the '68 election and the Democrats in 1970. All that nevertheless should not be allowed to obscure the fact that the parties are now running against not just each other but also some strong historical currents. Faced generally with only a Republican and Democratic choice, most voters have thus far proved willing to choose between the two. But it cannot be taken for granted that a more and more independent, educated, and alienated electorate will go on doing this indefinitely. Even more theatening than the drift out of the two parties is the widespread disenchantment with the political process itself. Twenty years ago, 80 percent of the persons surveyed said they thought that voting was the most efficient way to influence governmental action. Recently barely over half have felt that way.

It should also be remembered that the parties, as the main operative embodiments of the present politics, have lost most of their once-dominant big-city organizations, state machines, and vast governmental patronage. Fairly tightly held state and local organizations were the immediate building blocks Roosevelt and Farley used to put together the last really effective working majority in this country. Now most city and state political groups are little more than letterheads. A few real organizations still exist, but even they are on the defensive. Most candidates and campaign managers still like to think they have at their command great waves of workers, but fewer and fewer neighborhoods are covered by doorbell ringers and phone callers. As 1968 showed, the principal source of campaign workers now is young people, and they are hardly available to, or desired by, parties and candidates bearing the onus of orthodoxy. Students were supposed to be politically turned off in 1970. But surveys found 15 percent of the student community took some part in the campaigns that year. That is over three times the portion of the adult society which took even the least part in those campaigns.

The huge array of federal programs enacted in the last ten years and the annual multi-billion-dollar assortment of defense contracts offer new political opportunities for the party controlling the White House. These have already been used that way by both Democratic and Republican administrations much more than the American people or any would-be muckrakers have paid attention to. Despite that, these programs are still not as readily utilized for direct election purposes as old-fashioned patronage could be harnessed. In addition, the newer programs have been used by John Kennedy, Lyndon Johnson, and Richard Nixon much more for personal Presidential effect than for building up their parties. That may seem an illusory difference, but the increasingly distinct self-interest of Presidents from that of their parties tells much about the changing nature of our politics.

Other important factors in the erosion of the major parties are the mandate of television to "vote the man, not the party" and the parties' loss of support in the last half-dozen years among many of the politically most aware and involved elements of the electorate. These groups are not dropping out of the voter pool like many marginal voters of middle America, but rather are turning on to resist the prevailing politics from an independent base or even from within one of the major parties, as in the '68 Democratic Presidential primaries. In reaction to that loss, many older politicians seem to have decided that their last, best hope of long incumbency and the salvation of the country lies not in the politically aroused but in "the great majority" indifferently beyond. In effect, a special premium is being put on apathy rather than activism—but that hardly bodes well over the long run for party vigor or a popularly based political system.

Besides the decline of the parties and of partisan ties among voters, a loose stalemate has been building between the two major parties for the last quarter of a century, as reflected in the election results. Not since F.D.R. has either party really been able to dominate the country for long. Truman had to work with Republican majorities in two of the three Congresses elected while he held the White House, and his own surprise victory in 1948 was gained with less than 50 percent of the vote. Eisenhower had Democratic majorities in both wings of the Congress for six of his eight years as President and reigned more than ruled. The total popular vote cast for members of the House of Representatives in 1956, when Ike was easily re-elected, suggests the close division existing in the nation in that decade: 29 million votes for all the Democratic Congressional candidates compared to 28.7 million votes for all the GOP candidates. During the 1960s, two of the three Presidential elections were decided by less than one-half of 1 percent of the vote. The lopsided other contest, in 1964, was quite outside the pattern of the last twenty-five years, and the Democratic advantage that it produced in the Congress was largely nullified in the next off-year elections.

The political situation at the very outset of the 1970s provided almost a caricature of the country's over-all stalemate. The nation gained a Republican President who won by under one-half of 1 percent and the smallest portion of the vote in a half century, balanced against divided Democratic majorities in both houses of the Congress. The number of Democratic and Republican congressmen from outside the South in 1970 was almost exactly the same— 160 Democrats, 162 Republicans. And the make-up of the southern Congressional delegations has been moving in the direction of also producing a stand-off between the parties. A majority of the state governors that year were Republican, but the Democrats and Republicans each controlled twenty state legislatures, with eight others divided between the two parties and two others nominally nonpartisan. The 1970 election results tipped the state-level balance in the Democrats' favor, with the Democrats controlling twenty-three legislatures, the Republicans seventeen, and ten states having divided houses. But the national government remained split between a Republican President and a Democratic Congress which is itself divided even more closely in ideological than partisan terms.

In *The Deadlock of Democracy*, James MacGregor Burns traced how this country has been run from almost its outset by four major and quite distinct political "parties": two amorphous Presidential parties and two confederacies of Congressional and state-level parties. He concluded that the U.S. is suffering from a surfeit of political as well as constitutional checks and balances. But those long-existing drags on social and political change are fairly formalistic and modest in their effect compared to the drift toward stalemate.

A closer look is needed, however, at the major parties now.

The Republican Party has revealed fairly good electoral strength during the last half-decade in the more rapidly growing parts of the nation, and those may be a good testing ground for the period ahead. The GOP recaptured control of the governorship of the most populous state, California, in 1966, and has continued its base-building in the South, which gave Nixon a larger plurality in 1968 than did the rest of the country despite the special appeal of George Wallace in the region that year. The party has also demonstrated impressive strength in the now critically important suburbs. In '68 Nixon received almost half of all the ballots cast in suburbia —a strong contrast to the slightly over one-third he drew in the thirty-five largest cities. Further, Republicans have surpassed the Democrats by a margin of roughly two to one in the number of new senators, congressmen, and governors elected in the last half-decade.

GOP strategists have produced a barrage of statistics to show that what impends is an emerging Republican majority, as Kevin Phillips summed it up in his book of that title. But neither the recent election results nor the declared party ties of the overwhelming majority of voters gives much encouragement to the thesis. In fairness, it should be noted that Phillips' rationale is really a strategy for a GOP Presidential victory rather than for anything broader. Even then, both as a historical analysis and as a battle plan, his approach has basic flaws. He argues that the black "revolution" and "related bias of the Democratic party" are now the cleaving dynamic of national politics, and they unite conservatives in the North and South while dividing the Democrats from a number of their key past sources of strength. It is unquestionably correct that the racial factor has become a more pressing political factor than it has been in most of the nation's history, but it is only one of a number of influential developments. There must also be taken into account the shifting age mix of the electorate and the educational and economic upgrading going on as well as more short-term considerations, such as the contending personalities, the state of the economy, the appearance of the international scene, and much more. Any of those could be decisive against the background of the small margins by which two of the three Presidential elections in the 1960s were decided. In terms of the 1968 election alone, it is worth noting that a 2 or 3 percent shift in the vote of a half-dozen of the larger states would have more than wiped out Nixon's entire Southern and border-state advantage.

At another level of critique, to build on the racial division for national political purposes is to exacerbate one of America's most dangerous wounds. The maneuver ignores the not-so-latent want among many voters, including large numbers not really so sympathetic to blacks, for a social solution based on national and individual self-respect that can bring genuine civil calm. At a minimum, Republican tacticians must walk a tightrope, for they dare not forget the defection of millions of middle-of-the-road Northern and Western Republicans from Goldwater's 1964 campaign with its fairly blatant appeal to an all-white South. That combined with the Arizonan's military views to make him vulnerable to the charge of flirting with domestic and foreign extremism. Nixon has veered more Southward than any Republican President ever has, but the stratagem contains peril as well as promise.

What is really working on the GOP is the temptation to try to gather in the twelve million people who voted for Wallace in '68. The Republican Party may gain a considerable part of that group. But even with the racial vehemence which abounds among many of those voters, a substantial number are politically conventional, even strongly Populist in an economic sense, and can break from the Democratic label to an independent candidate more readily than they can cross over to the GOP. Another consideration in 1972 is that with a Republican in the White House, the GOP will be carrying much of the burden of the political establishment as far as this deeply estranged sector is concerned. In addition, Wallace or someone like him will likely be running; that troubled cause would be more experienced and better funded than ever before, even if it also appeared somewhat warmed over and already once plucked. If the racial climate heats up, to the further detriment of the Democrats, it is questionable whether the national Republican ticket could compete with a classic nativist candidate's demagoguery without losing more votes than it gained. Again, the room for even the crassest kind of maneuver has its political limits.

The future of the Republican Party, however, surely needs to be considered in terms besides the racial question. The main historical, educational, and economic constituencies of the GOP are weakening more than has generally been noted. The rapidly increasing college-educated sector has slowly but steadily switched from a very heavy preference for the GOP in the past to a somewhat narrower Republican margin in Presidential elections—from two to one in the 1950s, and usually more than that earlier, to five to four in the 1960s, including 1968. The party's standing with this group would still have been only three to two if all the Wallace voters in the sector in '68 were given to the GOP. For the first time in history, a majority of the college-educated group actually voted Democratic in the 1964 Presidential election.

The grammar-school-educated voting group—traditionally a Democratic bastion—shifted slightly further that way in the 1960s. Almost all of the Wallace support in '68 in this particular sector came from normally Republican votes. Nixon, in fact, received a smaller portion of the group than any GOP Presidential candidate in the last twenty-five years. The most that can be generalized about the high-school-educated voting group is that it swings wide or narrow with the over-all election results. In 1968, for instance, the group split 43 percent for Nixon to 42 percent for Humphrey.

In terms of economic groupings, the Presidential election results show that the GOP was off throughout the 1960s, including 1968, compared to the 1950s among those groups historically most staunchly Republican: the professional and managerial segment, the rest of the middle-class vote, and farmers. Democrats made perceptible inroads into those groups in '60 and '64, then lost their gains in '68. Significantly, however, the GOP did not return in '68 to its pre-1960 strength. Instead, Wallace gained a bloc roughly as large as that which had come unstuck from the Republican Party. In net effect, the GOP has been down almost 10 percent among these three groups for over a decade.

There has been much talk in recent years about the GOP gaining a beachhead in the blue-collar group, and that may come to pass under the pressure of the racial problem. But the contention has negligible support in the statistics of the three Presidential elections of the 1960s or a Gallup study of this group in the 1970 elections. There is slightly more evidence from the last ten years, in fact, that the Democrats are moving up the economic ladder than that Republicans are effectively moving down it. Gallup commented after the 1970 elections that one of the tactical mistakes the GOP made that year was in trying so hard for tough-to-get blue-collar or hard-hat votes when the party should have been stressing its appeal to the white-collar group, where the pickings could have been better.

Another warning sign for the GOP is the fact that the factionalism which chronically wracks the Democrats is now opening up within the Republican Party again. The ultraconservative elements which have long made their home in the Republican Party are rallying in many Northern states as well as in the South, and they have been attempting to shift the center of power within the party state by state. That problem has recurrently affected the GOP since before the turn of the century, but it has been especially acute since 1964 and flared virulently in a number of states in 1970. What has been happening is reflected in California, where the long reign of liberal Republicans like Earl Warren and then Thomas Kuchel gave way in the last half of the sixties to militant conservatives like Ronald Reagan. Since then, however, the GOP has lost two Senate seats there to the Democrats. And, sooner or later, a bitter internal struggle could break out in the state, pitting the Reagan wing against a still newer crop of Republican leaders like State Comptroller Hugh Flournoy and Congressman Paul McCloskey, with Robert Finch likely to be trying to straddle the two wings as a deft political technician. That party-wrenching test still lies ahead, but the last time it occurred it opened the way for eight years of Democratic rule.

The conservative leverage working within the GOP can also be traced in New York. A new Conservative Party was organized there in 1962 by a few apostles of William Buckley to pressure the state's Republican Party more to the right. The growth of that cause since has been dramatic. In 1962 the Conservative candidate for governor attracted 142,000 votes. In 1964 the Conservative candidate for the U.S. Senate received 212,000 votes. In 1966 the Conservative candidate for governor drew 510,000 votes. In 1968 the Conservative candidate for the U.S. Senate garnered 1,139,000 votes. In 1969 Conservative votes denied liberal Republican incumbent John Lindsay the GOP nomination for mayor of New York City, and he finally had to win re-election as a third-party candidate. In 1970 the Conservative Party candidate, James Buckley, won roughly two and a third million votes and a seat in the Senate, while the GOP candidate was a poor third. The objective of the Conservative drive, as David Broder has written, "is to neutralize, if not completely reverse the liberal influence of the New York Republican Party. When one remembers that it is this party which has been at the center of every national liberal Republican effort from Wendell Willkie to Rockefeller in 1968, one realizes what is at stake."

Over-all, the Republican prospect nationally may not be fairly bad over the short run. For the longer range, prospective needs to be kept on the small proportion of the electorate identifying itself as Republican, the party's heavy reliance on voters in their fifties or older, and the fact that the GOP is eroding among those educational and economic groups which have historically provided its staunchest support. Ironically, that last weakening is occurring just as some of the main groups on which it relied in recent decades are expanding faster than ever before. Equally ominous, the pressures from the party's own right and the lure of the South are rising just as the new generation of voters generally already to the left of the GOP is starting to flood into the electorate. From a long-term point of view, the pull of the right and to the South probably could not be worse timed for Northern Republicanism, especially since so much of the new generation has shown that it would quickly take an alternative to the Democratic Party if given any encouragement.

Polls show that young people tend to respond to the visibility of an incumbent President somewhat more than does the rest of the populace, and Nixon could pick up among younger voters between '68 and '72. But so far, Nixon's Southern strategy and square personal style are badly minimizing a historic opportunity for the GOP among the young. A party reduced to less than a third of the electorate in terms of more or less lasting loyalties needs to use its period in power to rebuild a long-range base. Otherwise, when the political pendulum inevitably swings and carries the Republicans out of the White House, the party could be in serious trouble. It is not at all inconceivable that by the end of the 1970s the GOP could claim barely over a fifth of the electorate as a hard-core base. That would be a party deeply in trouble in a historical sense.

But this does not quite complete the Republican range of prospects. With the nation's younger generation moving into the electorate in huge numbers by the middle seventies, the last real chance for the GOP right wing to take over the party and consolidate its influence over America for a long time to come may be in 1972. It may not be likely, but neither is it beyond the schemes of men that Nixon could be challenged for renomination that year from the right, or bluffed out by events and developments within his own party. This possibility could be more of a pressure on the perceptive politician who now occupies the White House than the national press or surface events have yet made clear. If the right wing feels that the Republican Party happens to get into a particular strong position not long before the next Presidential election or if Nixon falters, it is conceivable that some key ultraconservatives will decide the time is ripe to try to extend the hold on the GOP exerted in the historic 1964 convention. Nixon in '68 was a convenience, not a commitment, for this group, and the reallocation of votes to enhance the strength of the South in the last convention provides the precedent for putting a still stronger squeeze on the party.

Old-style politicians and commentators will argue that it is all but impossible for a party to turn out an incumbent President from its own ranks, but malcontent Democrats in 1968 showed that it is not impossible to attempt the exercise. And it would be easier to undertake the maneuver within the GOP through quiet discussions in executive suites and private drawing rooms than out on the streets and campaign hustings, as the Democrats had to do. As a matter of historical record, it should also be noted that well over a half-dozen sitting Presidents have been denied or bluffed out of renomination by their own party. Curiously, that has happened more often within conservative than within liberal ranks despite the latter group's undeniable capacity for political self-immolation. An important if uncertain component of the politics of the seventies is the possibility that elements within each party might wound themselves even as they reach to prevail.

The record of the Democratic Party in recent decades, like that of the GOP, underscores the erosion of the principal political arrangements in this country. At the start of the 1970s, for the first time in four decades, the Democrats could no longer claim to be "the majority party." Not only had the White House been lost, but well under half of those surveyed by Gallup and Harris any longer identified themselves as Democrats. That was contrary to the situation even during the Eisenhower period. And the prospect is that the party will continue to lose some of the strength it has long had among the working-class sector, the South, and voters in their twenties and thirties. A mild recovery was made in the 1970 election results, but the party will almost certainly not settle down until the society as a whole does, and that is not likely at all soon. The principal tensions wracking the country are still coming to bear most directly among key groups recently in the loose Democratic coalition. For the purposes of Presidential politics, national Democratic leaders must slow the defection from their ranks and make the tough decisions as to which sources of support can be maximized and which may have to be let slide, even though desired and paid lip service to. Samuel Lubell has pointed up that a coalition party is in serious danger only when several segments spin off more or less at the same time. Individual defections or erosions often strengthen other parts of a party and even attract new elements.

The Democrats will, of course, need all the votes they can get from every source. But in the early seventies there may still be slightly more incremental votes available for them in the blue-collar sector than in the new generation and its growing upper-middle-class allies—at least the practical priority seems to be that way. By the middle of the decade, however, the situation will almost surely be the reverse. Like the GOP, the Democrats thus have to develop a rolling strategy to cope with the next half-dozen years and more, though the real pressure in politics is only on winning the next election. Even in just a short-term sense, since the working-class vote for the Democrats could suffer still further defections in '72, party leaders will have to make up for that loss from the newer and upper groups. With such multipronged, simultaneous demands, it is hardly surprising that candidates often end up looking like a rubber man out of a circus sideshow.

A closely related difficulty for the Democrats, with their dependence on coalition politics, has been suggested by Louis Harris. He said after the '68 Presidential election that he doubted "next time Americans will tolerate another choice of candidates of the major parties who take the umbrella approach to politics . . . of having many different and diverse groups and interests all under one umbrella." It seems hard to envisage, however, how the diversity of American society can be politically reconciled and multiparty politics minimized without the major parties seeking to pull together some of the incredible pluralism and, especially now, some of the older and newer elements. With imagination, developing a "shopping list" of fresh appeals which reinvigorate much of the eclectic Democratic coalition for at least the 1972 election should not be insurmountable, despite the sharp current antagonisms among various parts of this longtime political conglomerate.

More difficult than drawing up a policy agenda will be to reconcile the diverse styles to which the different segments of the coalition respond. Many political writers are preoccupied with substantive concerns or special-interest politics and deprecate the personal styles which public figures must communicate if they are to maintain wide popular support in a period when the visual medium is as influential as it is today. Public leadership, whether in a tribal village or a great nation, must help cope with the psychic as well as the economic needs of the human condition, particularly *en masse*. The current dilemma is that most blue-collar whites as well as young people and blacks seem to be drawn most readily to public figures with considerable vividness—a "hot style," "personal intensity," a "distinct profile" in the language of the communications theorists, while much of the rest of middle America and particularly the better-educated elements now want a "cooler," quieter figure. In a period of increasingly personalized and media-scrutinized leadership, politics and especially coalition politics will have to be concerned with reconciling not merely conflicting interests but clashing implications of style as well. This problem has always been latent in campaigns; but it is of growing importance as more and more of the electorate votes not just its pocketbook but also its psyche.

The scramble of both major parties to put together a broader base in the seventies will be running up against the possible further splintering of the political system itself. Thus, it is not at all incon-

ceivable that in 1972 or 1976 the country could have four significant Presidential candidates to choose from. There may be not only
a Republican, Democratic, and Wallaceite candidate but also one
for another important gathering most readily signified here by
Eugene McCarthy, John Lindsay, Mark Hatfield, J. Kenneth Galbraith, Kingman Brewster, John Gardner, or others, though these
individuals are suggested without regard to whether any of them
might actually run for President and despite inevitable protestations
in the meantime on their part about disinterest, party loyalty, and
other responsibilities. This latest coalescing would cut into both
Republican and Democratic sources of strength. It would most
likely be made up largely of younger professional and managerial
types, semiprofessional groups like teachers and technicians, suburbanites, and young people. There might be a fair proportion of
blacks—certainly more than can be found in the Republican Party.
As a whole, this potential grouping would be better-educated,
financially better off, and younger than the average in the major
parties. It would also be more sympathetic to stepped-up social
change and a more selective foreign policy. It would be concerned
with poverty and equal rights, but it would be even more emphatic
in its rhetoric about the abstraction of human excellence. The leadership would undoubtedly declare itself concerned first of all with
averting "the impending catastrophes" in the environment, in race
relations, in the nuclear buildup, and above all in the American
spirit. In a more critical vein, it could easily also come through to
many Americans, including much of the Negro community, as less
cool than cold, with an air of superiority, even slickness.

This group could raise almost as much money for a national
campaign as the Democrats, and do it starting from scratch less
than a year before a Presidential election. Vastly more money and
muscle are available even now for starting an independent party
than for reform of either of the major parties, as by the officially
appointed Reform Commission within the national Democratic
Party or by the articulate but small and intellectualized Ripon Society in the GOP. The potential grouping, though likely to be a
distinct political minority throughout the early to middle seventies,

might slip into power from its position between the two principal parties rather than on the left. At a minimum, it could be the most significant third-party movement since the Know-Nothings of the 1850s. The Wallaceites, interestingly enough, are the only important third-party force to develop to the right of the two major parties since the Know-Nothings. The suburban appeal of a Lindsaylike party would encourage it to minimize ideological attacks and maximize an image of freshness which would contrast with the old forms of the major parties and their possibly necessary but still corrupting compromises of continuity.

Just at the level of political mechanics, Wallace and his American Party showed in 1968 how easily new groups can now get a Presidential candidate on the ballot. The Alabaman, in fact, deserves more recognition than has generally been given him for breaking open the political system by going to court to get on the ballot in a number of states in '68. Some traditionalists may urge that qualifying for the ballot should be made more difficult for third, fourth, and fifth parties. But to constrict political expression and new groupings when large numbers of citizens are groping for an alternative to the two major parties could estrange even more of the public from the political system than has already occurred. It is American society, not just our politics, that is fragmenting. To seal off rather than vent the substantial pressures which are building invites even greater frustration and trouble.

Out of a three-way and perhaps four-way split in the Presidential politics of this decade, the U.S. might be on the way to a more or less lasting *multicandidate* system, especially under the impact of television. That is more likely in the short run than a genuine *multiparty* arrangement. Such a development could produce a volatile, vivid, often vehement brand of politics. Certainly the increased political activism in diverse parts of U.S. society could be pointing in that direction. A more likely alternative, however, is that out of the prospective three- or four-way division, one of the two major parties will be reconstituted and major realignments will evolve.

Traditionalists may rightly say that such a prospect is a dangerous passage, with dogmatic thinking and overheated feelings running easily to authoritarianism on both left and right. But fluctuating multimovement politics might also lead to more direct assaults than would otherwise be possible on the overriding problems of our time, including the nuclear threat, the ruin of the natural environment, the racial controversy, and other basic problems which the present arrangements are proving to be incapable of significantly coping with before it may be too late to do anything except succumb—quite literally. How to minimize the profound peril which both the present course and that other political prospect offer is a central question for this society. But it should also be remembered that the purpose of politics is to try to solve public problems, not just (or even necessarily) maintain the existing parties and political relationships.

In the period ahead, the principal political institutions and movements will rise or fall on the basis of whether they show they can help people to gain a larger sense of direction over their lives and future. At a minimum, there is need to respond to the want among a rapidly growing and influential sector of American society, though still a decided minority, for a greater role or way of participating in the ruling processes. Herman Kahn, a blunt and articulate spokesman, has argued that the dominating problems have become too complex and dangerous to be left to the nonexpert and the general society. But the rooted convictions and growing pressures in millions of Americans will probably allow little surcease or lasting political success for any party or figure until the contemporary power struggle is resolved in favor of further empowering rank-and-file citizens. And that is but the latest in a long, uneven broadening of the power base of this society.

An abiding irony about the present situation, however, is that key segments of the citizenry, especially the activists of the new generation, are becoming more politicized not just to gain power—which is the usual historical ploy—but in order to restrain and put down the political system itself. They seem to have concluded that political power, as the English writer Alex Comfort has argued, "has developed into a hostile and uncontrollable environmental force of its own." Yet as almost a self-contradiction, the earliest way that people can regain a measure of influence over that force is through politics. Those who refuse to be involved, whether through apathy or disgust, nevertheless remain subject to the workings of this force and are, in fact, helping to perpetuate its prevailing sway by their inaction.

How to give effect to the spreading desire for greater involvement or self-determination, beyond just talk or street demonstrations or small tasks in the hierarchical structure of organized politics and government, is not proving an easy problem to solve. One modest starting point would be to develop local and symbolic national equivalents of the old town meeting—neighborhood meetings in local schools scheduled the same week throughout the country for public discussion of urgent social, political, and other problems, with politicians not there to talk but to listen, and with high-level outlets like the White House helping to build such forums several times a year as genuinely open and meaningful grassroots events. The infrequent "White House conferences" in Washington are no longer adequate. Discussions among some national opinion leaders and a symbolic acting out of a subject for the purposes of public education used to be enough to satisfy the more interested members of the general public about the openness and quality of the governing process. Now genuine and very broadbased participation by a growing sector of the citizenry is sought; the demand (despite the discomfort of such affairs for Presidents and other politicians) is likely to increase in a democracy with rising levels of education and other sophistication.

In the more overtly political arena, important parts of the public may not be willing too much longer just to be spectators while Presidents and other politicians engage in televised but frustratingly superficial and histrionic press conferences or, at campaign time, hold televised question-and-answer sessions with carefully constructed studio audiences who meekly submit to well-rehearsed replies to readily anticipated inquiries. Those overly structured responses by politicians to the TV era are now badly dated. They are, in fact, as old as the '68 Presidential campaign. A fuller and franker two-way relationship with more of the public is going to have to be attempted.

Nor can proffered solutions to public questions indefinitely continue to be packaged mostly as more and more governmental programs, with the attendant bureaucracies then cramping the daily life of people and costing more and more in taxes, subsidies, loopholes, or services which end up aiding mostly the already established groups after a few years, anyway. As just one possible alternative, the old Homestead Act is a remarkable model worth pondering. It set certain ground rules, provided some incentives, and pointed toward goals but then let society "go at it." The same approach needs to be considered to motivate neighborhoods, particular economic brackets, and social groups. The Land Grant College Act, also enacted during Lincoln's administration, is another useful model. It helped establish semiautonomous and sometimes almost competing public institutions to carry out specific functions and counter some of the thrust toward federal centralization.

Even within hierarchical structuring, much can be done to open up and enliven the present political parties. Participation and representation in party councils, for example, could be assured for the various economic, racial, and age groups, with spokesmen selected separately by each such sector, not by those already entrenched. That would help assure a better approximation of political democracy than now exists within the parties. At the same time, the step would tie those groups more enthusiastically to a party by bringing them into its decision-making. Though not likely, the present national committees of the two major parties might be reorganized to place the party chairman and professional staff under the policy guidance of a national biennial assembly made up of representatives from various social and economic groups plus a democratically elected party member from each Congressional district in the

country. Such steps would introduce more debate and reduce dic-
tation from above. Politicians generally object to such developments, but a broader, more open political system has long been a
basic impulse of American society. Politicians must keep relating
to that underlying and ultimately determining surge.

Beyond structural changes, political organizations may have to
become at least a little more akin to social-action movements over
the long term—that is, perform specific community projects and
national services. Those could help mobilize opinion and pull together working cadres between campaigns as well as prove the
worth and vigor of the parties themselves. As a small beginning, the
national offices of the major parties, and especially the party out
of power, could sponsor a wide range of new endeavors. Thus,
merely by way of illustration, a consumer gadfly such as Ralph
Nader or Bess Myerson Grant; a full-time political economist like
Walter Heller or Milton Friedman; a foreign *rapporteur* such as
W. Averell Harriman or Cyrus Vance; perhaps even a social satirist
like Allen Ginsberg; several qualified ombudsmen to visit industrial
areas, ghettoes, and campuses, then draw conclusions about grievances which should be articulated and acted on before further
strains develop; some flying squads of diversely skilled individuals
to provide illustrative services to model cities and suburbs from
time to time; and a staff of lawyers to bring some major test cases
in the consumer, safety, environmental, educational, and other
fields. All that could be done on a volunteer basis and would be
separate from the essential registration work, media counseling,
fund-raising, and more conventional efforts of the present national
party organizations.

Ultimately, of course, practical politics must focus on the lone
voter who is endlessly buffeted by personal problems and petty
concerns but gives only passing attention to politicians and public
issues. At the same time, actual campaigns must seek to discern
the general public mood at the time and try to distill a clear
and persuasive set of invigorating responses. Those seemingly simple goals of politics, however, are increasingly complicated by the
sweeping changes all about us, and "he that will not apply new

remedies," as Francis Bacon wrote long ago, "must expect new evils; for time is the greatest innovator." Unfortunately, as has been noted by Richard Goodwin (sort of a Francis Bacon of the current American Left), most politicians—like most generals—are usually trying to refight the last battle just one more time.

CHAPTER 11

Looking Forward

The net consequences of the many contradictory forces coming to bear on American society must still be determined in the politics and events of the coming period. It is quite possible that the nation will be moving in this decade through a desultory period part-Republican, part-Democratic toward a domestic testing unrivaled for over a century. Almost an entire generation of young blacks and a sizable portion of the huge, approaching generation of young whites are being (in considerable part have already been) radicalized, or "sensitized" as the process is called by many who experience it. At the same time, a much larger number of people who constitute the traditional mainstream are becoming (in considerable part have already become) repressive in their social and political reaction to many of the changes taking place. In this polarization, anger and absurdity, violence and viciousness abound and have already been working their will.

The pressure on the moderates in between will almost surely remain fairly intense for most of this decade, for the forces of social change causing the unsettlement are basic, swift, and continuing. In the past, almost the entire middle sector of American society, including much of the intellectual community, has recurrently "adjusted" to the right to ride out periods of avenging conservatism; the call for another such move can be heard today. Some cautious middle-aged commentators, for instance, invoking the specter of Senator Joseph McCarthy's rampages in the late 1940s and the first half of the 1950s, implicitly counsel that the country must disavow social dissent and further slow, not speed, black

progress—must in effect seek to co-opt reaction by giving up critical ground to it. Similarly, there is counsel that the U.S. cannot
pull out of Viet Nam too fast or let any of our client's countries in
Southeast Asia topple without risking a rightest reaction here at
home and even the danger of our military being infected like French
generals after that nation gave up Algeria. But today's left is also
relentlessly mobilizing, and it must be reckoned with even in a
passage of possibly severe reaction. The militant blacks and radical
young whites are generally less economically encumbered and more
freely, even orgiastically, politicized than those who previously
propelled the cause of political and social change.

Moderates dare not drift right and abandon their role of reconciliation in this highly plural society without accelerating the division and danger for both themselves and the nation. They may,
even perhaps will, forfeit much of their usual mediating function
—but the consequences could be very damaging for practically
everyone.

If the nation takes a really sharp political turn in the seventies,
the balance of power unmistakably indicates it will be further into
repression, not revolution. The forces of reaction have much larger
masses of people and capital resources potentially available to them
as well as some essential enforcing agencies. The possible recruits
for an actual early uprising on the left, in contrast, are few, and
there is more bravado than deliberateness even about them. Individuals here and there may be capable of adapting the lessons of
guerrilla warfare, particularly from the Western European resistance movements of World War II (more than from Mao or Ché) to
make sporadic strikes which disrupt the fragile order of this technological time. But even that kind of operation is questionable for very
long in a highly organized, electronically scanned society. The
more realistic prospect is a continuing rash of difficulties like campus disturbances, ghetto troubles, and isolated acts of senseless
retribution. These, however, hardly constitute a true revolution on
any national scale, nor do they seem capable of leading to a general
one in the foreseeable future.

The remote hope of such few real revolutionaries as there may be is that there will actually be repression and that it will be the sulfurous catalyst for serious national resistance. In the meantime, the more sophisticated of the rebels (as distinguished from the glandular hotheads) are likely to stay loose, unorganized, and non-violent while the reaction festers, realizing that efforts to bait a Götterdämmerung could prematurely abort both their immediate efforts and their deeper aims.

Who's Radical? Who's Conservative?

This country, with its constitution, belongs to those who live in it. Whenever they shall grow weary of the existing government, they shall exercise their right of amending it or their revolutionary right to dismember or overthrow it.
— Abraham Lincoln

Violence breeds violence. Revolutionary violence breeds fascist tyranny.
— Allen Ginsberg

We don't want to overthrow the government. We just want to create a condition in which it gets lost in the shuffle.
— "The Crazies"

The streets of our country are in turmoil. The universities are filled with students rebelling and rioting. Communists are seeking to destroy our country. Russia is threatening us with her might. And the Republic is endangered. Yes, danger from within and without. We need law and order! Yes, without law and order our nation cannot survive. . . . We shall restore law and order.
— Adolf Hitler, 1932

In the developing setting, the difficult task for American society will be to de-escalate all outbreaks of force immediately, whether by private citizens or the police, and get on with rational discussion to work out the underlying causes of the social strain as quickly as possible. Those who look primarily to government in the present circumstances—and that ironically includes more and more conservatives—would do well to ponder the conclusion of

Hannah Arendt, one of the most perceptive analysts of the modern state, that governing is not ultimately based on force but on power, and that when physical violence is necessary to maintain authority, then power has already been lost. For the young activists, both white and black, their special testing will be less whether what they raise up will prevail—the mere running of the years should accomplish a modest part of that and submerge the rest—than whether, in their war with the prevailing arrangements, they eventually become what they now rail against. Inevitably they will grow middle-aged, and they will slow. But will the young existentialists also finally become the philistines they now decry? And will the militants of black pride and brotherhood give meaning to pride and brotherhood only in rhetoric or also in their day-to-day lives? The destructive, dehumanizing qualities which so many people are now aroused against can win out again merely by the nature of the struggle the "outs" wage within themselves.

If there is neither all-out repression nor revolution in this decade (and American society has proved itself able to avoid a grave breakdown of its democratic processes all but once), what seems most likely to happen is perhaps best suggested by a historical analogy. It allows for a look at the processes of change free, for the most part, of contemporary antagonisms. The current over-all circumstances are probably most analogous, out of all the nation's history, to those in the 1840s and 1850s—with the former very roughly similar to the 1960s and the latter perhaps to the 1970s. These two eras can obviously be only very loosely compared, but the analogy still provides striking insights for pondering the present period.

That long-ago time was also one of sweeping unsettlement and population movement. The westward tide of people was full, with the Midwest filling up, Texas at last being securely populated by Americans, and the great flood into California and the Pacific Northwest getting under way. A vast technological transformation was also taking place. The building of the railroads was in full swing, the industrialization of the North was moving ahead at a record pace, and major technological breakthroughs like the invention of the telegraph and the popularization of the McCormick reaper were having their effect. The racial issue became rancorous, with the Abolitionists mobilizing, the South unrelenting, and the nation's political mainstream stalemated over what to do about the problem. The Mexican war came along in the middle of the 1840s and was just about the most unpopular in the country's history until the Vietnam involvement.

At the same time, however, the forces of manifest Americanism felt deeply threatened. Religious and cultural conflicts broke out as Irish and Catholic Germans arrived in unprecedented numbers. The Roman Catholic Church had only the fifth largest number of American communicants in 1840 but the most by 1850, a ranking it has held ever since. Bloody anti-Catholic riots broke out in city after city. "The Kennedys came to America at just that time before the Civil War," Theodore White wrote, "handkerchief migrants, outcasts in snow-cold Boston. And there, with the rest of the Irish, they suffered and shivered, hungered and strove, and rioted their way up to the light."

We talk now of a population explosion, but then the American populace was doubling every twenty-three years—more than a third faster than at present. The numbers were much fewer then, but the social stresses were about as severe, or possibly worse. Even with all the wide open spaces, there was overurbanization, with major cities unable to keep up with their water, sewage, crime, and housing problems. A great educational boom spread and strongly reinforced the drive for further democratization. At the same time, violence and drunkenness became markedly more pervasive. A number of religious sects splintered, and usually toward greater liberality. The women's rights movement was formally organized. Wilderness utopias—early hippie havens—flourished and failed, being symptoms rather than sources of the vast forces at work. Yet they were often attacked as dangerous.

The strongly wrought political battle lines of the earlier Jackson era had already faded. The two major parties, the Democrats and the Whigs, had both become divided, vacuous and vacillating, particularly on the overriding issue of slavery and its implications for the nation. The immediate campaigns of that time, however, were fought out with even more vehemence and packaged bunting than previously, from the Whigs' successful hard-cider and torch-light Presidential campaign of 1840, when the country chose General William H. ("Tippecanoe") Harrison, a candidate notable mostly for the obscurity of his views (the Whigs refused even to set forth a platform), to "Abe the Railsplitter" and the portable log cabin in 1860. Unable to cope with the major problems or channel the basic turmoil of the time, the politics of that period instead fashioned the hoopla which has marked almost all Presidential campaigns ever since.

The generally more conservative of the two principal parties, the Whigs, won the Presidency twice during the 1840s but then quickly disintegrated, a casualty of the political splintering of the time and the party's reliance for too many years on tactical opportunism instead of offering a clear sense of direction for the country. In the party's second occupancy of the White House, from 1848 to 1852, the Whigs had not done such a bad job as to deserve their sudden fate; they lost the fairly close election of 1852 mostly by some pedestrian campaign mistakes. Yet within three years the main body of the party had dissolved. The Democrats were just as divided and desultory on the fundamental problems of the period, but they were more widely based—perhaps too much so in such an acrimonious climate. They stalemated as they sought to hold their divergent ranks together and helped hurry the apocalypse.

The nativist uprisings against the Catholic influx coalesced in the late 1840s in the Order of the Star Spangled Banner, which developed shortly into the formidable American, or Know-Nothing, Party—a tag derived from the secretiveness of many of its labors against "the Papist intrusion." A few years after the American Party was unveiled, still another grouping sprang up: the Republican Party. It drew in part from the Whigs but also from the newer forces all around. It was a heady mixture of fresh faces, established figures like New York's antislavery Senator William Seward and lesser-known political veterans like Illinois' ex-Congressman Abraham Lincoln, formerly a Whig himself. It refused to espouse the biases of the Know-Nothings and risked having its developing strength cut into as a result. The Know-Nothings garnered over 20 percent of the vote in 1856. But the Republican Party benefited handsomely in its formative years from Democratic Senator Stephen Douglas' key but unpopular role in having driven through the Congress the historic Kansas-Nebraska Act, which handled the slavery issue as a political rather than moral question, as more and more people were coming to view the issue. From some scattered, spontaneous local starts in 1854, the Republican Party became the principal challenger of the prevailing Democrats in 1856 and even elected a Republican Speaker of the House of Representatives after that election. Four years later, never really a third party, it captured the White House—almost as much by luck as hard work.

During the 1840s and fifties, first two, then three major candidates contended for the Presidency in the same election. Finally, in 1860, there were four. No man was able to hold onto that office for more than a single term between 1840 and 1860. Indeed, not a single Chief Executive during those twenty years of change and upheaval was even renominated by his own party! One took himself out of consideration before the end of his term—Polk, of the Mexican war; the other four incumbents (two of them Vice-Presidents who had succeeded through tragedy to the White House) simply were sacked at the end of their term. The victors in the 1856 and 1860 Presidential elections were elected by considerably less than a majority of the votes cast. Lincoln gained the White House by the smallest percentage in the nation's history: 39.8 percent, almost 4 percent less than Nixon in 1968. More basically, all seven men who served as Chief Executive during the 1840s and fifties largely backed and filled on the overhanging dilemma of the time, the slavery issue. Three owned slaves; another was of "the first families of Virginia" and "understanding" about the institution though a resident of Ohio; one was a New Hampshire Democrat selected almost entirely because he was sympathetic to the South; two were nobodies tapped for the ticket because their views were vague enough to be broadly acceptable.

Most of the other major figures, as well as the popular majorities of that era, were also unable or unwilling to move deliberately and effectively against the problem and the sectional, economic, moral, and martial passions pent up in it. The politicians and vast majority of private citizens were preoccupied with their own pursuits and, insofar as they acknowledged a larger stake, with the "manifest destiny" of American expansion, which then was reaching out for the first time across the Pacific Ocean. When, rarely, the public process had to face up to the racial controversy and any action was taken, it was equivocal or backsliding, as in the Kansas-Nebraska Act, the Fugitive Slave Law, and the Dred Scott decision. The political hallmark of the period, in fact, was drift and division—and that course led straight into the Civil War, the seedbed of total modern warfare.

Now the nation's mainstream politicians mostly drift and duck and delay again on the really fundamental issues. But the problems this time are potentially even graver. Not only is the racial controversy resurgent; generational tensions, environmental contamination, and international perils of the most profound kind are piling up, all long overdue for substantial further action, each by itself more destructive in its possibilities than the slave issue ever was. The Praetorian guards of the prevailing order keep telling the newer forces to work within the system, but evidence accumulates that the dominant groups are not really willing to open up the system institutionally for the new, or even for some of the disenchanted older element. The major parties pay lip service to the young and black and poor but still usually load up committees, caucuses, conventions, laws, and legislative appropriations almost entirely in favor of the already established and empowered. Seemingly the refrain to "work within the system" really is an invitation into impotence—or, in the language of the young, "Up against the wall, baby!" At the same time, millions of other Americans—including many conventional-minded Democrats and Republicans as well as George Wallace's yeomen—feel increasingly isolated and overwhelmed by the huge institutions which dominate our national life and much of our daily lives. Yet those same institutions continue to grow steadily larger and more ponderous, whether governmental or privately run, and whether a Republican or a Democrat sleeps in the White House.

How close may we be to another grisly national showdown? Can we break through to a new public era which really moves on the massive problems of this time other than through tragedy? We may try to cling to outdated forms and attitudes and relationships, as in the antebellum period and with Herbert Hoover, when sweeping transformation was also already under way but the political leadership resisted, ignored, equivocated, or moved too slowly. Or we may move on partially to empower the new forces and values, as in the American Revolution and with Franklin Roosevelt. The historical record indicates that the latter course is the more hopeful one. Yet can and will this society now consciously accept that lesson for the seventies?

If an inconclusive drift, as well as eventual all-out repression or revolution, is to be avoided, then the history of the United States in this decade will doubtless have to emerge out of a broad-based Two-Stage Unfolding. First is the current conservatism or stalemate, depending on one's point of view, extending in power until 1972 or possibly the middle seventies. The unwitting purveyors could be a Democratic as well as a Republican administration. But sooner or later there should come a fairly major opening for the newer forces in American life as the huge wave of young people moving into their middle to latter twenties, and floods into the electorate in record numbers. Such should not be characterized as an opening to the left any more than to the right, but an Opening to the Future. That will be reinforced by rapidly rising levels of affluence, education, and cultural sophistication in substantial sectors of the present electorate. Along with that will also come hard-won breakthroughs by the gathering black move for political power in areas where Negroes are virtually a majority. Experience suggests that the more severe the reaction, the stronger the pendulum is likely to swing when it moves back in the other direction. True conservatives should particularly be the ones to press for moderation in the current phase, for example is probably the only persuasive way to build into the new generation and its allies a modicum of reasonableness and restraint for the second and longer phase to come.

A great depression, war, widespread drought, or other unpredictable event could, of course, have fundamental effect. But the new influences already at work or irreversibly moving in on American society have a substantial thrust of their own that great events could exaggerate or lessen, but most likely not completely dispel. The suggested two-stage unfolding could therefore still stand, though in a more stark or subdued outline as the unknowns come to bear.

In a substantive sense, the outcome of the many changes being fought over may someday be summed up as historian Allan Nevins described two earlier passages of national turbulence: "Roosevelt's so-called revolution, though unprecedentedly broad and swift, was like Jefferson's 'revolution'; it was simply a combination of numerous practical changes, the main test of which was whether or not it worked." As with the citizens of those periods, a central question for the seventies is whether we can and will assimilate a "revolution" without feeling threatened and insecure. The culture and politics and peace of the country will depend heavily on how that is resolved and on whether the resulting public mood is one of buoyancy or an enervating fear that things are coming unstuck.

It may well be that the main force shaping American society and particularly the public sector is profoundly changing. Prior to the 1930s, business—or, in the political simplification of that time, "Wall Street"—was dominant. Since Franklin Roosevelt, politics and government have displaced commerce to an important extent as the primary force working both on themselves and on the larger society. Commerce and politics are now losing very considerable power to what might broadly be characterized as cultural sources, and the implications for both our politics and the general society can only be far-reaching.

What different institutional arrangements might be sought? Surely not just more structuring for an epoch experiencing basic and continuing change and needing to attempt almost continuous adaptation. Certainly not more bureaucratization in either the private or the governmental sector, though this is undoubtedly absurdly wishful thinking. In fairness, it should be recognized that there has already been a considerable calling of special conferences and the appointment of committees and other minor mechanisms at different levels to "communicate" with blacks, young people, hard-hats, consumers, and others. The persisting problem is that such devices have generally been used thus far as a gesture or mostly for symbolic purposes, appearing to respond to various stirrings while actually shunting them far down the ladder of influence. What is still glaringly missing is a willingness by "in" groups and authorities significantly to empower the striving elements of people, if only through such conventional means as funding (subsidies, incentives, tax avoidance, and all the rest that the long-influential business community has gained), prominent and continuing semiofficial forums, expanded legal rights and remedies, increased autonomy, review access in the stream of decision-making and administration, and other concrete steps. In a more important sense, what is really needed is a more genuine spirit of national, social, and human community and equality among the principal "in" and "out" sectors, especially by the former toward the latter. Power is rarely shared willingly, but this country could risk the dangers of instability and repression for a very prolonged period if it does not open up and share much more than presently is the case.

We will not easily move on during this decade. But what could be blowing in the wind with the newer elements is a national reinvigoration that will occupy American society for much of the rest of this century. To bring that to fruition, we need to encourage and energize the younger and more vital human forces of this time and help provide better outlets for their fresh qualities and insights. Equally, we must recognize that, like ancient Ulysses, we all have been swiftly transported into strange new environments. We are creatures only recently out of caves, then rough farms and small towns and cities, now plopped increasingly in suburbs. At the same time, we have suddenly been swept into a whole new electronic grid and lashed to international girders, one with mankind. And at the same historical moment, the increasingly pervasive view of life has become less attuned to an industrialized world and more internalized. To cope with all that is happening, we must fairly quickly adapt ourselves, our social order, and our politics. Yet we are barely at the beginning of that experience. Whatever of the old persists (and most does from one epoch to the next) will prevail not by social rigidity and political stalemate but through adaptation and regeneration, two processes applying as much to a society and its politics as to nature and life itself.

Acknowledgments

For a book of this kind, I am indebted to many current sources, including particularly, among the press, the superb staffs of the *National Observer*, *The New York Times*, *The Wall Street Journal*, Washington *Evening Star* and Washington *Post*, and among periodicals, the *Congressional Quarterly*, *Daedalus*, *Dissent*, *Fortune*, *Look*, *Newsweek*, *New York Review of Books*, *The Public Interest*, *Time*, and *Saturday Review*. Special acknowledgment is due to the College, Field, Gallup, Harris, Yankowitch, and Kraft polls, which I have sometimes individually cited but often synthesized: the National Planning Association; and a number of academic monographs and government reports, especially those of the Bureau of Labor Statistics, Census Bureau, Civil Rights Commission, Federal Communications Commission, National Advisory Commission on the Suburbs, and National Commission on Urban Problems.

As to books, I am under obligation to many but especially these, in the order the discussion first involves use of them:

Kevin Phillips, *The Emerging Republican Majority*, Arlington House, 1969.

Richard A. Scammon and Ben Wattenberg, *The Real Majority*, Coward-McCann, 1970.

Robert Heilbroner, *The Future as History*, Harper, 1959.

Robert and Helen Lynd, *Middletown in Transition: A Study in Cultural Conflicts*, Harcourt, Brace, 1937.

Caroline Bird, *The Invisible Scar*, Pocketbooks, 1966.

W. Lloyd Warner, *Democracy in Jonesville*, Harper, 1949.

260

Arthur Schlesinger, Jr., *The Crisis of the Old Order*, Houghton Mifflin, 1957.

Daniel Bell (ed.), *Toward the Year 2000: Work in Progress*, Houghton Mifflin, 1968.

Oscar Handlin, *Race and Nationality in American Life*, Anchor, 1957.

Thomas Bailey, *The American Pageant*, Heath, 1956.

Samuel Lubell, *The Future of American Politics*, Harper, 1951, and *The Revolt of the Moderates*, Harper, 1956.

Ronald Freedman (ed.), *Population: The Vital Revolution*, Anchor, 1964.

Angus Campbell *et al.*, *The American Voter*, Wiley, 1960.

Peter Gay, *The Enlightenment*, Random House, 1966.

Marshall McLuhan, *Understanding Media*, Signet, 1964.

Eric Hoffer, *The Temper of Our Time*, Harper, 1967.

David Riesman and Christopher Jenks, *The Academic Revolution*, Doubleday, 1968.

Robert F. Kennedy, *To Seek a Newer World*, Doubleday, 1967.

Alvin Toffler, *Future Shock*, Random House, 1970.

Merle Severy (ed.), *Greece and Rome: Builders of Our World*, National Geographic, 1968.

Alexis de Tocqueville, *Democracy in America*, Knopf, 1951.

Brink and Harris, *Black and White*, Simon & Schuster, 1967.

Donald Mathews and James Prothro, *Negroes and the New Southern Politics*, Harcourt, Brace, 1966.

Stokely Carmichael and Charles V. Hamilton, *Black Power: The Politics of Liberation in America*, Random House, 1968.

Martin Luther King, *Where Do We Go from Here: Chaos or Community*, Harper, 1967.

James Baldwin, *The Fire Next Time*, Dial Press, 1963.

Hubert Humphrey (ed.), *Integration vs. Segregation*, Crowell, 1964.

C. Wright Mills, *The Power Elite*, Oxford, 1956, *Power, Politics and People*, Balantine, 1963, and *White Collar*, Oxford, 1951.

J. Kenneth Galbraith, *The New Industrial State*, Houghton Mifflin, 1967.

David Bazelon, *Power in America*, New American Library, 1967.

National Planning Association, "The Dimensions of U.S. Metropolitan Change," 1967.

David Riesman, *Abundance For What?*, Anchor, 1965.

Peter Drucker, *The Age of Discontinuity*, Harper, 1969.

Michael Harrington, *The Other America*, Penguin, 1964, and *Toward a Democratic Left*, Macmillan, 1968.

Ronald D. Laing, *The Politics of Experience*, Pantheon Books, 1967.

Joint Atomic Energy Committee staff report, "Biological and Environmental Effects of Nuclear War," U.S. Government Printing Office, 1959.

Herbert Alexander, "Broadcasting and Politics," *The Electoral Process*, Citizens Research Council, 1968, and other publications of the Council.

Herman Kahn and Anthony Weiner, *The Year 2000*, Macmillan, 1967.

James MacGregor Burns, *The Deadlock of Democracy*, Prentice-Hall, 1963.

Ripon Society, *The Lessons of Victory*, Dial, 1969.

Hannah Arendt, *The Origins of Totalitarianism*, Harcourt, Brace, 1951, and *On Revolution*, Viking, 1963.

Theodore White, *The Making of the President 1968*, Atheneum, 1969.

About the use of statistics: Numbers are often taken in our present culture, whether or not so intended by the individual using them, to indicate a precision which is misleading, especially when dealing with rapidly changing social and political circumstances. That is particularly true when the figures are generally cited, as here, to discern possible moving flows. In order to offset to some extent the almost inevitable implication of certainty, the statistics have been rounded off whenever that reasonably could be done. Gunnar Myrdal has best summed up the problem with his comment that facts in the social services are only weak indices of reality.

Finally, I am deeply grateful to many, many individuals whom I have learned from and worked with in politics and other public matters over the years, but who are too many to list. I have been especially indebted, however, to Adlai Stevenson, Pat Brown, John F. Kennedy, Robert Kennedy, and some exciting younger people from whom I have also had the good fortune to learn in recent years, especially at the University of California.

FREDERICK DUTTON

Washington, D.C., 1971

About the Author

Frederick Dutton was Secretary to the Cabinet and Special Assistant to President John F. Kennedy (1961), Assistant U.S. Secretary of State for Congressional Relations (1962–1964), Executive Assistant to California Governor Edmund G. Brown (1959–1960), Chief Assistant Attorney General of California (1957–1958), and has been a Regent of the University of California since 1962. He was Executive Director of the Robert F. Kennedy Memorial Foundation (1968–1970), served as organizing director of the John F. Kennedy Oral History Project, and has practiced law for a number of years in Washington, D.C., and California.

In the political arena, Mr. Dutton was a key personal aide to Senator Robert F. Kennedy in the 1968 Democratic Presidential primaries; executive director of the 1964 Democratic National Committee's Platform Committee and deputy chairman of the Democratic National Committee in charge of research and planning for the 1964 Democratic Presidential campaign; deputy national chairman of the Citizens for Kennedy and Johnson in 1960; and California campaign manager for the 1958 Democratic gubernatorial campaign. He has also, he says, "gone down the drain in some losing campaigns" in California, New York, and nationally.

A native of Julesburg, Colorado (1923), he is a graduate of the University of California at Berkeley and Stanford Law School, and served in the infantry in World War II, ending up a German POW, and in the Korean Emergency "fighting a desk" in Japan.